Hazardous Locations
By Tom Henry and Tim Henry

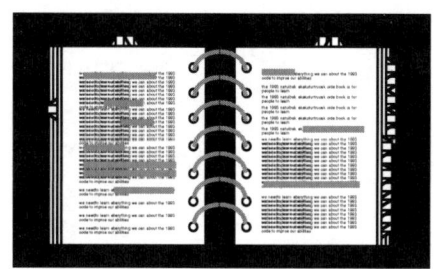

Based on the 2020 National Electrical Code

National Electrical Code® and NEC® are Registered Trademarks of the National Fire Protection Association, Inc., Quincy, MA.

ISBN 978-1-7350449-5-8

ENRY PUBLICATIONS SINCE 1985

**CODE ELECTRICAL
LEADER IN ELECTRICAL
EDUCATION WORLD WIDE**

Meet the authors

Tom Henry

•Certified Chief Electrical Inspector Building Officials of Florida
•Certified Chief Electrical Inspector Southern Building Code Congress
•Former Electrical Inspector Walt Disney World-EPCOT
•Registered Electrical Contractor State of Florida
•Licensed Master Electrician
•Member National Fire Protection Association (NFPA)
•Member International Association of Electrical Inspectors (IAEI)
•Owner of Code Electrical Classes Inc. Winter Park, FL
•Certified Vocational Instructor State of Florida
•Instructor of over 22,000 Electricians
•Author of Electrical Inspection Workbook
•Author of over 90 Electrical books
•Legal consultant involving Electrical fires and deaths
•Over 62 years experience in the Electrical field
•President of Tom Henry's "Learn to be an Electrician" program with over 2,000 enrolled from all 50 states and several foreign countries

Meet the Vice-President and Co-Author

Tim Henry

•Registered Electrical Contractor State of Florida
•Licensed Master Electrician
•Member National Fire Protection Association (NFPA)
•Vice-President over 30 years of Code Electrical Classes Inc. Winter Park, FL
•Instructor of over 12,000 Electricians
•Co-Author of over ten Electrical books
•Legal consultant involving Electrical fires and deaths
•Over 40 years experience in the Electrical field
•Electrical construction co-editor for the "*Informer*" newsletter
•Director of Tom Henry's "Learn to be an Electrician" program with over 1900 enrolled from all 50 states and several foreign countries

The secret of making something work in your lives is first of all, the deep desire to make it work; then the faith and belief that it can work; then to hold that clear definite vision in your consciousness and see it working out step by step, without one thought of doubt or disbelief.

We act as though comfort and luxury were the chief requirements of life, when all we need to make us really happy is something to be enthusiastic about.

CONTENTS

CONTENTS

Introduction

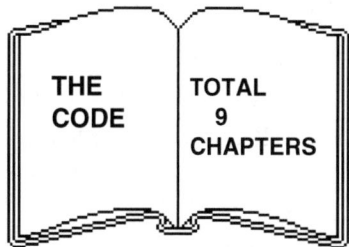

The most difficult task in preparing for the electrical exam is trying to "study" the Code.

The Code book is divided into nine chapters and then divided into articles, parts and sections.

The "meat" of the Code is the first four chapters. General wiring, grounding, services, motors, etc.

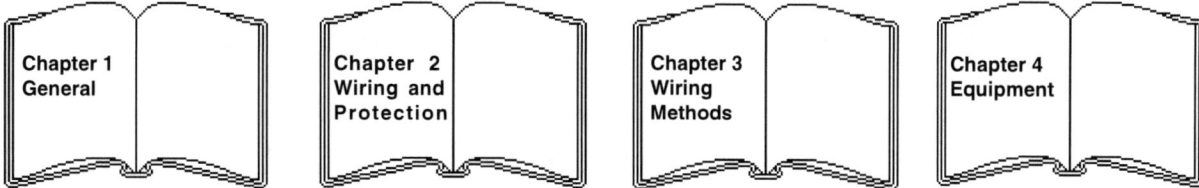

Chapters 5 through 9 are for special applications.

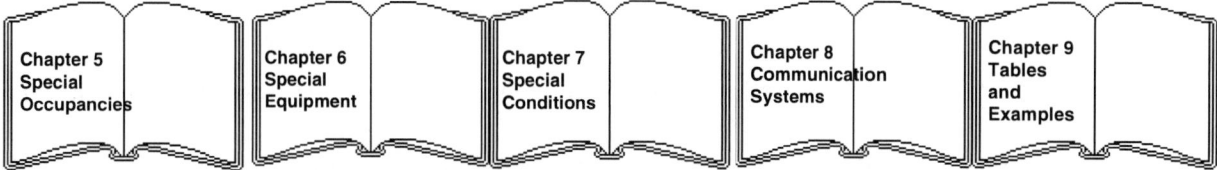

The following is an example of how the Code is divided: Flexible cords are not permitted as a substitute for fixed wiring of a structure per 400.8 of the Code.

The 400.8 is broken down to the 4 indicates Chapter 4.

The 400 is Article 400.

Article 400 is divided into three parts: Part I. General, Part II. Construction Specifications, Part III. Portable Cables over 600 Volts, Nominal.

400.8, the 8 is the section number.

Chapter 4, Article 400, Section 8 which is located in Part I of Article 400.

The latter part of each Article will contain the **over 1000 volts (high-voltage) section**.

Example: The definition of a fuse is located in the **over 1000 volts** Part II of Definitions Article 100 Chapter 1. Article 100 Definitions is listed in alphabetical order but fuse is not listed in Part I. Following the last Definition in Part I is the word wet location. Part II over 1000 volts starts after wet location. Fuse is defined in Part II of Definitions not Part I.

It is very helpful as we try to master the Code book to know how it is laid out in Chapters, Articles, Tables, Parts and Sections.

I

Author's note: There's a tremendous amount of work that must be done in electrical training. The one area I feel we are lacking in is "learning" the Code. You can't just read the Code book, it must be taught to you.

Most likely you've heard the expression, "A picture is worth a thousand words." I've always maintained a smile means the same in any language. A picture is like a poem without words. In my writing books, I take text and massage it and put it into a picture where possible.

Hazardous Locations *"The Pictorial Workbook of the Code"* is an excellent study guide for the apprentices, electricians, inspectors, technical schools and even for the electrical engineer that had zero hours of Code study at the University.

Once the area has been classified, the Code states what electrical equipment and wiring methods are the minimum required in the area of classification.

Hazardous Locations is a workbook requiring the student to use the National Electrical Code book in answering the questions from each Article. A final exam is included on all the Articles.

Explosionproof equipment is expensive more so than the nonhazardous electrical equipment. Careful attention should be made to locate much of the equipment in a less hazardous area, thus reducing the amount of special equipment required. The larger the equipment, the less likely explosionproof equipment will be available. Motors and generators suitable for Group C locations are quite limited in availability.

After installation, routine maintenance is still needed, mainly because many hazardous locations are also corrosive locations.

The weakest link in the total system can undermine the effectiveness of the best individual components.

The quality of American life depends upon the safety and effectiveness of electrical application.

Are you an electrician or are you an installer? The difference is education.

It's what we think we already know that often prevents us from learning.

As an electrician, It's what you know after you know it all that counts.

If you can read a book, thank a teacher. If you can read a book at night, thank an electrician.

I want to personally thank Appleton for providing photos of some of the equipment.

Appleton also offers a complete line of products for hazardous locations, fully tested to **IEC** and **CENELEC** standards. Ask your local Appleton representative about the ATX brand or visit the ATX web site at www.egsatx.com for details.

DEFINITION of ELECTRICIAN

ELECTRICIAN
A specialist in electricity
One who installs, maintains, operates or repairs electrical equipment

SPECIALIST
One who devotes himself to a special occupation or branch of learning

DEVOTE
To give to a cause, enterprise or activity
Devote means to set apart for a special and often higher end

SPECIAL
Distinguished by some unusual quality
Being in some way superior
Held in particular esteem
Readily distinguishable from others of the same category
Being other than usual

LEARNING
Knowledge or skill acquired by instruction or study

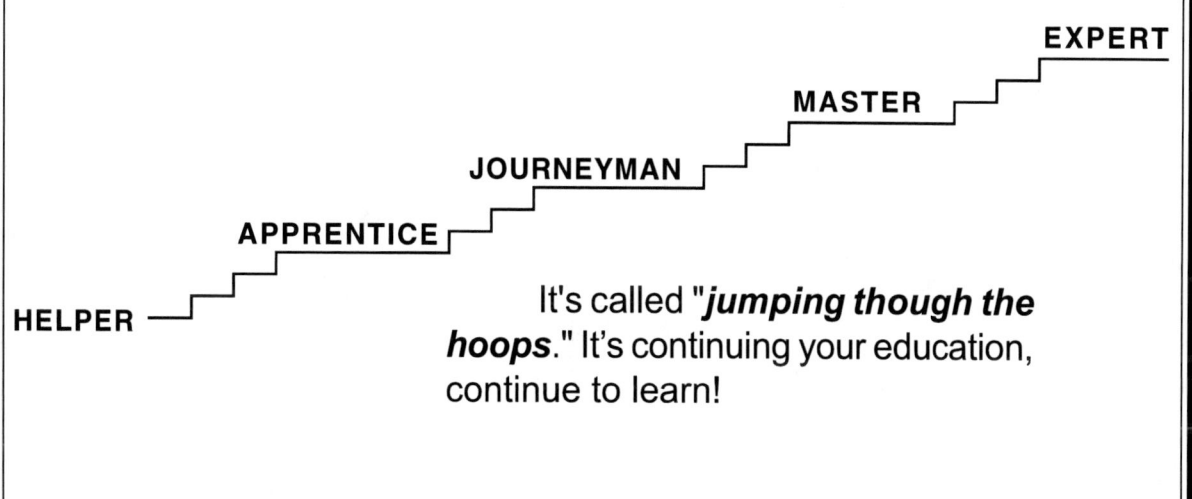

It's called "*jumping though the hoops*." It's continuing your education, continue to learn!

What must be understood with testing is the electrical industry has specialized categories just as the medical field has. You have a doctor who is a specialist for eyes, kidneys, bones, etc. It's the same situation in the electrical industry. We have electricians in construction wiring, service work, maintenance, inspection, designing, engineering, etc. The electrical exam may ask questions from a category you are not familar with so one must properly prepare in all categories to enhance passing the electrical exam.

ELECTRICAL

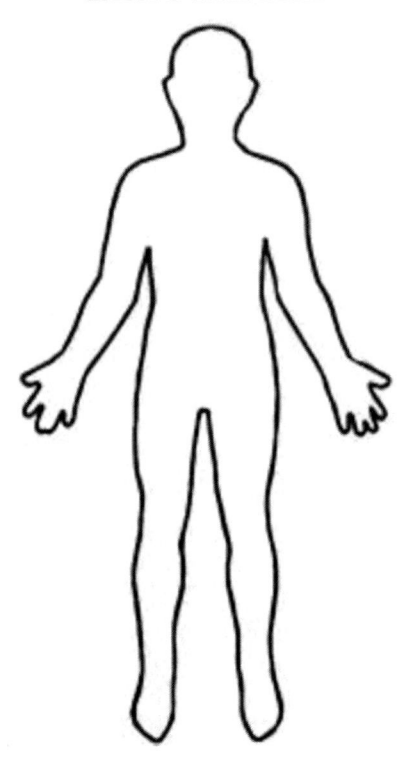

Engineer
Designer
Master
Journeyman
Residential
Commercial
Industrial
Maintenance
High Voltage
Lineman
Alarm System
Oil Field
Marine
Air Plane
Locomotive
Low Voltage
Sign

MEDICAL

Neuro Surgeon
Neurologist
Ophthalmologist
Cardiologist
Pulmonologist
Gastrologist
Hepatologist
Nephrologist
Proctologists
Urologist
Oncologist
Rheumatologist
Orthopedist
Surgeons
Dermatologist
Podiatrist

Type of Electrical Certificates

Electrical Contractor
Master Electrician
Journeyman Electrician
Apprentice Electrician
Maintenance Electrician
Low-Voltage/Limited
Limited Technician
Low Voltage License
Restricted Electrical Contractor
Beginning Electrician
HVAC Electrician
Electric Sign Electrician
Single Family Dwelling
Elevator Electrician
Fire Alarm System Electrician
Burglar Alarm System Electrician
Electrical Contractor Specialist
Electrical Contractor Specialist Fixture
Designated Master Electrician
Designated Master Electrician Specialist
Temporary Electrician
Journeyman Electrician Specialist
Escalator Electrician
Specialty Electrician
Apprentice/Trainee
Type "S" Journeyman
Grandfathered Electrician
Electrical Sign Apprentice
Electrical Sign Contractor
Journeyman Sign Electrician
Master Sign Electrician
Residential Wireman
Class "B" Electrician
Journeyperson Electrician
Lightning Protection Contractor
Specialty Electrician
Journey Worker
Lighting Maintenance Specialty
Limited Energy
Utility Line
Limited Special Electrician
Master Special Electrician
Limited Electrician

General Journeyman Electrician
Limited Journeyman Electrician
General Supervising Electrician
Limited Supervising Electrician
Limited Maintenance Electrician
Limited Residential Electrician
Limited Journeyman Stage Electrician
Limited Journeyman Elevator Electrician
Limited Journeyman Energy Electrician
Electrical Contractor Limited
Electrical Contractor Intermediate
Electrical Contractor Unlimited
Electrical Contractor Single Dwelling
Electrical Contractor Special
Cathodic Protection Electrician
Sound & Intercommunication Electrician
Telephone Communications Systems
Photovoltaics Electrician C-2g class
Integrated Ceilings Electrician C-2b class
Residential Journeyman , Type RW
Residential Electrician
Power Limited Technician
"A" Master Electrician
"A" Journeyman Electrician
"A" Installer   Electrician
"B" Installer   Electrician
Sign Specialty Apprentice Technician
Sign Specialty Contractor
Sign Specialist
Fire Alarm Apprentice Technician
System Contractor
Systems Technician
Journeyman-in Training Electrician
Electrical Company
Limited Electrician
Specialty Electrical Contractor
Supervising Electrician
General Electrician
Voice Data Video Technician
Fire/Life Technician
Nonresidential Lighting Technician
Air Conditioning Electrician
Hospital Electrician

ARTICLE 500

Hazardous (Classified) Locations, Classes I, II, and III, Divisions 1 and 2

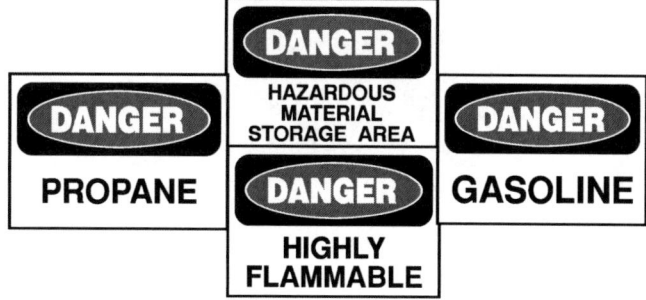

For hazardous locations, the Code rules become more complex and must be applied with an understanding of other items that must be considered in the design and installation. Code rules are not the only rules that must be followed. The NFPA and those of qualified testing laboratories also provide guidelines for the selection, installation, and operation of equipment to be used in hazardous locations.

The decision in the classification of a location is what is "normal" and what is "abnormal". This decision must be made by a team of experts, the safety engineer, the electrical engineer, the process engineer, the project engineer and the authority having jurisdiction which can be the electrical inspector, building official, fire inspector, insurance underwriters, etc. The decision would not be made by one person.

A thorough knowledge of equipment design fundamentals is necessary for proper selection and installation of electrical system components in a classified area.

Selection of equipment to be installed in hazardous locations requires an understanding of the Code rules involved.

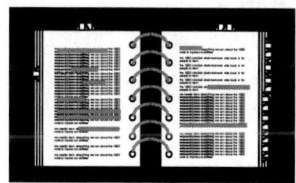

CHEMISTRY OF FIRE

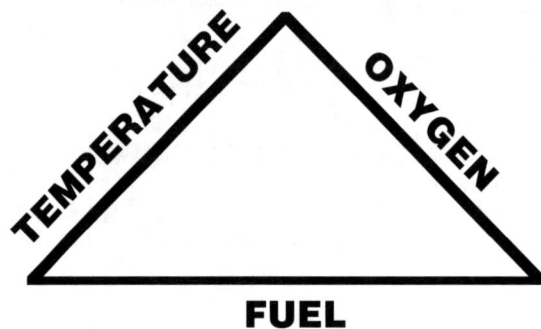

To have a fire, you must have three things present: Fuel, oxygen, and heat. Take away any one of those three and the fire will be extinguished.

There are many possible sources of heat capable of igniting flammable vapors.

•Arcs often created by switches, relay contacts, motor brushes.
•Sparks from static electricity, lightning, loose light bulb, bad splice.
•Surface temperatures of heaters, resistors, lamp with too high a wattage.
•Faults and failures from poor material, poor workmanship, poor design.
•Ferrous metals can cause sparking by striking them together.
•Tools striking concrete can cause a spark.

Flammable gases and vapors are the most common potential sources of an explosion.

Vapor is defined as any substance in a gaseous state, that under ordinary conditions is usually a liquid or solid. It could be gasoline, which is normally a liquid, within a container. Because of its low flash point temperature, a certain amount will evaporate in the form of a vapor and mix into the surrounding air. Gasoline is denser than air, thus, the vapor will collect above the surface of the liquid. If the ambient temperature is very cold and the mixture of gasoline vapor and air is too "thin," a source of ignition will not cause the mixture to explode. If the ambient temperature is high and the container is virtually full, the vapor-to-air ratio may be too "rich" for a source of ignition to cause it to explode. Between this upper and lower flammable (explosive) limits is the danger zone.

Gases and vapors are not the only items that have the potential for creating an explosion; dusts also can. Atmospheres containing combustible dusts such as grain, wood, and others such as plastics must be considered to be hazardous.

Flyings of certain fibers are included among those items that are potentially dangerous.

Hazardous locations are areas where some flammable material is, or may be, present in an easily ignitible state. These areas are classified by the type of material that will be handled, processed, or stored in the location. Article 500 defines the Classes as:

> Class I,   Division 1 or 2, gases and vapors
> Class II, Division 1 or 2, dust
> Class III, Division 1 or 2, lint or flyings

Class I locations are subdivided into Groups, A,B,C, and D. Group A contains acetylene the most dangerous.

Class II locations are subdivided into Groups, E,F, and G.

Class III has no Group subdivisions.

500.1 This section **Scope Articles 500 through 504** has four Informational Notes.

500.5. Where pyrophoric materials are the only materials used or handled, these locations shall not be classified.

Definition: **pyrophoric**. Igniting spontaneously, emitting sparks when scratched or struck with steel.   Each room, section, or area shall be considered individually in determining its classification.

500.5(B)(1). Class I, Division 1 is a location
(1) In which ignitible concentrations of flammable gases, flammable liquid produced vapors, or combustible liquid produced vapors can exist under normal operating conditions, or

(2) In which ignitible concentrations of such flammable gases, flammable liquid produced vapors, or combustible liquids above their flash points may exist frequently because of repair or maintenance operations or because of leakage, or

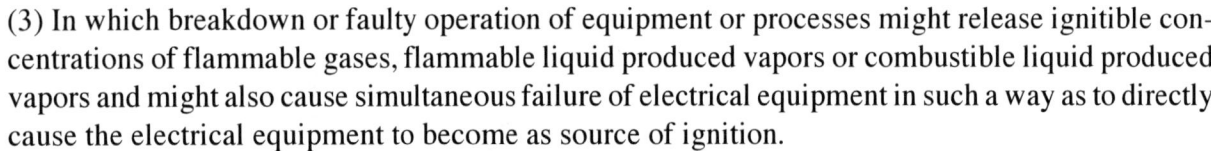

(3) In which breakdown or faulty operation of equipment or processes might release ignitible concentrations of flammable gases, flammable liquid produced vapors or combustible liquid produced vapors and might also cause simultaneous failure of electrical equipment in such a way as to directly cause the electrical equipment to become as source of ignition.

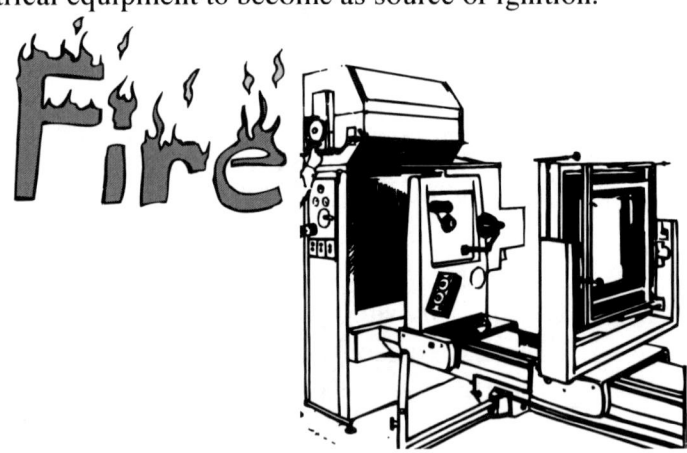

•*Note*: An **Informational Note** is a recommendation only and cannot be enforced by the authority having jurisdiction.

500.5(B)(2). Class I, Division 2 location is a location
(1) In which volatile flammable gases, flammable liquid produced vapors, or combustible liquid produced vapors are handled, processed, or used, but in which the liquids, vapors, or gases will normally be confined within closed containers or closed systems from which they can escape only in case of accidental rupture or breakdown of such containers or systems or in case of abnormal operation of equipment, or

(2) In which ignitible concentrations of flammable gases, flammable liquid produced vapors, or combustible liquid produced vapors are normally prevented by positive mechanical ventilation and which might become hazardous through failure or abnormal operation of ventilating equipment, or

(3) That is adjacent to a Class I, Division 1 location, and to which ignitible concentrations of flammable gases, flammable liquid produced vapors, or combustible liquid produced vapors above their flash points might occasionally be communicated unless such communication is prevented by adequate positive-pressure ventilation from a source of clean air and effective safeguards against ventilation failure are provided.

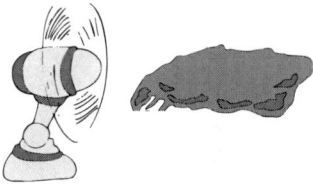

•**Author's note**: Mechanical sparks can occur wherever two objects strike each other. Some grain elevator dust explosions have been caused by mechanical sparks.

The use of nonsparking metals such as bronze and some aluminum alloys or nonmetallic materials can reduce the mechanical sparks.

500.5(C)(1). Class II, Division 1 location is a location

(1) In which combustible dust is in the air under normal operating conditions in quantities sufficient to produce explosive or ignitible mixtures, or

(2) Where mechanical failure or abnormal operation of machinery or equipment might cause such explosive or ignitible mixtures to be produced, and might also provide a source of ignition through simultaneous failure of electric equipment, through operation of protection devices, or from other causes, or

(3) In which Group E combustible dusts may be present in quantities sufficient to be hazardous.

Informational Note: Dusts containing magnesium or aluminum are particularly hazardous, and the use of extreme precaution is necessary to avoid ignition and explosion.

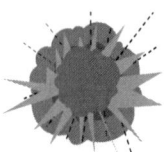

500.5(C)(2). Class II, Division 2 location is a location

(1) In which combustible dust due to abnormal operations may be present in the air in quantities sufficient to produce explosive or ignitible mixtures; or

DUE TO ABNORMAL CONDITIONS

(2) Where combustible dust accumulations are present but are normally insufficient to interfere with the normal operation of electrical equipment or other apparatus, but could as a result of infrequent malfunctioning of handling or processing equipment become suspended in the air; or

(3) In which combustible dust accumulations on, in, or in the vicinity of the electrical equipment could be sufficient to interfere with the safe dissipation of heat from electrical equipment, or could be ignitible by abnormal operation or failure of electrical equipment.

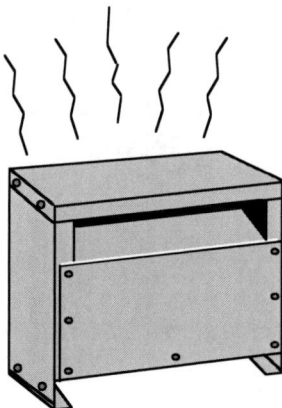

Informational Note #1: The quanity of combustible dust that may be present and the adequacy of dust removal systems are factors that merit consideration in determining the classification and may result in an unclassified area.

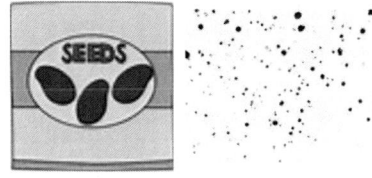
Informational Note #2: Where products such as **seed** are handled in a manner that produces low quantities of dust, the amount of dust deposited may not warrant classification.

500.5(D)(1). Class III, Division 1 location is a location in which easily ignitible fibers/flyings or where materials producing combustible flyings are handled, manufactured, or used.

There are no Group subdivisions in Class III locations. Sawdust in large quantities is a severe fire hazard. Wood flour which is the same basic material is a Class II material, because it can be in suspension in the air in the same way that finely divided dusts from grain can.

Informational Note #1: Such locations usually include some parts of rayon, cotton, and other textile mills.

Informational Note #2: Easily ignitible fibers/flyings include rayon, cotton, and other materials of similar nature.

500.5(D)(2). Class III, Division 2 location is a location in which easily ignitible fibers/flyings are stored or handled other than in the process of manufacture.

•**Author's note**: It's not difficult to determine the extent of a Division 1 or Division 2 in a Class III location as it depends on the use of the area rather than the amount of material present or likely to be present.

500.6. Flammable chemicals are widely used for various purposes. Testing is the only way to determine their degree of hazard (Group). Based on the outcome of tests, gases and vapors that have somewhat similar explosive characteristics have been placed in one of four Class I hazard categories (Groups).

Exception: Equipment identified for a specific gas, vapor, or dust.

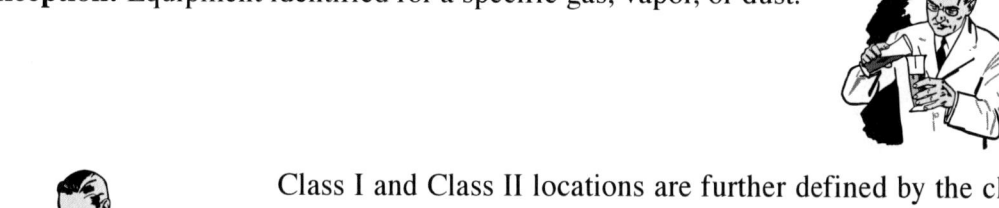

Class I and Class II locations are further defined by the chemical and/or physical nature of the material that poses the danger. According to their characteristics they are included within Groups having similar degrees of hazard. No Groups are given for Class III hazardous materials; they are classified according to their location in the process as either Class III, Division 1 or Class III, Division 2.

500.7. Protection Techniques.

(A) Explosionproof equipment is the predominant form of protective strategy against flammable gases and vapors and may be used in any Class I, Division 1 or 2 location for which it is approved.

(B) Dust-ignitionproof equipment may be used in any Class II, Division 1 or 2 location for which it is approved.

(C) Dusttight protection shall be permitted for equipment in Class II, Division 2 or Class III, Division 1 or 2 locations.

(D) Purged and pressurized protection can be used in any hazardous location for which it is identified.

(E) Intrinsically safe apparatus and wiring approved for the location are permitted. •*Intrinsically safe will be explained in detail in Article 504.*

(F). Nonincendive circuits that are incapable of igniting the specified flammable gas/vapor and air mixture are allowed in those Class I, Division 2, Class II, Division 2, and Class III, Division 1 or 2 locations for which they have been approved.

(G) Nonincendive equipment shall be permitted for equipment in Class I, Division 2, Class II, Division 2, and Class III, Division 1 or 2 locations for which they have been approved.

(H) Nonincendive component shall be permitted for equipment in Class I, Division 2, Class II, Division 2, and Class III, Division 1 or 2 locations for which they have been approved.

(I) Oil-immersed current-interrupting contacts of the general-purpose type having a 2" minimum immersion of power contacts, or a 1" immersion for control contacts are permitted in Class I, Division 2 areas.

(J) Hermetically sealed devices that prevent the entrance of an external atmosphere is permitted for current-interrupting contacts in Class I, Division 2, Class II, Division 2, or Class III, Division 1 or 2 locations.

(K) A combustible gas detection system shall be permitted as a means of protection in industrial establishments with restricted public access and where conditions of maintenance and supervision ensure that only qualified persons service the installation.

(K)(2) Inadequate Ventilation. A location, enclosed space, or building that is classified as a Class I, Division 1 location due to inadequate ventilation, that is provided with a combustible gas detection system shall be permitted to utilize electrical equipment, installation methods, and wiring practices suitable for Class I, Division 2 installations.Sensing a gas concentration of not more than 40% of the lower flammable limit or a gas detection system malfunction shall activate an alarm (audible or visual, or both, as most appropriate for the area.)

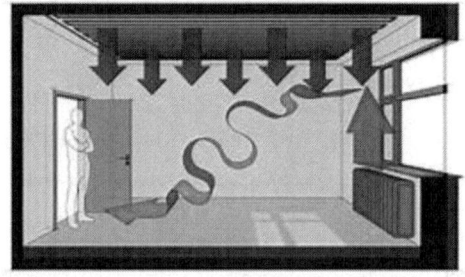 

(K)(3) Interior of a Building or Enclosed Space. Any building or enclosed space that does not contain a source of flammable gas or vapors that is located in, or with an opening into, a Class I, Division 2 hazardous (classified) location that is provided with a gas detection system shall be permitted to utilize electrical equipment, installation methods, and wiring practices suitable for unclassified installations under all of the following conditions:

(1) An alarm shall be sounded at not more than 20% of the lower flammable limit.

(2) Sensing a gas concentration of not more than 40% of the lower flammable limit.

(3) The power disconnect shall be suitable for Class I, Division 1 if located inside the building.

(4) Inside the interior of a control panel containing instrumentation or other equipment utilizing or measuring flammable liquids, gases, or vapors, which is provided with combusstible gas detection equipment shall be permitted to utilize electrical equipment, installation methods, and wiring practices suitable for Class I, Division 2 installations.

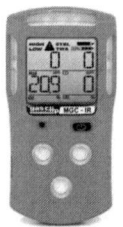 

500.8. Articles 500 through 504 require equipment construction and installation that ensure safe performance under conditions of proper use and maintenance.

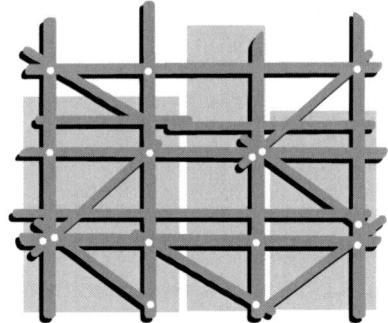

UNDER CONSTRUCTION

Hazardous locations have a higher level of danger requiring the design and installation to be done in particularly strict compliance with the instructions given in the product standards.

Informational Note #1: Urges designers, installers, inspectors, and maintenance personnel to "exercise more than ordinary care" for hazardous location work.

500.8(A). Suitability of identified equipment shall be determined by any of the following:

(1) Equipment listing or labeling

(2) Evidence of equipment evaluation from a qualified testing laboratory or inspection agency concerned with product evaluation

(3) Evidence acceptable to the authority having jurisdiction such as a manufacturer's self-evaluation or an owner's engineering judgement

500.8(B)(1). Requires that all equipment in hazardous locations be approved not only for the class of location but also for the particular type of hazardous atmosphere such as Group A, B, C, or D for locations involving gases or vapors, or Group E, F, or G if the atmosphere involves combustible or flammable dusts.

Class I equipment shall not have any exposed surface that operates at a temperature in excess of the ignition temperature of the specific gas or vapor.

Class II equipment shall not have an external temperature higher than allowed for the Group of the dust involved.

Class III equipment shall not exceed the maximum surface temperatures: 165°C (329°F) for equipment not subject to overloading, and 120°C (248°F) for equipment that can be overloaded such as motors and power transformers.

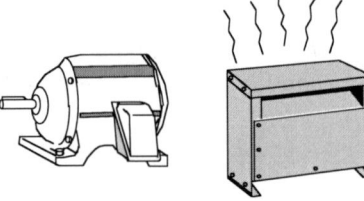

Informational Note: Luminaires and other heat-producing apparatus such as switches, breakers, and receptacles are potential sources of ignition and are investigated for suitability in classified locations.

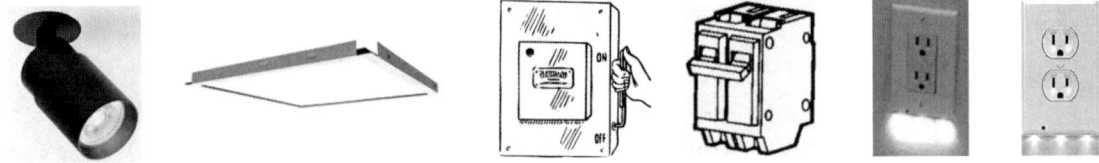

Fixed wiring, however, may utilize wiring methods that are not evaluated with respect to classified locations. Cable, raceways, boxes, and fittings are not marked as being suitable for Class I, Division 2 locations.

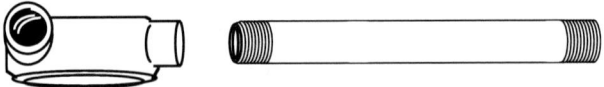

500.8(B)(2). Equipment identified for a Division 1 location is permitted to be installed in a Division 2 location of the same Class or Group.

(a) Intrinsically safe apparatus having a control drawing requiring the installation of associated apparatus for a Division 1 installation shall be permitted to be installed in a Division 2 location if the same associated apparatus is used for the Division 2 installation.

•**Author's note**: Intrinsically safe circuits will be clearly explained in detail in Article 504.

(b) Equipment that is required to be explosionproof shall incorporate seals in accordance with 501.15(A) or (D).

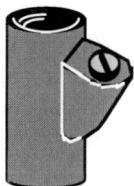

500.8(B)(3). Where permitted by Code rules, equipment in general-purpose enclosures can be installed in Division 2 locations if the equipment does not constitute a source of ignition under normal operating conditions.

•**Author's note**: Section 501.10(B4) states that boxes and fittings are not required to be explosionproof in a Class I, Division 2 location except as required in 501.105(B1), 501.115(B1), and 501.150(B1).

What is not clear is "under normal operating conditions," unless the phrase applies to the equipment instead of the surrounding atmosphere. Equipment that is operating normally might not pose a threat of ignition, but a ground fault or short circuit in the equipment, which is not a normal operating condition, could ignite a combustible atmosphere that might exist in a Division 2 location.

With respect to equipment approval, great care must be taken to understand clearly the rules on hazardous locations equipment as covered in the electrical standards of OSHA of the U.S. Department of Labor. Those rules constitute federal law on this matter.

OSHA standard, 1910.307, Hazardous (Classified) Locations, is listed as one of totally retroactive sections that apply to *all* electrical systems, both new ones and old ones, no matter when they were installed.

Underwriters' Laboratories, Inc. ® ●

Listed Electric Lighting Fixtures For Hazardous Locations

Class I   Serial No.   Class II
Group C D   Group E F G

Listed For Locations Having Deposits Of
Readily Combustible Paint Residue

Caution: To Prevent Ignition Of Hazardous
Atmospheres. Disconnect The Fixture
From The Supply Circuit Before Opening.
Keep Tightly Closed When In Operation. ●

500.8(C)(4). Approved equipment must be marked to show the Class, Group, and operating temperature or temperature range referenced to a 40°C ambient. Equipment not marked to indicate a Division means that it is acceptable in both Division 1 and Division 2 applications.

Electrical equipment suitable for ambient temperatures exceeding 40°C must be marked with both the maximum ambient and the operating temperature or temperature range at that ambient temperature.

Equipment approved for both Class I and Class II locations must be marked with the maximum safe operating temperature, as determined by simultaneous exposure to the combinations of Class I and Class II locations.

Temperature Class (T Code)	Maximum Surface Temperature	
	Degree C	Degree F
T1	450	842
T2	300	572
T2A	280	536
T2B	260	500
T2C	230	446
T2D	215	419
T3	200	392
T3A	180	356
T3B	165	329
T3C	160	320
T4	135	275
T4A	120	248
T5	100	212
T6	85	185

Exceptions to the marking rules are:

Junction boxes, conduit, fittings, and similar nonheat-producing type equipment having a maximum temperature not more than 100°C (212°F) are not required to have a marked operating temperature or temperature range.

Fixed lighting fixtures marked for use in Class I, Division 2, or Class II, Division 2 locations, only are required to be marked with the Group.

Fixed general-purpose equipment (other than fixed lighting fixtures) that is acceptable for Class I, Division 2 locations is not required to be marked with Class, Group, Division, or operating temperature.

Fixed dusttight equipment (other than fixed lighting fixtures) that is acceptable for Class II, Division 2 and Class III locations is not required to be marked with Class, Group, Division, or operating temperature.

500.8(D). Temperature markings are to be used to judge the suitability of the equipment for the atmosphere in which it is to be installed.

In Class I locations the temperature of the equipment must not exceed the ignition temperature of the specific gas or vapor that will be encountered. Ignition temperatures observed under one set of conditions may vary substantially by a change of conditions, including a change in a test method. Ignition temperatures should be looked upon only as approximations.

In Class II locations the temperature markings must be less than the ignition temperature of the specific dust that will be encountered. For organic dusts that may dehydrate or carbonize, the temperature markings must not exceed the lower of either the ignition temperature or 165°C (329°F).

Informational Note: See NFPA 497-2017, Recommended Practice for the Classification of Combustible Dusts and of Hazardous (Classified) Locations for Electrical Installations in Chemical Process Areas, for minimum ignition temperatures of specific dusts.

500.8(E). All conduit must be threaded with a NPT (National Standard Pipe Taper) standard cutting die. The conduit and fittings must be made up wrenchtight to minimize sparking when fault current flows through the conduit system, and to ensure the explosionproof or dust-ignitionproof integrity of the conduit system. Threaded entries into explosionproof equipment shall be made up with at least five threads fully engaged.

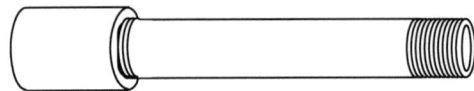

Exception: Listed explosionproof equipment, factory threaded NPT entries shall be made up with at least 4 1/2 threads fully engaged.

•**Author's note**: When tightening a threaded pipe, one must understand the importance of tightening, a water pipe is tightened to prevent a leak at a joint while under pressure. But, there is a world of difference when it comes to tightening a threaded electrical conduit. The electrical pressure is so much higher, it's actually an explosion of current when a **ground fault** occurs sending several thousand amperes through the raceway system that is being used as the **equipment grounding conductor**.

Tests have been made using 2 1/2" rigid conduit with #4/0 copper conductors applying a fault current of 10,000 amperes. This high-current test produced a shower of sparks from about half the couplings in the conduit run. From one coupling came a blowtorch stream of sparks which burned out many of the threads. The conduit run had been installed by a crew regularly engaged in such work and they gave assurance that the joints had been pulled up to normal tightness and perhaps even a little more.

The bad showing of the conduit joints in throwing fire when conducting high current is due entirely to improper assembly or unsuitable fittings. In every case involving couplings, they found the coupling loose or conclusive evidence of previous looseness.

Another test was made using two 2 1/2" couplings at 8,500 amperes. The current was maintained for approximately two seconds. Uncleaned factory threads were employed in each case. The joints were assembled by one man utilizing 24" pipe wrenches. In the two couplings (four threads) tested, no sparking resulted in this tight condition. No sparking, resulted when the joints had been loosened one turn. However, in all cases, when the threads were backed off two turns, which is equivalent to "hand-tight," extensive sparking resulted.

During a 450 ampere test on #4/0 conductors in a 1 1/4" conduit, which was not cleaned before joining, one of the joints became blue because of the high resistance at that point.

Many electricians assume that the conduit is used essentially for mechanical protection and do not realize the likelihood of sparking when the conduit is called upon to carry fault currents.

The circuit breaker that has an AIC (ampere interrupting capacity) of 10,000 amperes must trip instantaneously which requires the conduit system to have a good conductivity path to carry the current to the circuit breaker and prevent damage and fires.

Threaded conduit in a hazardous (Classified) location is required to have seals at certain points and threads fully engaged.

ARTICLE 501

Class I Locations

•Author's note:

When installing seal fittings in a Class I location, they are installed to prevent the transmission of hazardous gases or vapors from one part of a conduit system to another part of the system, and to contain an explosion that occurs within an enclosure from affecting the rest of the system

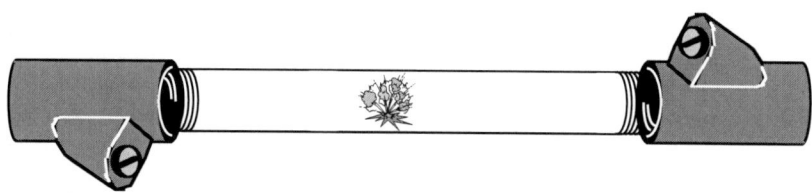

Sealing compound must be of a type approved for the conditions and use and must not have a melting point of less than 93°C (200°F). Sealing compound must expand while it hardens to close all voids. It must also develop enough mechanical strength to withstand the force of explosions.

An explosionproof enclosure is an apparatus enclosed in a case that is capable of withstanding an explosion of a specified gas or vapor that may occur within it and of preventing the ignition of a specified gas or vapor surrounding the enclosure by sparks, flashes or explosions of the gas or vapor within, and that operates at such an internal temperature that a surrounding atmosphere will not be ignited thereby.

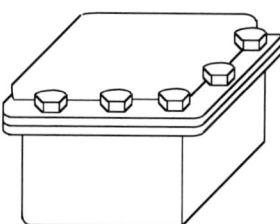

Basically, explosionproof equipment must provide: strength, joints that will not permit flame or hot gases to escape; and cool operation to prevent ignition of surrounding atmosphere. UL standards require that explosionproof enclosures must withstand a hydrostatic test of four times the maximum explosion pressure developed inside the enclosure. Such enclosures are not gas tight.

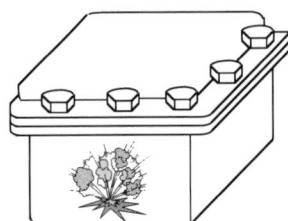

Since it is expected that hazardous gases in the ambient atmosphere will enter them either through normal breathing from heating and cooling cycles of the equipment or when maintenance is performed on the enclosed equipment.

Motors and light fixtures are typical of heating and cooling cycles

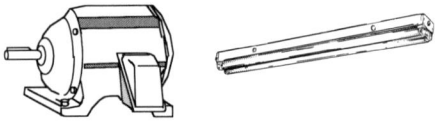

The energy generated by the explosion with an enclosure must be permitted to dissipate through the joints of the enclosure under controlled conditions. There are two recognized joint designs to provide this control "threaded and flat."

5 THREADS

0.0015"

When an explosion occurs inside a threaded enclosure, the flame and hot gases create an internal pressure against the cover, thus locking the threads and forcing the gases out through the helical path of the threads. By the time the gases reach the outside hazardous atmosphere, they have cooled to a point below the atmosphere's ignition temperature. This is the main reason the Code requires a minimum of five fully engaged threads into the fitting is to provide enough of a path to cool this heat.

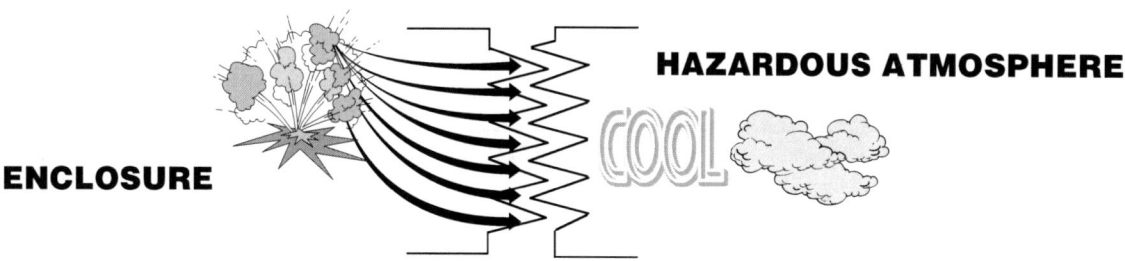

A flat joint is constructed by accurate grinding or matching of the mating surfaces of the cover and body. The flat joint works in a fashion similar to the threaded joint. The two surfaces are bolted together, and as the flame and hot gases are forced through a narrow opening (0.0015"), they are cooled by the mass of the metal enclosure, and only cool gas enters the hazardous atmosphere.

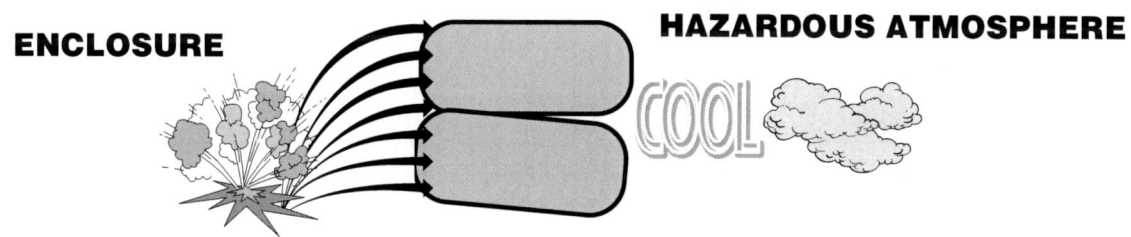

UL requires a maximum clearance of 0.0015" between the body and cover on small enclosures. This gap is known as the maximum experimental safe gap, or MESG. All cover screws must be secured tightly and to make sure no foreign particle is between the enclosure and the cover that could allow a flame to pass into the hazardous atmosphere before cooling.

Part I. General

501.1. Article 501 contains specific regulations that control the selection of equipment and the installation techniques required where flammable mixtures of gases, vapors or liquids either exist or can occur are identified as Class I locations.

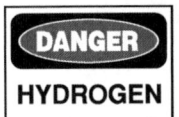

CLASS I
Flammable gases, vapors, or liquids

DIVISION 1	DIVISION 2

•Exists under normal conditions
•May exist because of:
  -repair operations
  -maintenance operations
  -leakage
•Released concentration because of:
  -breakdown of equipment
  -breakdown of process
  -faulty operation of equipment
  -faulty operation of process that
   causes simultaneous failure of
   electrical equipment
	•Liquids and gases are in closed containers or the systems are:
	  -handled
	  -processed
	  -used
	•Concentrations are normally prevented by positive mechanical ventilation
	•Adjacent to a Class I, Division 1 location

GROUP A: Atomspheres containing acetylene

GROUP B: Atmospheres such as butadiene, ethylene, oxide, propylene oxide, acrolein, hydrogen, or gases or vapors equivalent in hazard to hydrogen, such as manufactured gas.

GROUP C: Atmospheres such as cyclopropane, ethyl ether, ethylene, or gases or vapors equivalent in hazard.

GROUP D: Atmospheres such as acetone, alcohol, ammonia, benzine, benzol, butane, gasoline, hexane, lacquer solvent vapors, naphtha, natural gas, propane, or gases or vapors equivalent in hazard.

•Note: The major reason Group A (acetylene) is separate from Group B materials (such as hydrogen) is that the pressure generated when acetylene-air mixtures explode are greater than the pressures generated when hydrogen-air mixtures explode.

501.5. Equipment "listed and marked" for installation in Zone 0, 1, and 2 locations may be used, provided it is suitable for the location as determined in accordance with 505.9(C)(2)

Part II. Wiring

501.10(A)(1). Class I, Division 1 wiring rules are:

(1) Threaded rigid metal conduit or threaded steel intermediate conduit.

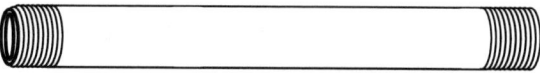

Exception: Type PVC conduit, Type RTRC conduit, and Type HDPE conduit shall be permitted where buried 24" and encased in 2" of concrete.

(2) MI cable terminated with fittings. Although MI cable is not "explosionproof" by definition, the magnesium oxide acts as both an electrical insulator for the conductors and as a continuous seal. Standard Type MI cable fittings are not permitted in Class I, Division 1 locations. Special explosionproof Type MI cable fittings are required, because the unthreaded joints between the outside of the cable and the inside of the fitting must be explosionproof.

(3) Metal clad cable Type TC-ER-HL listed for Class I, Zone 1 or Division 1 where installed in industrial buildings with restricted public access and where only qualified persons service the installation.

(4) In industrial establishments with restricted public access, where the conditions of maintenance and supervision ensure that only qualified persons service the installation, listed Type P cable with metal braid armor, with an overall jacket, terminated with fittings listed for the location, and installed in accordance with 727.4.

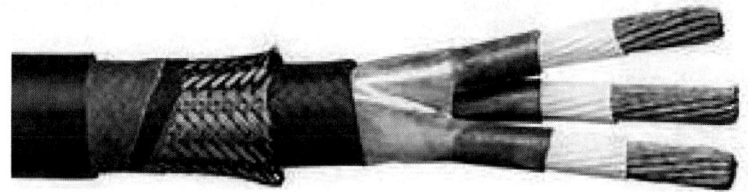

501.10(A)(2). Where it is necessary to employ flexible connections, as at motor terminals, flexible fittings listed for the location, or flexible cord in accordance with 501.140 terminated with cord connectors listed for the location, must be used.

501.10(A)(3). All boxes and fittings shall be approved for Class I, Division 1.

501.10(B)(1). In Class I, Division 2 locations, the following wiring methods shall be permitted:

(1) Rigid metal conduit (RMC) and intermediate metal conduit (IMC) with listed threadless fittings.
(2) Enclosed gasketed wireways and busways.
(3) Type PLTC and PLTC-ER cable per Article 725 including installations in cable tray systems.
(4) Type ITC and ITC-ER cable per 727.4.
(5) Type MC, MV, TC, or TC-ER cable including installations in cable tray systems.
(6) Listed reinforced thermosetting resin conduit, RTRC, all fittings marked with the suffix -XW.
(7) Optical fiber cable.
(8) Cablebus.
(9) In industrial establishments with restricted public access, where the conditions of maintenance and supervision ensure that only qualified persons service the installation, listed Type P cable with or without metal braid armor, with an overall jacket, terminated with fittings listed for the location, and installed in accordance with 337.10.

501.10(B)(2). Where provisions must be made for limited flexibility, one or more of the following shall also be permitted:

(1) Listed flexible metal fittings.
(2) Flexible metal conduit with listed fittings.
(3) Liquidtight flexible metal conduit with listed fittings.
(4) Liquidtight flexible nonmetallic conduit with listed fittings.
(5) Flexible cord listed for extra-hard usage and terminated with listed fittings. An additional conductor for grounding shall be included in the flexible cord.
(6) Flexible cord listed for extra-hard usage.
(7) For elevator use, an identified elevator cable.

501.10(B))(3). Nonincendive field wiring is permitted using any of the wiring methods permitted for unclassified locations.

Separate nonincendive field wiring circuits shall be installed in accordance with one of the following:

(1) In separate cable.
(2) In multiconductor cables where the conductors of each circuit are within a grounded metal shield.
(3) In multiconductor cables or raceways, where the conductors of each circuit have insulation with a minimum thickness of 0.01".

Author's note: We need to understand about the meaning and application of nonincendive circuits in Division 2 locations. It is important to understand what the term means.

Most equipment that has been tested and listed as being nonincendive are *battery-operated* self-contained items. They are permitted to be used in a Class I, Division 2 location because a hazardous condition is not likely to exist in such an area except under *abnormal* circumstances.

A piece of nonincendive equipment is not permitted to be used in a Class I, Division 1 location because if damaged, the equipment could possibly ignite a hazardous gas or vapor present there. But the probability of a hazardous atmosphere being present in a Class I, Division 2 is low. The probability of such catastrophic failure of the nonincendive circuit is also low.

A nonincendive component is one having contacts for making or breaking an incendive circuit and the contacting mechanism constructed so that the component is incapable of igniting the specified flammable gas or vapor air mixture.

A nonincendive circuit is one in which any arc or thermal effect produced, under *intended operating conditions* of the equipment or due to opening, shorting, or grounding of field wiring, is not capable, under specified test conditions, of igniting the flammable gas, vapor, or dust-air mixture.

Many of the items listed as nonincendive involve hand-held instruments and process control and instrumentation.

The word "nonincendive" is not found in very many dictionaries. It means **not** capable of causing ignition under *normal* conditions of operation.

501.10(B)(4). Boxes, fittings, and joints are **not** required to be explosionproof **except** when explosionproof enclosures are required because they contain control devices, circuit breakers, motor starters, alarms, or similar devices that have make-and-break contacts.

501.15. When installing electrical equipment in a Class I location, it is usually necessary to use seal fittings to prevent the transmission of hazardous gases or vapors from one part of the system to the other, and to contain an explosion (pressure piling) that occurs within an enclosure from affecting the rest of the system. If the explosionproof enclosure does not house an ignition-capable part, and the conduit system is 1 1/2" or smaller, a seal is not required at the enclosure.

501.15(A)(1). In Class I, Division 1 locations, conduit seals shall be located in each conduit entry into an explosionproof enclosure where either of the following apply:

(1) The enclosure contains switches, breakers, fuses, relays, or resistors that exceed 80% of the autoignition temperature, in degrees Celsius, of the gas or vapor involved in normal operation.

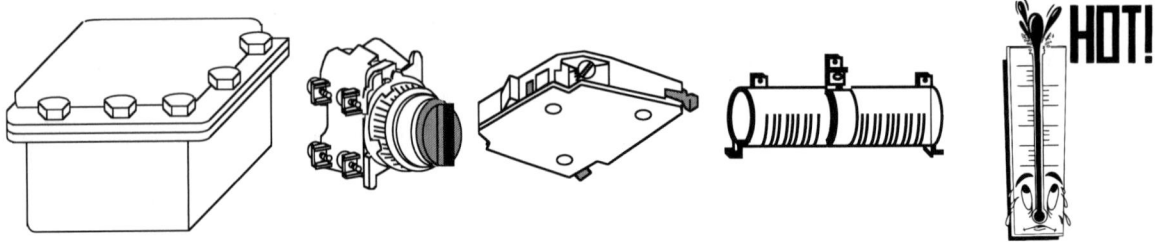

501.15(A)(1)(1). High temperatures shall be considered to be any temperature exceeding 80% of the autoignition temperature in degrees Celsius of the gas or vapor involved.

80%   HOT! IGNITION °C

(2) The conduit entry is 2" or larger and the enclosures contains terminals, splices, or taps.

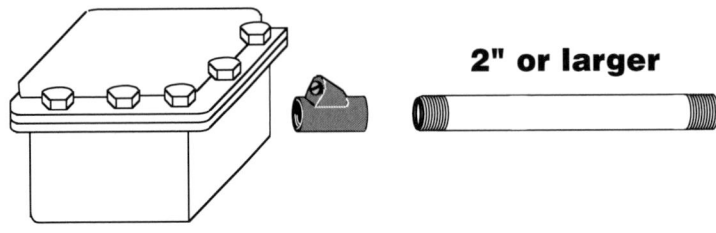

2" or larger

501.15(A)(1) Exception. The exception states seals are not required for conduits entering enclosures with switches, relays, breakers, fuses, or resistors with one of the following:

(1) Are enclosed within a chamber of hermetically sealed against the entrance of gases or vapors.

(2) Are immersed in oil.

(3) The switch, circuit breaker, fuse, relay, or resistor is enclosed within an enclosure, identified for the location, and marked "Leads Factory Sealed," or "Factory Sealed," "Seal not Required," or equivalent.

(4) Are in nonincendive circuits.

Factory-sealed enclosures shall not be considered to serve as a seal for another adjacent explosionproof enclosure that is required to have a conduit seal.

501.15(A)(2). Conduit seals shall be installed within 18" of the enclosure.

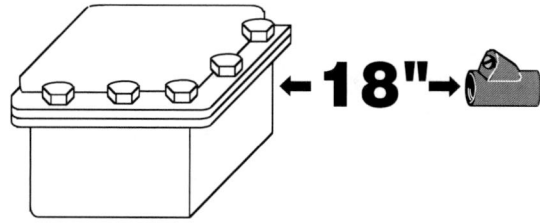

Only threaded couplings, or explosionproof fittings such as unions, couplings, reducers, elbows, capped elbows, and conduit bodies similar to L, T, and Cross types that are not larger than the conduit are the only enclosures or fittings permitted between the seal and the enclosure.

501.15(A)(2). A conduit seal must be placed in each conduit entering a pressurized enclosure where the conduit is not pressurized as part of the protection system. The seal must be within 18" of the enclosure.

501.15(A)(3). Where two explosionproof enclosures are connected by a conduit not over 3' in length, a single seal is permitted provided if it is in the center of the 3'.

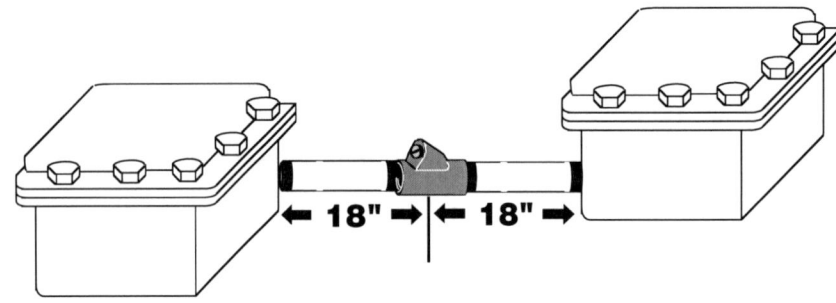

Note: According to UL Hazardous Location Equipment Directory, no splices are permitted within a seal.

501.15(A)(4). This section requires a seal in each and every conduit that leaves the Class I, Division 1 location, whether it passes into a Division 2 location or into a nonhazardous location. This required seal may be installed on either side of the boundry and within 10' of the boundry.

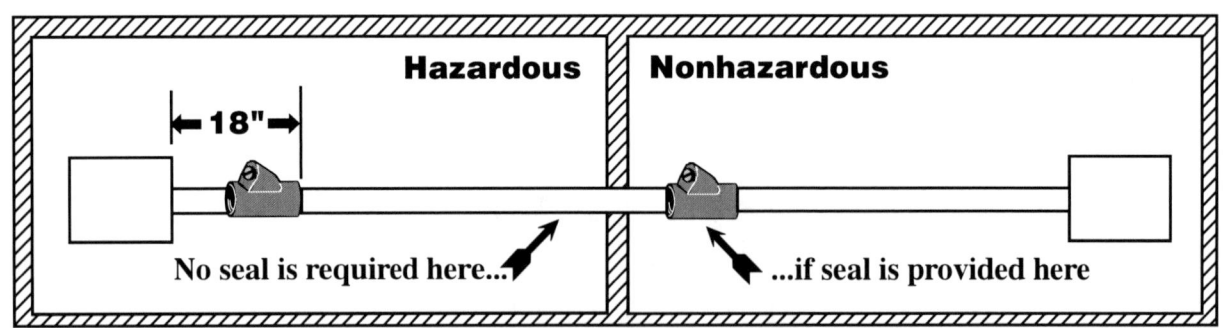

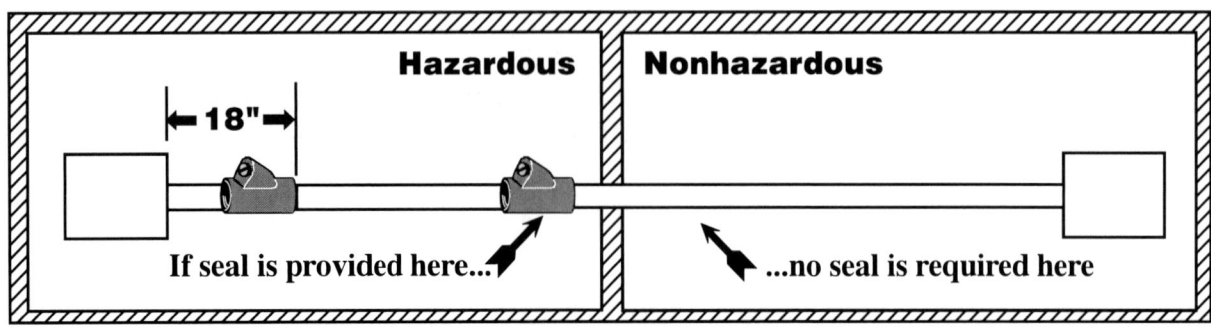

501.15(A)(4) Exception 1. This exception covers the installation where a metal conduit system passes from a nonhazardous area, runs through a Class I, Division 1 hazardous area, and then returns to a nonhazardous area. This is permitted without installing a seal at either of the boundries where it enters or leaves the hazardous area provided the conduit has no unions, couplings, boxes, or fittings extending 12" into each nonhazardous area.

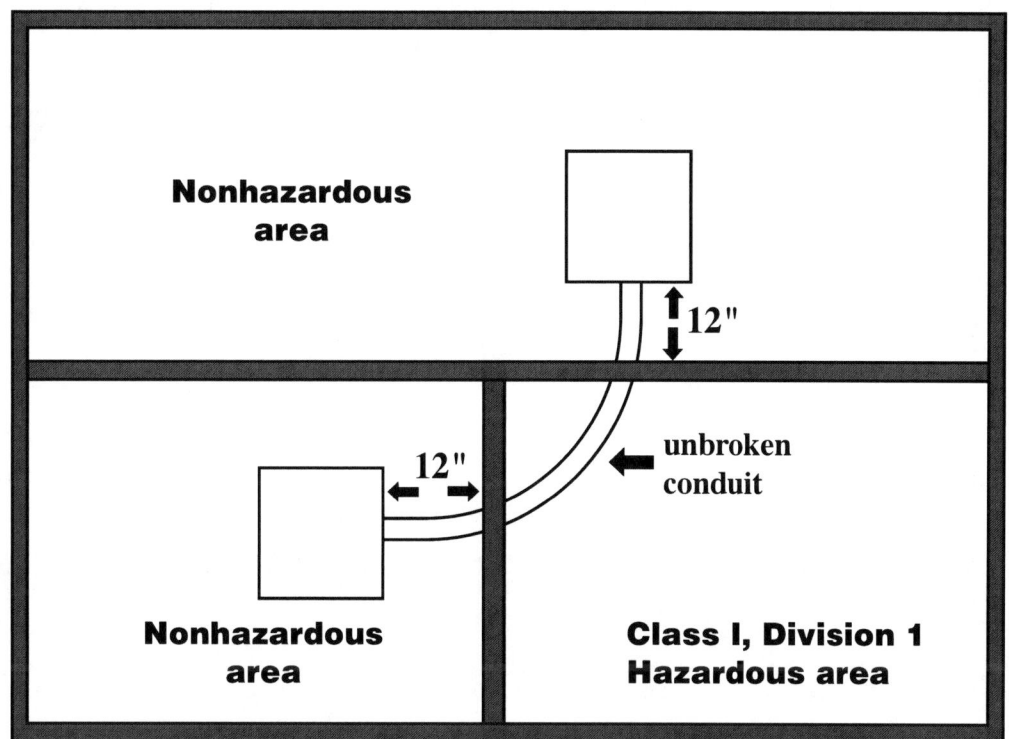

 •**Author's note**: Explosionproof enclosures often use special high-strength bolts. Substitution of an equivalent size bolt of a different strength can reduce the effectiveness of the enclosure. The bolt strength is usually indicated by a coded marking on the head of the bolt. A bolt must be replaced with a bolt of the same size and *strength*.

Routine maintenance is always required because many hazardous locations are also corrosive locations.

501.15(A)(4) Exception 2. For underground conduit installed where the boundry is below the grade, the sealing fitting shall be permitted to be installed after the conduit emerges from below grade, but there shall be no union, coupling, box, or fitting, other than explosionproof reducers at sealing fittings, in the conduit between the sealing fitting and the point at which the conduit emerges from below grade.

The exception is provided due to the impossibility of being able to install and fill a seal underground. Where the boundary with Class I, Division 1 is below the grade, the Code permits the sealing fitting to be installed after the conduit emerges from below grade.

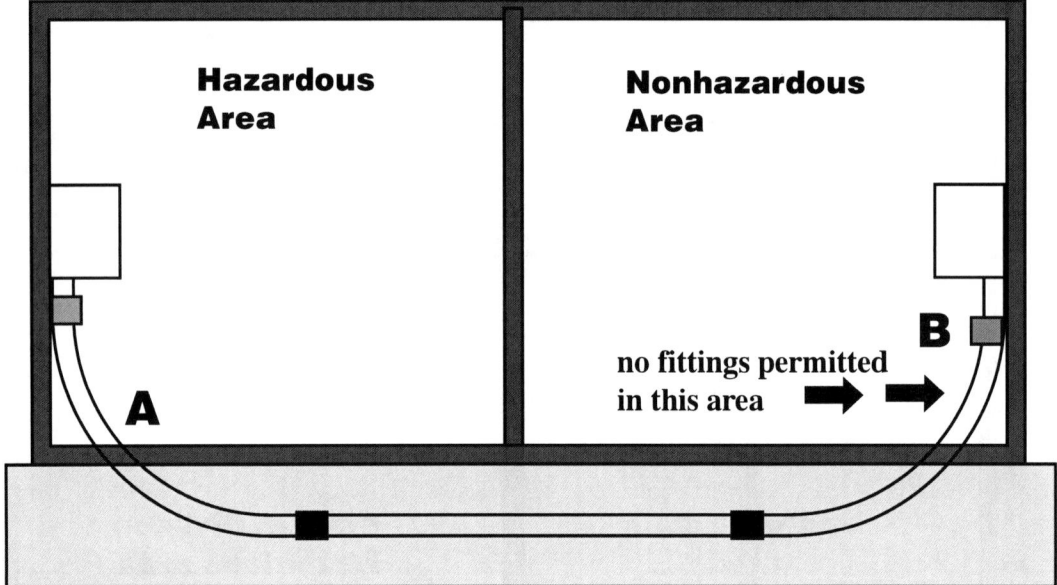

Hazardous Area

Nonhazardous Area

B

no fittings permitted in this area ➡ ➡

A

Author's note: The Code provides no definition of *boundary*. The inspection authority should be consulted in cases not covered by the Code. Always remember, there are no provisions in the Code that prohibit the use of seals, when in doubt, install a seal. Some authorities may require seals at both **A** and **B**. With a seal at **A** and not at **B**, a heavier-than-air gas or liquid (such as gasoline) might penetrate a crack in the floor, enter the conduit through a coupling, and pass into the enclosure in the nonhazardous area.

Or, a seal at **B** but not at **A** might not prevent vapor in the conduit from entering the nonhazardous area through a coupling in the concrete and then through a crack in that floor. That has happened in the past.

With the sketch above, the argument could be made, it would be best to install a seal at both locations **A** and **B**.

A   **B**

501.15(B)(1). Class I, Division 2, connections entering enclosures that are required to be explosionproof are required to have a seal installed under the same rules as Class I, Division 1.

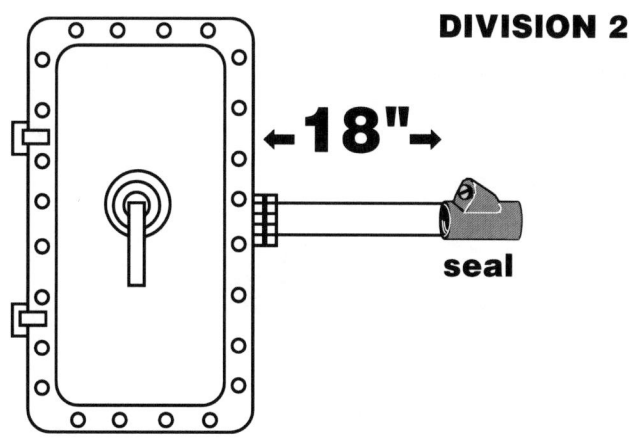

DIVISION 2

←18"→

seal

501.15(B)(2). Class I, Division 2 boundary, the seal is permitted on either the Division 2 or nonhazardous side of the boundary. It must be installed in a manner that will minimize the gas or vapor that can enter the conduit system within the Division 2 location and be communicated beyond the seal.

Rigid metal conduit or threaded IMC conduit must be used between the sealing fitting and the point at which the conduit leaves the Division 2 location.

A threaded connection must be used at the sealing fitting, and no fittings, unions, etc. except an explosionproof reducer at the sealing fitting can be installed between the sealing fitting and the point at which the conduit leaves the Division 2 location.

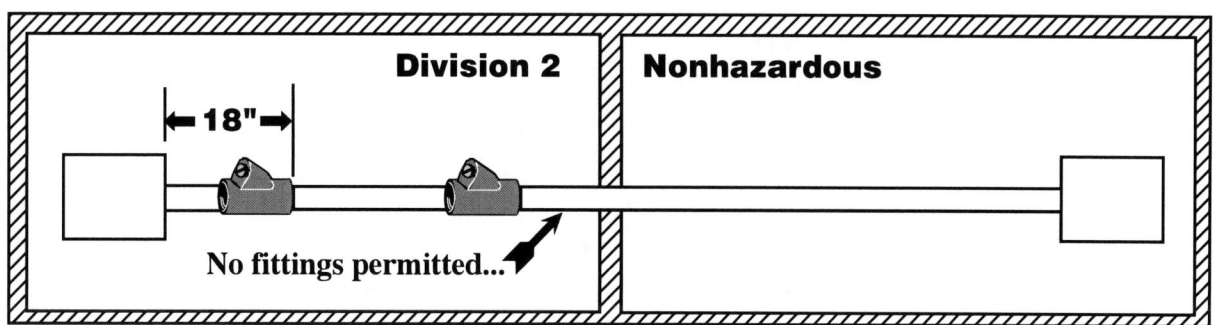

Division 2   Nonhazardous

←18"→

No fittings permitted...

501.15(B)(2) Exception 1. A continuous run of metal conduit passing completely through a Class I, Division 2 location without any fittings within the Division 2 location, and not less than 12" beyond each of the boundaries, is not required to be sealed if both ends are in nonhazardous locations.

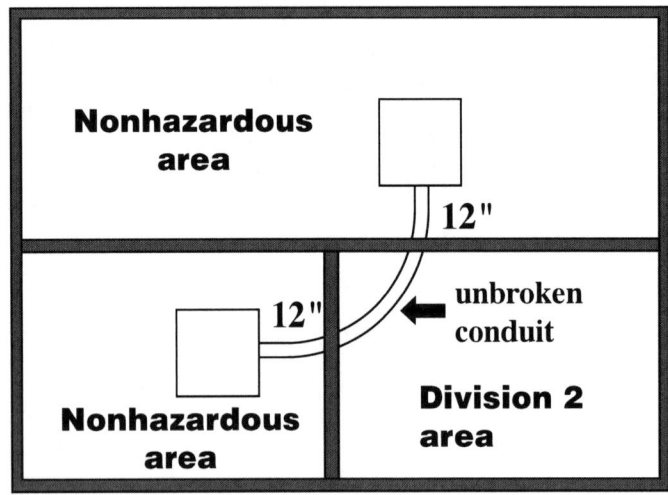

501.15(B)(2) Exception 2. No seal is needed in the conduit run from a Division 2 to a nonhazardous area where a transition is made in the nonhazardous location from a conduit to cable tray, cablebus, ventilated busway, Type MI cable or open wiring.

The principle here is that a Division 2 location is one that seldom contains the hazardous atmosphere. This, in combination with an outdoor termination to a wiring method that is incapable of serving as a means of conducting the hazardous agent, means that chance of ignition is very slight.

No seal is required where the transmission is made *indoors* if the conduit system is in *one room* and the conduit does not terminate in an enclosure containing an ignition source.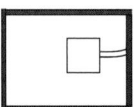

This assumes that only part of a large room is classified as Division 2 and the rest of the room is nonhazardous. Here, the transmission of the hazardous atmosphere in case of accidental release is not limited by walls, by not having a seal would not contribute greatly to the increased hazard in the nonhazardous area.

501.15(B)(2) Exception 3. Conduit systems passing from an enclosure or room that is nonhazardous as a result of pressurization into a Class I, Division 2 location shall not require a seal at the boundary.

501.15(B)(2) Exception 4. Segments of aboveground conduit systems shall not be required to be sealed where passing from a Class I, Division 2 location into an unclassified (nonhazardous) location if all of the following conditions are met:

(1) No part of the conduit system passes through a Class I, Division 1 location where the conduit contains unions, couplings, boxes, or fittings *within 12" of the Division 1 location.*

 **←12"→ Class I**

(2) The conduit system segment in the unclassified (nonhazardous) location is run entirely in outdoor locations.

(3) The conduit system is not directly connected to canned pumps, process or service connections for flow, pressure or analysis measurement instruments that depend on a single compression seal, diaphragm, or tube to prevent flammable or combustible fluids from entering the conduit system.

(4) The conduit system contains only threaded metal conduit, unions, couplings, conduit bodies, and fittings in the unclassified (nonhazardous) area.

(5) The conduit system segment is sealed at its entry to each enclosure or fitting housing terminals, splices, or taps in the Class I, Division 2 locations.

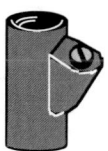

501.15(C). Class I, Divisions 1 and 2 seals shall comply with the following:

(1) Where sealing is required, approved sealing fittings or sealing fittings built into enclosures must be used. The sealing fitting must be listed for use with one or more specific compounds. The sealing fittings must be installed in an accessible location,

LISTED 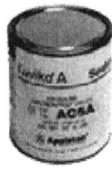 **ACCESSIBLE**

(2) The sealing compound must be of a type approved for the conditions of use and must not have a melting point less than 93°C (200°F). Unless otherwise specifically indicated in the instructions with the product, a sealing compound made by a manufacturer **A** should not be used with a sealing fitting made by a manufacturer **B**.

(3) Except for listed cable sealing fittings, in a completed seal, the thickness of the sealing compound must not be less than the trade size of the conduit, and in no case less than 5/8".

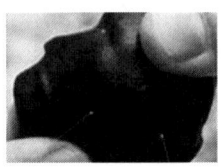 **5/8" MINIMUM**

(4) The Code prohibits splices and taps from being located within a sealing fitting.

VIOLATION

(5) Assemblies consisting of an enclosure containing items that may produce arc, sparks, or high temperatures, and a separate compartment for splices and taps, and an integral seal where conductors pass from one compartment to the other, must have the entire assembly approved for Class I locations. Seals must be provided in 2" or larger conduit connections to the compartment containing splices or taps. The sealing fitting must be located within 18" of the compartment.

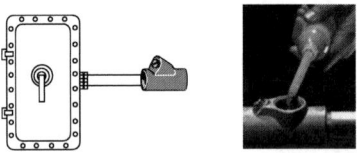

(6) The cross-sectional area of the conductors permitted in a seal must not exceed 25% of the cross-sectional area of the rigid metal conduit of the same trade size as the trade size of the sealing fitting, unless the sealing fitting is specifically approved for a higher percentage of fill. This Code rule exists because it is very difficult to force sealing material between conductors in a seal when the percentage is only 25%, and it is almost impossible when the the percentage of fill is higher.

25% CSA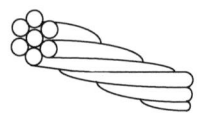

501.15(D). Class I, Division 1 cable seals. Multiconductor Type MC-HL cable with a gas/vaportight continuous corrugated metallic sheath and an overall jacket of suitable polymeric material must have the jacket and sheath removed, an approved fitting installed, and sealing compound poured to surround each individual insulated conductor in a manner that will minimize the passage of gas or vapor at all terminations.

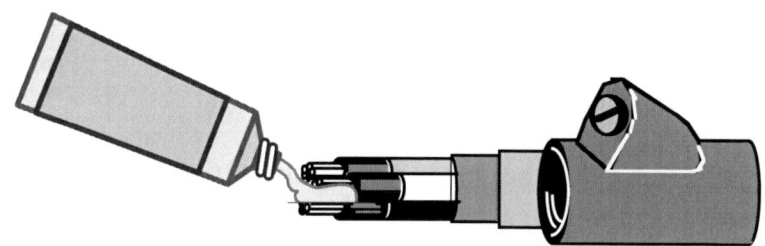

Multiconductor cable in conduit having a gas/vaportight continuous metallic or nonmetallic sheath capable of transmitting gases or vapors through the cable core, must be sealed in a Class I, Division 1 location after removing the jacket and any other coverings so that the sealing compound will surround each individual insulated conductor and the outer jacket.

Seals for cables entering enclosures shall be installed within 18" of the enclosure or as required by the enclosure marking. Only explosionproof unions, couplings, reducers, elbows, and capped elbows that are not larger than the trade size of the enclosure entry shall be permitted between the sealing fitting and the enclosure.

When several multiconductor cables are installed in a conduit, each is considered to be a single conductor if the cables are incapable of transmitting gases or vapors through the cable core. Also, a cable is permitted to be treated as a single conductor if: the cable is sealed in the conduit within 18" of the enclosure; and the cable end within the enclosure is sealed by an approved means to minimize the entrances of gas or vapor and prevent the propagation of flame into the cable core.

501.15(D)(1) Exception: Shielded cables and twisted pair cables do not require that the shield be removed or that the twisted insulated conductors be separated.

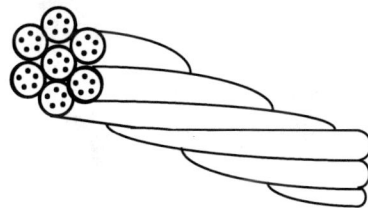

501.15(E). Class I, Division 2 cable seals. The requirements for cable sealing in Division 2 are somewhat more complex than Division 1, because other cable wiring systems are permitted. Consideration must be given to cable not in conduit as well as cable in conduit.

Cables permitted in Class I, Division 2 locations include cables capable of transmitting gases or vapors through the core of the cable and those not so capable.

When sealing individual conductors in a conduit, the sealing compound is poured around the conductor insulation. Because there are spaces between each strand of a stranded conductor, called the *interstices* (voids) of the conductor strands, a conduit seal does *not* act as a complete block for gases and vapors. It reduces the passage of gases and vapors to a manageable level, provided the end of the conductor is not pressurized so as to force the gas or vapor through the interstices of the strands.

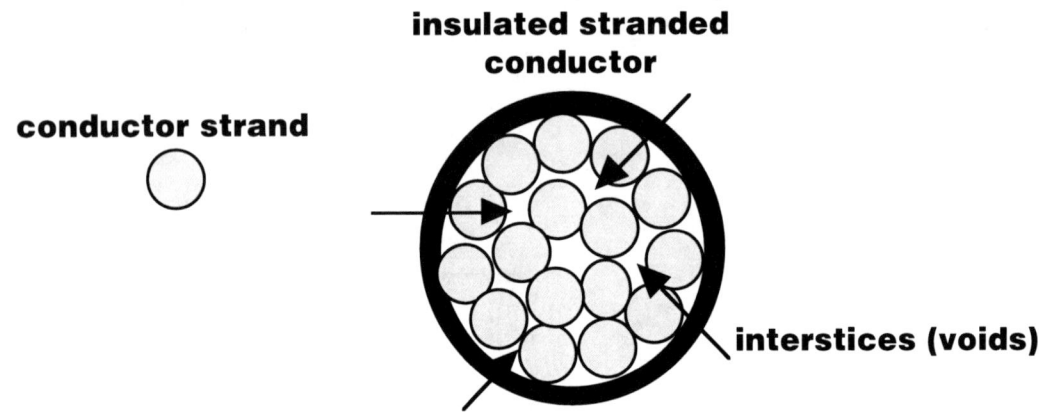

Conductors larger than #2 have sufficient space in the interstices of the strands that can allow an appreciable amount of vapor to escape and even cause small explosions. The strands must be sealed to prevent this vapor escape.

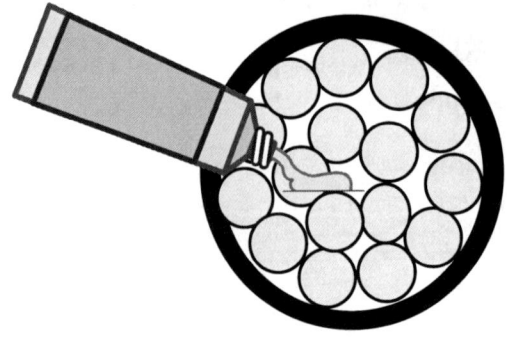

Cable with a continuous sheath either gas/vaportight metal or nonmetallic, that will *not* transmit gases or vapors through the cable core in excess of the quantity permitted for seal fittings, is not required to be sealed where it enters a general-purpose enclosure. The cable core does not include the interstices of the conductor strands. The cable core may be closed up by other elements of the cable, such as fillers to make the cable round. The cable may be capable or incapable of transmitting gases or vapors through the cable core.

multiconductor cable

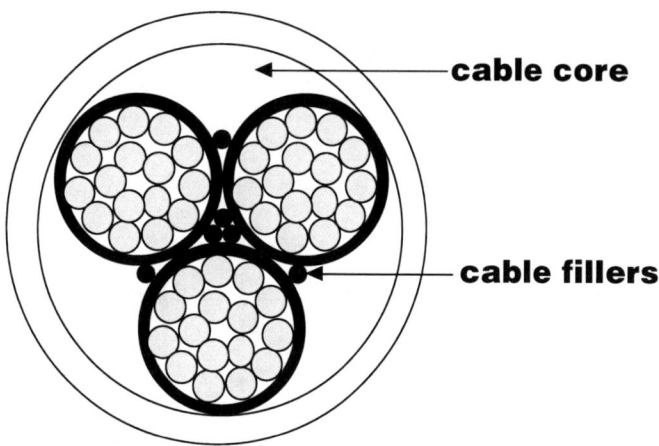

cable core

cable fillers

The minimum continuous length of cable that can be used for a run is the length that limits the gas or vapor flow through the cable core to the permitted rate through seal fittings.

Even sheathed cable that is capable of transmitting gases or vapors is not required to be sealed unless it is attached to process equipment or devices that may cause a pressure in excess of 6" of water (1500 pascals) to be applied to the cable end. If the pressure is higher, a seal, barrier, or other means must be provided to prevent the migration of flammables into an nonhazardous location.

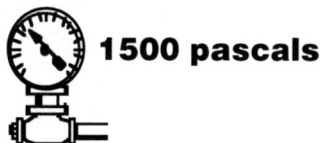

1500 pascals

If the cable is constructed in such a manner, or the installation has a number of bends and clamps in a vertical or horizontal run, that will actually make the core equivalent to a conduit seal, the cable is considered a gas-blocking cable not capable of passing gases or vapors through its core. Some cables are specifically designed and listed as gas-blocking cables.

•The definition of **pascal**: a unit of pressure in the meter-kilogram-second system equivalent to one newton per square meter.

In Class I, Division 2 locations, a seal at the boundary of the Division 2 and nonhazardous location is not required if the cable is sealed at the enclosure and has a continuous gas/vaportight sheath.

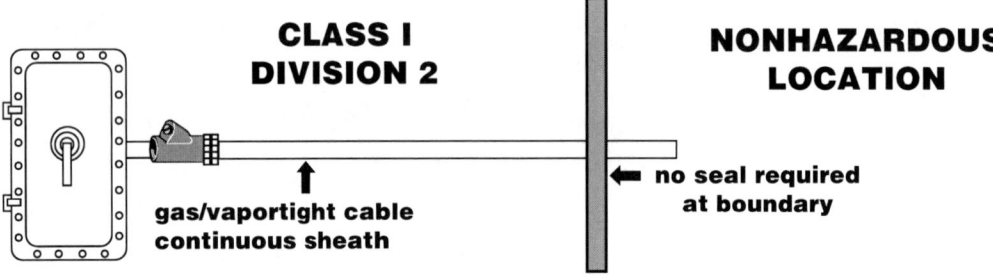

If the cable does *not* have a continuous gas/vaportight sheath, for example, Type MC cable, the seal is required at the boundary.

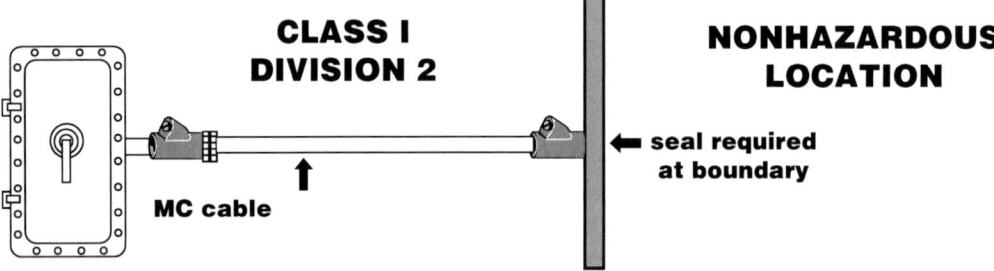

If the cable is capable of transmitting gases or vapors through the cable core, and the end of the cable is pressurized in excess of 1500 pascals, a seal is required between the enclosure and the boundary.

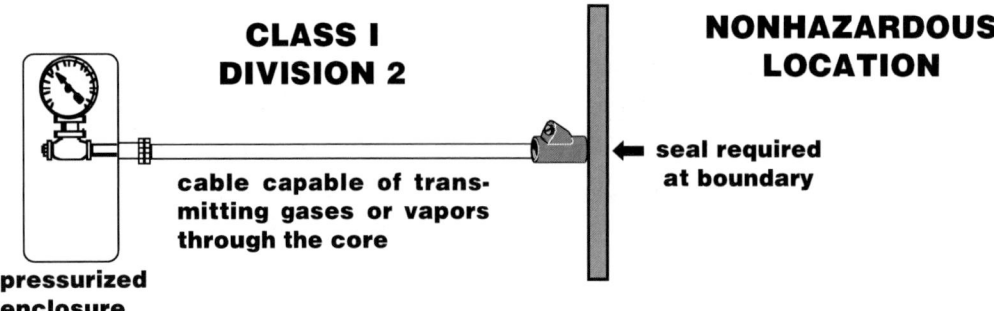

501.15(F)(1). No conduit system with fittings and enclosures is completely airtight. Air will be drawn into it and pushed out periodically due to thermal expansion and contraction of the enclosed air due to changes in the ambient temperature and the heat from the current carrying conductors.

Where there is probability that liquid can be trapped within control equipment enclosures or in conduit systems, approved drain fittings must be installed to permit the enclosure to be drained periodically.

Drain breather installed to drain water formed by condensation

501.15(F)(2). Where there is a probability in the judgement of the authority having jurisdiction that a liquid could accumulate within motors or generators, joints and conduit systems must be arranged to minimize its entrance. Drains must be provided at the time of manufacture and are considered to be an integral part of the machine.

501.17. For instrumentation, canned pumps, pressure switches, thermocouple, or other process instrumentation that depend upon a single compression seal, diaphragm, or tube, must have a drain installed beyond the sealing fitting, barrier or other means used to prevent transmission of flammable of combustible process fluids from entering an attached electrical conduit or cable system.

501.17(1). There shall be a vent or drain between the single process seal and the suitable barrier. Indication of the single process seal failure shall be provided by visible leakage, an audible whistle, or other means of monitoring.

Author's note: Accumulation of condensed water in conduit systems can be reduced by properly sloping all conduits and install drain fittings at the low points. A drain fitting can be installed on the bottom of an enclosure as a drain, or on top of an enclosure to provide ventilation.

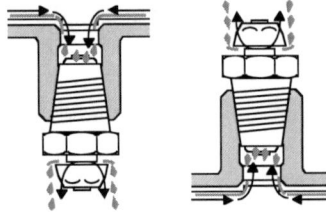

501.20. In Class I, Divisions 1 and 2, it is important to use conductor and cable insulations that will **not** be attacked by the process fluids. Where condensed vapors or liquids may collect on, or come in contact with, the insulation must be of a type identified for the conditions used. The insulation may be required to be protected by a lead sheath or other approved means.

501.25. There shall be no uninsulated exposed parts, such as conductors, buses, terminals, or components, that operate at more than 30 volts (15 volts in wet locations.)

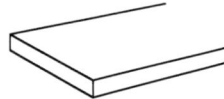

501.30. Grounding and bonding in Class I, Division 1 and 2 locations shall be grounded as specified in Article 250 and:

(a) In hazardous locations it is mandated that bonding jumpers with proper fittings, or other approved means of bonding, be used. Double locknuts and locknut-and-bushing combinations are *not* permitted to be depended upon for this purpose.

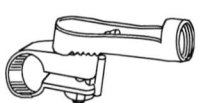

(b) Where flexible metal conduit or liquidtight metal conduit is relied upon as the only **equipment grounding path**, properly sized internal or external bonding jumpers must be run with each conduit.

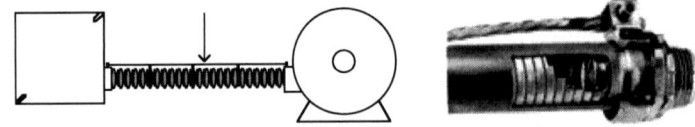

Exception: In Class I, Division 2 locations, the bonding jumper can be omitted where the following are met:
(1) Listed liquidtight flexible metal conduit 6' or less in length.
(2) Overcurrent protection is 10 amps or less.
(3) The load is not a power utilization load.

 **Author's note**: All connections of conduit to boxes, enclosures, etc. must be made to secure a permanent and **effective grounding path** to prevent the possibility of arcs or sparks. This form of installation is not only necessary in the areas classed as hazardous, but should also be carried out back to the point where the connection for grounding the conduit is made to the grounding electrode system serving the premises.

In nonhazardous areas outside the hazardous area, threaded connections should be used for conduit, unless bonding techniques are used for connections to knockouts in sheet metal enclosures. Any conduit emerging from a Class I, Division 1 or 2 location must have a bonding path of **equipment grounding** from the hazardous location back to the bonded service equipment, to the bonded secondary of a transformer that supplies the circuit into the hazardous location, or, as covered in the exception, under certain conditions, to the bonded main building disconnect.

This requires *service bonding* throughout the length of a continuous path from the raceway and equipment in a hazardous location all the way back to the *first* point at which the system neutral is bonded to the system equipment grounding terminal and both are connected to a grounding electrode, either at the transformer or at the service equipment if there is no voltage change in the system.

This means that every raceway termination in the ground return path to the service must be a threaded metal conduit connection to a threaded hub. Any connection to a sheet metal knockout must use one of the following methods:

(1) A locknut outside with a bonding locknut inside where connection is made to a *clean* knockout. A clean knockout is one with *no* concentric or eccentric rings.

 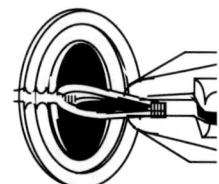

(2) A bonding bushing with a bonding jumper to a grounding terminal within the enclosure, on a knockout that is clean *or* has concentric or eccentric rings left in the wall.

(3) A bonding bushing that does not require a jumper when used on a clean knockout.

501.35. Surge arresters (and surge protective devices and capacitors) in Class I, Division 1 locations must be mounted in enclosures approved for Class I, Division 1 locations.

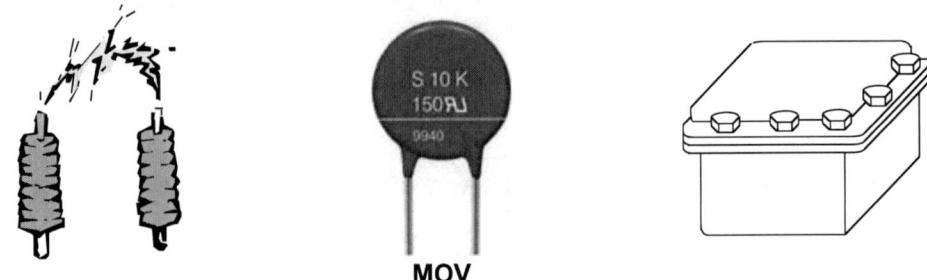

MOV

Surge arresters in Class I, Division 2 locations must be of the non-arcing type such as metal-oxide varistors (MOV) and sealed types. They must be mounted in enclosures that can be of the general-purpose type. Surge arresters other than the non-arcing types must be mounted in enclosures approved for Class I, Division 1 locations.

Part III. Equipment

501.100(A)(1). Transformers or capacitors containing a liquid that will burn shall be installed only in vaults that comply with section 450.41 through 450.48 and as follows:

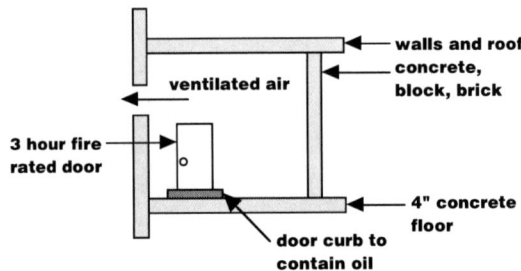

walls and roof concrete, block, brick

ventilated air

3 hour fire rated door

4" concrete floor

door curb to contain oil

(1) No door or other communicating opening is allowed between the vault and the Division 1 location.

(2) Ample ventilation must be provided for the continuous removal of flammable gases or vapors.

(3) Vent openings or ducts must lead to a safe location outside the building.

(4) Vent ducts and openings must be of sufficient area to relieve explosion presures within the vault, and all portions of vent ducts within the buildings must be reinforced concrete construction.

501.100(A)(2). If the liquid contained will not burn, the transformer either must be installed in a vault, or must be approved for Class I locations.

501.105(A). In Class I, Division 1 locations, instrumentation such as ammeters, relays, kWH meters, resistors, rectifiers, etc. are permitted only in explosionproof or purged-and-pressurized enclosures. Often these items are grouped together on control panelboards and enclosure doors. Rules for installation of wiring methods, seals, and others contained in Article 501 must be rigorously applied to the whole system.

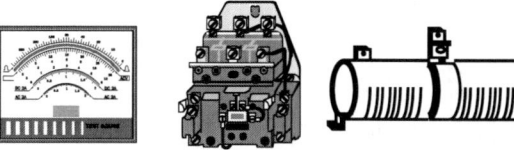

501.105(B). Class I, Division 2 instrumentation shall comply with the following:

(1) Contacts of switches, breakers, and make-and-break contacts of pushbuttons, relays, etc. shall comply with 501.105(B)(2) through (B)(6).

Exception: General-purpose enclosures shall be permitted if current-interrupting contacts comply with one of the following:

(1) Are immersed in oil.

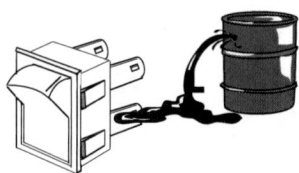

(2) Are enclosed within a chamber that is hermetically sealed against the entrance of gases or vapors.

(3) Are in nonincendive circuits.

(4) Are listed for Division 2.

501.105(B)(3) Exception. Resistors, rectifiers, and similar devices in control or communication circuits are treated similarly to those of power circuits. They must be in enclosures identified for Class I, Division 1 locations unless they are without make-and-break or sliding contacts, and the maximum operating temperature of any exposed surface will not exceed 80% of the ignition temperature of the gas or vapor involved, or have been tested and found incapable of igniting the gas or vapor.

501.105(B)(4). Control transformer windings, impedance coils, solenoids, and other windings that do not have sliding or make-and-break contacts are permitted in general-purpose type enclosures.

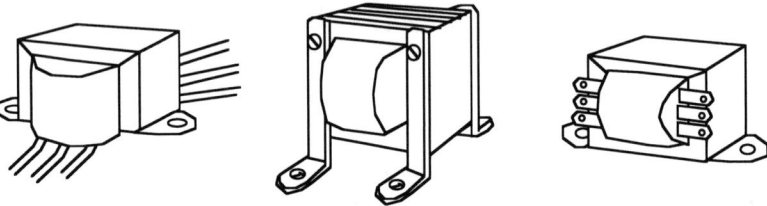

501.105(B)(5). Where general-purpose enclosures are used for fuses in protection of instrument circuits, the fuse shall be preceded by a switch.

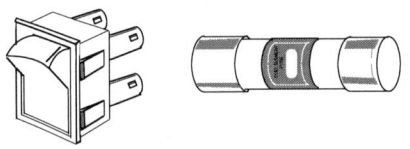

501.105(B)(6). To facilitate replacements, process control instruments shall be permitted to be connected through flexible cord, by means of attachment plug, and receptacle, providing that all of the following conditions apply:

(1) The attachment plug and recptacle are listed for use in Class I, Division 2 locations and listed for use with flexible cords and shall be of the locking and grounding type.

Exception: A Class I, Division 2 listing is not be required if the circuit involves only nonincendive field wiring.

(2) The power-supply cord cannot exceed 3', must be approved for extra-hard usage (or hard usage if protected by location).

(3) Only immediately necessary receptacles must be provided. In other words, no receptacles are to be mounted in anticipation that an instrument will be located there in the future.

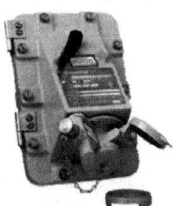

(4) The attachment plug and receptacle are interlocked mechanically or electrically, or otherwise designed so that they cannot be separated when the contacts are energized and the contacts cannot not be energized when the plug and socket are separated, a switch complying with 501.105(B)(2) is provided so that the attachment plug or receptacle is not depended on to interrupt current.

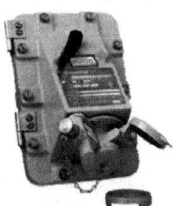

Exception: The switch shall not be required if the circuit is nonincendive field wiring.

501.115(A). Class I, Division 1 locations, switches, breakers, fuses, motor controllers, pushbuttons, relays and similar devices that interrupt current, are potential arc-producing devices and thus potential hazards when installed in Class I locations. This equipment must be in an enclosure approved for use in Class I locations.

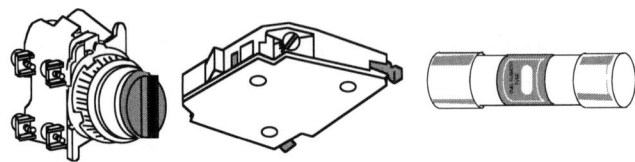

501.115(B)(1). Class I, Division 2 locations. Breakers, motor controllers, and switches that interrupt current in a normal performance must be installed in enclosures approved for Class I, Division 1 locations.

These devices are also permitted to be installed in general-purpose enclosures if:
(1) The interruption of current occurs within a chamber that is hermetically sealed against the entrance of gases and vapors.

(2) The make-and-break contacts are oil-immersed and the contacts that interrupt power circuits have a 2" minimum immersion, 1" for contacts that interrupt control circuits.

(3) The interruption occurs within a factory-sealed explosionproof chamber approved for the location, and marked "Leads Factory Sealed," or "Factory Sealed," "Seal not Required," or equivalent.

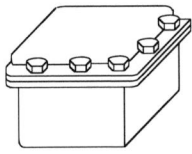

(4) The device is solid-state (without contacts) and its surface temperature does not exceed 80% of the ignition temperature in °C of the gas or vapor involved.

80%   **HOT!**   **IGNITION °C**

501.115(B)(2). In Division 2 locations, disconnects and isolating switches, fused or unfused, that are not intended to interrupt current of transformers or capacitor banks in normal performance of the function for which they are installed, are permitted to have a general-purpose enclosure.

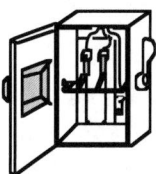

501.115(B)(3). In Division 2 locations, standard plug or cartridge fuses for the protection of motors, appliances, lighting, etc., are required to be within an enclosure approved for Division 2 locations. They are permitted to be installed in a general-purpose enclosure if the operating element is immersed in oil or other approved liquid; the operating element is enclosed within a chamber that is hermetically sealed against the entrance of gases and vapors; or the fuse is a nonindicating, filled, current-limiting type.

 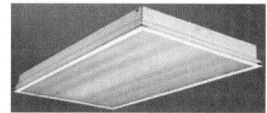

501.115(B)(4). Approved cartridge fuses are permitted as supplementary protection within luminaires.

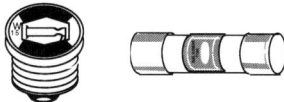

501.120(A). In Class I, Division 1 locations control transformers, resistors, impedance coils, etc., are often in control circuitry. By themselves, they are not current interrupting devices, but may have associated arcing devices. The control transformers and other devices, along with any switching mechanisms associated with them, must be installed in an enclosure approved for a Class I, Division 1 location.

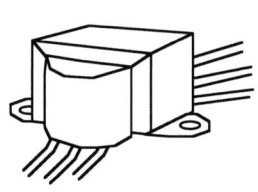 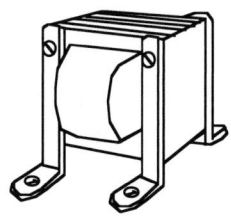 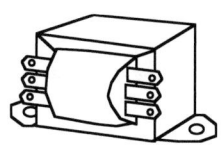 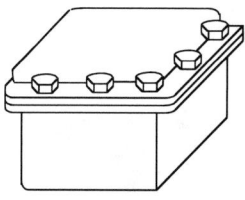

501.120(B)(1). In Class I, Division 2 locations, switching mechanisms must be approved for Division 1 locations.

501.120(B)(2). Coils and windings are permitted to be in a general-purpose type enclosure.

501.120(B)(3). Resistors must be provided with enclosures. The assembly must be approved for Class I locations unless the resistance is nonvariable and the maximum operating temperature in °C will not exceed 80% of the ignition temperature of the gas or vapor involved or it has been tested and found incapable of igniting the gas or vapor.

501. 125(A). In Class I, Division 1 locations, motors, generators, and other rotating electric machinery shall be one of the following:
(1) Identified (not just approved) for Class I, Division 1 locations.

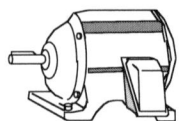 **IDENTIFIED CLASS I DIVISION 1**

The definition of identified (as applied to equipment) is: Recognizable as suitable for the specific purpose, function, use, environment, application, and so forth, where described in a particular *Code* requirement.

Note: Some examples of ways to determine suitability of equipment for a specific purpose, environment, or application include investigations by a qualified testing laboratory (listing and labeling), an inspection agency, or other organizations concerned with product evaluation.

 **IDENTIFIED**

 **Author's note**: Manufacturers have found that it is impractical to build electric motors and generators for use in Group A and Group B locations, not only for the small demand, but maintaining the extremely close tolerance between the rotating shaft and the housing is impractical. This does not mean they can't be designed. Motors and generators suitable for Group C and D locations are quite limited also. Due to the cost of explosionproof equipment, it is desirable to design an installation so that a minimum of explosionproof equipment is needed.

501.125(A)(2). Motors that are totally enclosed with positive-pressure ventilation from a source of clean air with discharge to a safe area. The Code does not include a specific definition of purged or pressurized equipment. The Code description is: The controls must be arranged so that the unit cannot be energized before it has been purged with at least 10 volumes of air, and automatically de-energizes the unit when the air supply fails. Clean air is the most common gas used where a continuous flow is maintained. The surface temperature of the unit while operating must not exceed 80% of the ignition temperature of the gas or vapor involved, and must be automatically de-energized or an alarm must sound if there is an increase above that limit. The auxiliary devices must be of a type identified for the location in which they are installed.

501.125(A)(3). Motors of the totally enclosed inert gas-filled type must be supplied with a reliable source of inert gas for pressurizing the enclosure. Controls must be provided so the unit will be automatically de-energized if its gas supply fails or does not maintain a positive pressure in the enclosure.

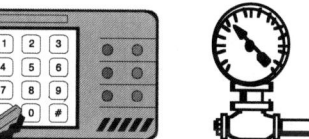

501.125(A)(4). For machines that are for use only in industrial establishments with restricted public access, where the conditions of maintenance and supervision ensure that only qualified persons service the installation, the machine is permitted to be of a type designed to be submerged in a liquid that is flammable only when mixed with air, or in a gas or vapor at a pressure greater than atmospheric and which is flammable only when mixed with air. The controls of the machine must be arranged so that it cannot be energized before it has been purged with the liquid or gas to exclude air, and will automatically de-energize the equipment when the supply of liquid, gas, or vapor fails or its pressure is reduced to atmospheric.

AIR

501.125(B). Class I, Division 2 motors with sliding contacts, centrifugal switches, integral resistance devices, or similar items, must be *identified* for Class I, Division 1 locations unless the contacts are provided with an enclosure *identified* for a Division 2 location.

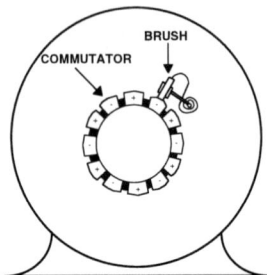

Space heaters used to prevent condensation of moisture during shutdown periods must have an exposed surface that does not exceed 80% of the ignition temperature (in °C) of the gas or vapor involved when operated at rated voltage.

The installer must check the motor nameplate, which must be marked with the maximum surface temperature based on 40°C (104°F) of the heater when operating at rated voltage, and the maximum space heater surface temperature (based on a 40°C or higher marked ambient) shall be permanently marked on a visible nameplate mounted on the motor. Otherwise, a heater *identified* for a Class I, Division 2 location must be used.

Nonexplosionproof motors in Class I, Division 2 locations are permitted provided they do not contain brushes, switching mechanisms, or similar arc-producing devices. An example would be a squirrel-cage induction motor.

SQUIRREL CAGE

Author's note: Before installing a motor in a Class I, Division 2 location, it is important to consider the temperature of internal surfaces that could be exposed to the flammable atmosphere.

Ignition due to arcing and overheating between adjoining sections of large induction motors and generators is possible. Such equipment may require equipotential bonding jumpers between sections and to ground.

Definition of equipotential: having the same potential: of uniform potential throughout.

Where the presence of ignitable gases or vapors is possible, clean air purging prior to and during start-up periods should be considered.

501.130(A)(1). When installing luminaires in a Class I, Division 1 location, the installer should verify that each luminaire is *identified* for the Class I, Division 1 location and marked to show the *maximum wattage* permitted for the lamps in the luminaire.

CLASS I, DIVISION 1

MAXIMUM WATTAGE

501.130(A)(2). Each luminaire shall be protected against physical damage by a suitable guard or by location of the luminaire.

501.130(A)(3). Pendant luminaires are subject to specific rules in mounting. Either threaded rigid metal conduit or threaded IMC stems must be used to support the luminaires. Threaded joints must be provided with setscrews or other effective means to prevent loosening. Stems over 12" long must have permanent and effective bracing against lateral displacement that must be provided at a level not more than 12" above the lower end of the stem or a fitting or flexible connector *identified* for Class I, Division 1 locations must be provided not more than 12" from the point of attachment to its supporting box or fitting.

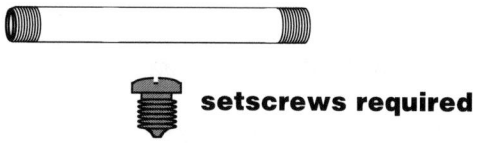

setscrews required

501.130(A)(4). Boxes, box assemblies, or fittings used for the support of luminaires shall be identified for Class I locations.

501.130(B)(1). Class I, Division 2, where lamps are of a size and type that may reach a surface temperature under normal operating conditions exceeding 80% of the ignition temperature (in°C) of the gas or vapor involved, luminaires that are *identified* for a Class I, Division 1 location shall be installed.

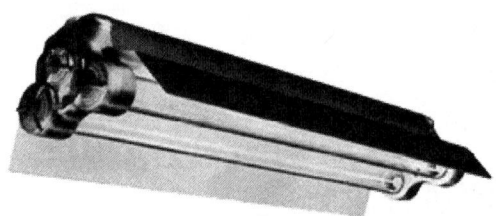

501.130(B)(2). Class I, Division 2 luminaires must be protected from physical damage by suitable guards or by location. Where there is a danger that falling sparks of hot metal from the lamps or luminaires might ignite localized concentrations of flammable vapors or gases, suitable enclosures or other effective means must be provided.

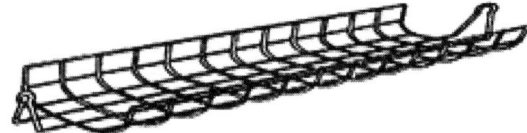

501.130(B)(3). Class I, Division 2 pendant luminaire rules are similar to those for Division 1 locations except they can be suspended not only from threaded rigid conduit or threaded steel IMC, but also by other *approved* means.

Security, bracing and flexibility requirements generally remain the same, except the setscrew requirement for threaded joints is *not* included. Also, flexibility can be provided with an approved fitting or flexible connector that does *not* have to be identified for a Division 1 area.

 **Author's note:** Luminaires in Class I, Division 2 locations are treated somewhat differently from other equipment in Class I, Division 2 locations.

Luminaires are a source of heat and it may be difficult for the installer or inspector to determine if the lamp temperature will exceed the ignition temperature. This was not as difficult years ago as only fluorescent and incandescent luminaires were used, but today we have mercury vapor luminaires involved also.

501.130(B)(4). Portable lighting equipment used in Class I, Division 2 locations must be identified for Class I, Division 1 locations.

Exception: Where portable lighting equipment is mounted on movable stands and is connected by flexible cords, it shall be permitted where protected from physical damage by suitable guards or by location. Where there is a danger that falling sparks of hot metal from the lamps or fixtures might ignite localized concentrations of flammable vapors or gases, suitable enclosures or other effective means must be provided.

501.130(B)(5). Class I, Division 2 switches that are a part of a luminaire or of an individual lampholder shall comply with 501.115(B)(1).

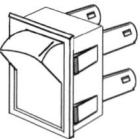

501.130(B)(6). Starting and control equipment for electric-discharge lamps shall comply with 501.120(B).

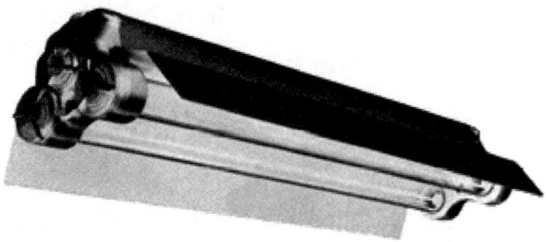

Exception: A thermal protector potted into a thermally protected fluorescent ballast if the luminaire is *identified* for the location.

501.135(A). Class I, Division 1 utilization equipment. This section covers devices that utilize electrical energy other than light fixtures and motors or motor-operated equipment. All equipment must be identified for Class I, Division 1 locations.

501.135(B). In Class I, Division 2 locations, all utilization equipment shall comply with:

(1) Electrically heated utilization equipment must not exceed 80% of the ignition temperature (in°C) of the gas or vapor involved when energized by a voltage of 120% of the heater nameplate rated voltage. An alternative is the heater can be *identified* for a Class I, Division 1 location.

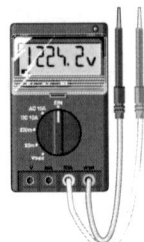

120% of nameplate

Exception 1: An exception is made for motor space heaters used to prevent condensation.

Exception 2: Exempts heaters on circuits containing current-limiting devices that will limit the current in the heater to less than required to raise its surface temperature to 80% of ignition temperature.

Heaters that do not meet the preceding conditions must be *identified* for Class I, Division 1 locations. The exception recognizes electric resistance heat tracing *identified* for Class I, Division 2 locations.

(2) Motors of motor-driven utilization equipment shall comply with 501.125(B).

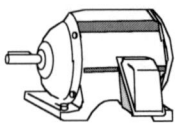

(3) Switches, breakers, and fuses shall comply with 501.115(B).

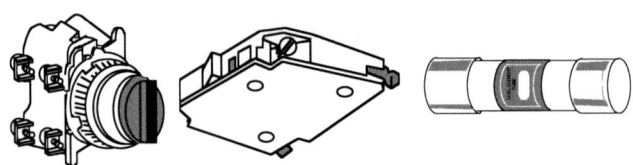

501.140(A). Class I, Divisions 1 and 2 flexible cord shall be permitted:

(1) For connection between portable lighting equipment or other portable utilization equipment and the fixed portion of their supply circuit.

(2) For that portion of the circuit where fixed wiring methods cannot provide the necessary degree of movement for fixed and mobile electrical utilization equipment, and the flexible cord is protected by location or by suitable guard from damage and only in an industrial establishment where conditions of maintenance and engineering supervision ensure that only qualified persons install and service the installation.

Definition: **Qualified person.** One who has skills and knowledge related to the construction and operation of the electrical equipment and installations and has received safety training on the hazards involved.

(3) For electric submersible pumps with means for removal without entering the wet-pit. The extension of the flexible cord within a suitable raceway between the wet-pit and the power source shall be permitted.

(4) For electric mixers intended for travel into and out of open-type mixing tanks or vats.

(5) For temporary portable assemblies consisting of receptacles, switches, and other devices that are not considered portable utilization equipment but are individually listed for the location.

501.140(B). Where flexible cords are used in a Class I, Divsion 1 or 2 location, they shall comply with all of the following:

(1) Be of a type listed for extra-hard usuage.

(2) Contain an **equipment grounding conductor** having a continuous identifying marker readily distinguishing it from other conductors in the cord.

(3) Be supported by clamps or other suitable means in such a manner that there is no tension on the terminal connections.

(4) In Division 1 and Division 2 locations where boxes, fittings, or enclosures are required to be explosionproof, the cord shall be terminated with a cord connector or attachment plug listed for the location or a cord connector installed with a seal listed for the location. In **Division 2 locations** where explosionproof equipment is not required, the cord shall be terminated with a listed cord connector or listed attachment plug.

(5) The cord shall be in a continuous length. For temporary portable assemblies, the cord shall be in a continuous length from the power source to the temporary portable assembly and from the temporary portable assembly to the utilization equipment.

501.145(B). Class I, Division 1 and 2 receptacles and attachment plugs shall be of the type providing for connection to the **equipment grounding conductor** of a flexible cord and shall be identified for the location.

501.150(A). In Class I, Division 1 locations, all apparatus and equipment of signaling, alarm, remote-control, and communications systems, regardless of voltage, shall be identified for Class I, Division 1 locations.

501.150(B). In Class I, Division 2 locations signaling, alarm, remote-control, and communications systems shall comply with:

(1) Switches, breakers, and make-and-break contacts shall have enclosures identified for Class I, Division 1 locations.

Exception: General-purpose enclosures shall be permitted if current-interrupting contacts comply with one of the following:

(1) Are immersed in oil.

(2) Are enclosed within a chamber that is hermetically sealed against the entrance of gases or vapors.

(3) Are in nonincendive circuits.

(4) Part of a listed nonincendive component.

(2) Resistors, resistance devices, thermionic tubes, rectifiers, and similar equipment shall comply with 501.105(B)(3).

(3) Enclosures shall be provided for lightning protective devices and for fuses. General-purpose type is permitted.

(4) All wiring shall comply with 501.10(B), 501.15(B) and 501.15(C).

Articles 500 - 501   Quiz #1   -   Open Book

•*Circle your choice of answer and **write the Code section where it was found**.*

1. Class II locations are those that are hazardous because of _____.

(a) the presence of combustible dust
(b) over 8' depth of water
(c) flammable gases or vapors may be present in the air
(d) easily ignitible fibers are stored or handled

2. In a Class I, Division 2 area, bonding can be accomplished by ____.

I. double locknuts   II. locknut-bushings

(a) I only   (b) II only   (c) both I and II   (d) neither I nor II

3. Where are conduit seals **NOT** required in a Class I installation?

(a) Where metal conduit passes completely through the Class I area with no fittings less than
     12" outside any classified area.
(b) Where a conduit less than 36" in length connects two enclosures.
(c) Where the conduit enters an explosion-proof motor.
(d) Where the conduit exits the Class I area.

4. Pendant fixtures shall be suspended in a Class I location by rigid non-metallic conduit if ____.

I. not more than 12" long   II. braced if over 12" long

(a) I only   (b) II only   (c) both I and II   (d) neither I nor II

5. Class III locations are those that are hazardous because of ____.

(a) the presence of combustible dust
(b) over 8' depth of water
(c) flammable gases or vapors may be present in the air
(d) the presence of easily ignitible fibers or flyings

6. The minimum thickness of the sealing compound in Class I, Division 1 and 2 locations shall not
be less than the trade size of the conduit and in no case less than ____.

(a) 3/16"   (b) 3/8"   (c) 1/2"   (d) 5/8"

Articles 500 - 501 Quiz #1 - Open Book

7. Class I locations are those that are hazardous because of _____.

(a) the presence of combustible dust
(b) over 8' depth of water
(c) flammable gases or flammable liquid produced vapors are or may be present in the air
(d) the presence of easily ignitible fibers or flyings

8. For limited flexibility for motor connections in a Class I, Division 2 location, flexible conduit _____.

(a) must be explosion-proof
(b) must be liquid-tight flexible conduit or equal
(c) may be standard flexible metal conduit with listed fittings
(d) shall not be used

9. Locations where ignitible fibers are stored are designated as _____.

(a) Class II, Division 2
(b) Class III, Division 1
(c) Class III, Division 2
(d) non-hazardous

10. In Class I, Division 1 locations, the Code requires conduit seals adjacent to boxes containing splices if the conduit is equal to or larger than _____.

(a) 3/4" (b) 1 1/2" (c) 1" (d) 2"

11. For general wiring in Class I Division 1, locations it is permissible to use _____.

(a) rigid metal conduit (b) EMT (c) flexible metal conduit (d) all of these

12. Locations where combustible dust is normally in heavy concentrations are designated as _____.

(a) Class I, Division 2   (b) Class II, Division 1
(c) Class II, Division 2   (d) Class III, Division 1

Articles 500 - 501   Quiz #2 - Open Book

•*Circle your choice of answer and* **write the Code section where it was found**.

1. Sealing compound is employed with mineral-insulated cable in a Class I location for the purpose of ____.

(a) preventing passage of gas or vapor
(b) excluding moisture
(c) limiting a possible explosion
(d) preventing escape of powder

2. Totally enclosed motors of Types specified in 501.125(A)(2) or (A)(3) shall have no external surface with an operating temperature in degrees Celsius in excess of ____ of the ignition temperature of the gas or vapor involved.

(a) 100% contained   (b) 80%   (c) 75%   (d) none of these

3. In a Class I, Division 2 location a conduit passing through into a nonhazardous location, the sealing fitting shall be permitted ____.

(a) no seal required under the conditions   (b) on either side of the boundary
(c) on both sides of the boundary   (d) at the first fitting

4. All conduit referred to herein shall be threaded with a/an ____ National Standard Pipe Taper thread.

(a) rigid   (b) NPT   (c) metal   (d) American

5. The Code provides that in Class I, Division 1 locations, conduit seals shall be placed not farther from spark-producing devices than ____ inches.

(a) 18   (b) 24   (c) 12   (d) 30

6. The minimum depth of oil over the power contacts in an oil immersion type switch for use in a Class I, Division 2 location is ___ inches.

(a) 1   (b) 1 1/2   (c) 2   (d) 3

7. In Class II locations, ____ dust may dehydrate or carbonize making them even more dangerous.

(a) plastic   (b) coal   (c) organic   (d) metallic

8. A receptacle is permitted in a Class I, Division 2 circuit if _____.

I.   attachment plug is not depended on to interrupt current
II. current does not exceed 3 amps at 120 volts nominal
III. cord does not exceed 3 feet
IV. only necessary receptacles provided

(a) I and II only   (b) I and IV only   (c) I, II and III only   (d) I, II, III and IV

9. A Class II, Division 1 location is a location in which _____ combustible dusts may be present in quantities sufficient to be hazardous.

(a) Group D   (b) Group E   (c) Group B   (d) Group C

10. The cross-sectional area of the conductors permitted in a seal shall not exceed _____ percent of the cross-sectional area of a rigid metal conduit of the same trade size unless it is specifically identified for a higher percentage of fill.

(a) 25%   (b) 30%   (c) 45%   (d) 50%

11. Enclosures for isolating switches in Class I, Division 2 locations _____.

(a) may be of general-purpose type   (b) must be explosionproof type
(c) must have interlocking devices   (d) may not have doors in hazardous area

12. In a cotton mill, rayon would be classified as a _____.

(a) Group F   (b) Group E   (c) Group A   (d) there are no Groups in Class III locations

ARTICLE 502

Class II
Locations

Part I. General

502.1. Class II locations are where hazardous concentrations of dust exist or can exist. The classification of Class II locations can be considerably more difficult. Dusts do not readily disperse in the same way that gases or vapors tend to.

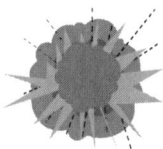

Class II locations are subdivided into three groups. They are based on the electrical resistivity of the dusts, commonly encountered dust particle sizes, and the thermal blanketing effect of dust layers on electrical equipment. The type of material involved is the most important factor, the other is electrical resistivity.

•**Group E**, atmospheres containing metal dust. Conductive metal dusts are more hazardous than carbonized dust. Any accumulation of metal dust presents a conductive short circuit path and arcing.
There are no Division 2 areas for metal dust groups.

•**Group F**, atmospheres containing carbon black, coal dust, or coke dust. Coal is a carbonaceous material that can be explosive in powdered form. The hazard exists in mines and processing facilities.

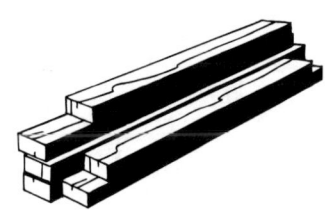

•**Group G**, atmospheres containing combustible dusts not included in Groups E or F, including grain dust, such as in grain elevators, flour, wood, plastic and chemicals. Group G dusts are less abrasive and less likely to cause electrical insulation breakdowns. Group E has metal dust which are generally electrically conductive.

Equipment installed in Class II locations must be able to function at full rating without developing surface temperatures that are high enough to cause excessive dehydration or gradual carbonization of organic dust that is deposited on it. Very dry dusts are subject to spontaneous ignition.

The intent of the Code is to prevent arcs and sparks from coming into contact with the dusts, and to prevent equipment surfaces from being hot enough to cause drying, carbonizing, or ignition.

A dust-ignitionproof enclosure does not have to be strong enough to withstand the internal pressures resulting from an explosion, and explosionproof equipment is not necessarily dust-ignitionproof.

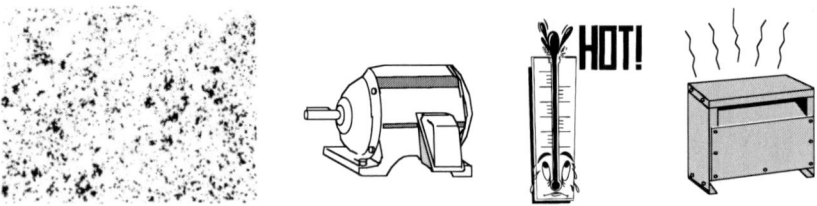

Class II enclosures are different from Class I area enclosures. There are several types of enclosures for use in an atmosphere containing dust. Some enclosures carry several different NEMA number identifications.

• *Dustproof*, are constructed or protected so dust *will not interfere* with its successful operation.

•*Dusttight*, are constructed so that dust *will not enter* the enclosure.

•*Dust-ignitionproof*, are for use in Class II hazardous locations. Dust-ignitionproof equipment is enclosed in a manner to exclude ignitible amounts of dust which will not permit arcs, sparks, or heat inside the enclosure.

Author's note: One must remember that a device that is approved for a Class I location is not necessarily approved for a Class II location. Some devices have been tested and found suitable for both locations. However, equipment that is suitable for both environments may also be unsuitable if materials with low autoignition temperatures are in use. Equipment that is layered with dust may produce higher temperatures than it would in the unlayered condition.

Such a condition could limit the use of the device in the Class I environment. To be acceptable, the device must have a maximum surface temperature that is not capable of igniting either atmosphere.

Any one of four hazards, or a combination of two or more, may exist in a Class II location:
•An explosive mixture of air and dust.
•The accumulation of conductive dust on and around live parts.
•Overheating of equipment from deposits of dust interfere with the normal radiation of heat.
•The possible ignition of deposits of dust by arcs or sparks or static electricity.

Remember, grain dust will ignite at a temperature below that of many Class I flammable vapors.

Housekeeping should be based on the amount of dust that a process generates. Some processes require several cleanings per shift. Do not used compressed air as it is an extremely dangerous cleaning process as it generates a dust cloud and static electricity which have resulted in explosions. If housekeeping becomes infrequent, the area may require a change in classification from a Division 2 location to a Division 1 location.

I can recall when I worked as an electrician on diesel locomotives, the insulators on the traction motors and generators would accumulate carbon dust from the carbon brushes which at higher voltages causes a current flow through the dust, causing the dust to heat. This has caused ignition of the dust layer. This phenomenon is known as tracking or a "worm".

Tracking (worms) is an electrical discharge phenomenon caused by electrical stress on insulation. Tracking develops in the form of arcs on the surface of the insulation. A common sign of tracking is one or more irregular carbon lines in the shape of tree branches.

Insulation and insulators must be kept clean and dry. A tracking pattern has been known to develop from moisture droplets in a heavy layer of dust which forms a carbon track which can often be hidden by later deposits of dust.

Although dusts such as aluminum rapidly form oxides, the oxides can be broken down, rendering the dust conductive. As the oxides begin to break down, a current flows through the dust, causing the dust to heat. This may cause ignition of the dust layer.

Part II. Wiring Methods

502.10(A)(1). Class II, Division 1 wiring methods are:
(1) Threaded rigid metal conduit or threaded steel IMC.

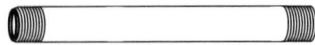

(2) Type MI cable with termination fittings listed for the location and installed so that no tensile stress is placed on them.

(3) Permitted in industrial establishments is Type MC-HL cable listed for use in Class II, Division 1 locations, and having a gas/vaportight continuous corrugated metallic sheath, an overall jacket of suitable polymeric material, separate equipment grounding conductors, and termination fittings listed for the application. Use is permitted only where the facility has limited public access and where maintenance and supervision ensure only *qualified persons* will service the installation.

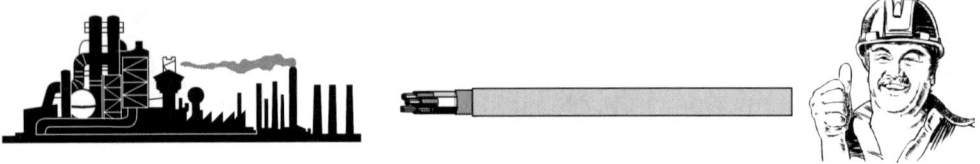

(4) Optical Fiber cable.

(5) In industrial establishments with restricted public access, where conditions of maintenance and supervision ensure that only qualified persons service the installation, listed Type ITC-HL cable with a gas/vaportight continuous corrugated metallic sheath and an overall jacket of suitable polymeric material, and terminated with fittings listed for the application, and installed in accordance with the provisions of 727.4.

(6) In industrial establishments limited to 600 volts.

(7) In industrial establishments with restricted public access that only qualified persons service the installation, listed Type P cable with metal braid armor installed in accordance with 337.10.

502.10(A)(2). Where flexibility is necessary, the following can be used:
(1) Dusttight flexible connectors.
(2) Liquidtight flexible metal conduit with listed fittings.
(3) Liquidtight flexible *nonmetallic* conduit with listed fittings.
(4) Interlocked armor Type MC cable having an overall jacket of suitable polymeric material and provided with termination fittings listed for Class II, Division 1 locations.
(5) Flexible cord listed for extra-hard usage, terminated with listed dusttight fittings, and having a grounding conductor. It must be connected and supported by suitable means so no tension will be exerted on the connections.

(6) For elevator use, an identified elevator cable of Type EO, ETP, or ETT, shown under the "use" column in Table 400.4 for "hazardous (classified) locations" and terminated with listed dusttight fittings.

(7) In industrial establishments limited to 600 volts.

(8) In industrial establishments with restricted public access that only qualified persons service the installation, listed Type P cable with metal braid armor installed in accordance with 337.10.

502.10(A)(3). Fittings and boxes installed must have threaded bosses (or hubs) for connection of conduit or cable terminations, close-fitting covers, and no holes through which dust could enter or sparks or burning material could escape. They must be identified for Class II locations if they contain taps, joints, or terminal connections, or where located in an area containing electrically conductive combustible dust.

An electrical enclosure or fitting with a "boss" has integral threads, usually five or more. A typical conduit body or FS box are boss type. It must be an integral part of the enclosure.

Cable trays are not recognized in Class II, Division 1 locations because they are considered "dust collectors" and difficult to keep clean. They are recognized in Class II, Division 2 locations.

502.10(B)(1). Wiring methods in Class II, Division 2, the following can be used:
(1) All wiring methods that are permitted in Class II, Division 1 locations.

(2) Rigid metal, steel IMC, with listed threaded or threadless fittings.

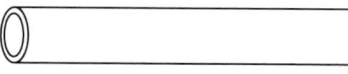
THINWALL

(3) Type EMT or dusttight wireways.

(4) Type MC, MV, TC, or TC-ER cable, including installation in cable tray systems.

(5) Types PLTC and Type PLTC-ER in cable trays, terminated with listed fittings.

(6) Types ITC and Type ITC-ER as permitted in 727.4 and terminated with listed fittings.

(7) Where metal conduit will not provide sufficient corrosion resistance, any of the following (a) through (d) shall be permitted.

(8) Optical fiber cable.

(9) Cablebus.

(10) In industrial establishments with restricted public access that only qualified persons service the installation, listed Type P cable with metal braid armor installed in accordance with 337.10.

502.10(B)(2). Where flexibility is necessary, the requirement of section 502.10(A)(2) Class II, Division 1 are required.

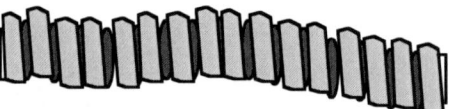

502.10(B)(3). Nonincendive field wiring shall be permitted using any of the wiring methods permitted for unclassified (nonhazardous) locations. Nonincendive field wiring systems shall be installed in accordance with control drawing(s). Simple apparatus, not shown on the control drawing, shall be permitted in a nonincendive field wiring circuit, provided the *simple apparatus* does not interconnect the nonincendive field wiring circuit to any other circuit.

 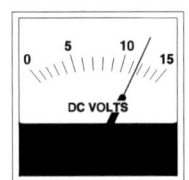 **1.5 volts or less**

Definition: Simple apparatus is an electrical component or combination of components of simple construction with well defined electrical parameters that does not generate more than 1.5 volts, 100 milliamps, and 25 milliwatts, or a passive component that does not dissipate more than 1.3 watts and is compatible with intrinsic safety of the circuit in which it is used.

Informational Note: Simple apparatus is defined in Article 100 Part III.

Separate nonincendive field wiring circuits shall be installed in accordance with one of the following:
(1) In separate cables.
(2) In multiconductor cables where the conductors of each circuit are within a grounded metal shield.
(3) In multiconductor cables or in raceways where the conductors of each circuit have insulation with a minimum thickness of 0.01 inch.

.01"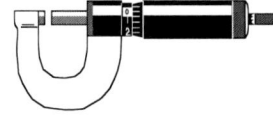

502.10(B)(4). Wireways, fittings, and boxes containing taps, joints, or terminal connections must minimize the entrance of dust, be provided with telescoping or close-fitting covers or other means of preventing the escape of sparks or burning material, and have no opening through which sparks of burning material might escape or through which adjacent combustible material might be ignited. All boxes and fittings shall be dusttight.

502.15. Sealing in Class II, Division 1 and 2 locations. Where a raceway provides communication between a dust-ignitionproof enclosure and one that is not, suitable means shall be provided to prevent the entrance of dust into the dust-ignitionproof enclosure through the raceway. One of the following means is permitted:

(1) A permanent and effective seal.

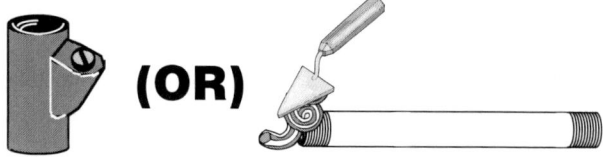

(2) A horizontal raceway not less than 10' long.

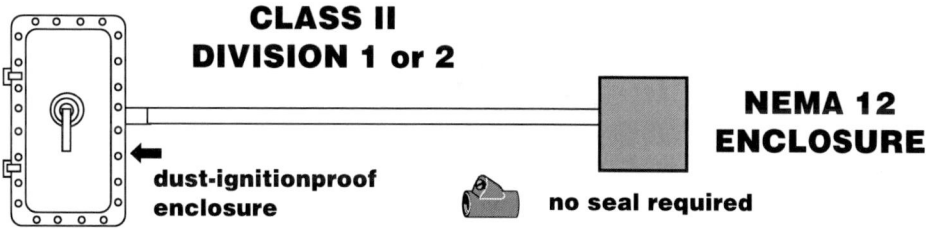

(3) A vertical raceway not less than 5' long and extending downward from the dust-ignitionproof enclosure.

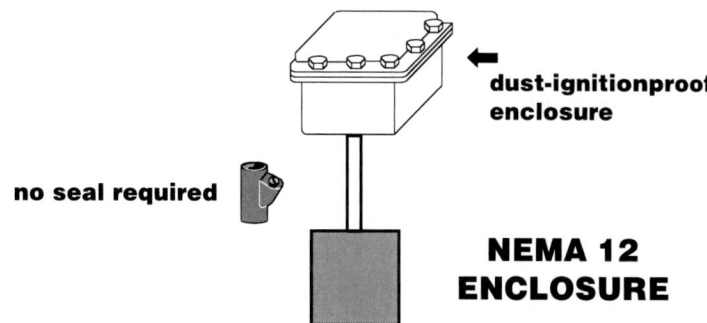

(4) A raceway installed in a manner to (2) or (3) that extends only horizontally and downward from dust-ignitionproof enclosures.

Seals are not required where a raceway provides communication between a dust-ignitionproof enclosure and an enclosure in a nonhazardous (unclassified) location.

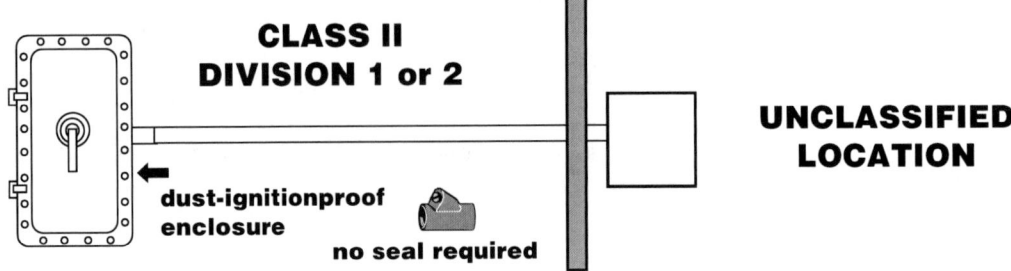

Sealing fittings shall be accessible.

Definition: **Accessible (as applied to wiring methods)**. Capable of being removed or exposed without damaging the building structure or finish or not permanently closed in by the structure or finish of the building.

Seals are *not* required to be explosionproof.

Informational Note: Electrical sealing putty is a method of sealing.

Author's note: One must note that a Class I location is one of gases and vapors, whereas a Class II location is one of **dust**. The surface temperature of equipment is more critical in Class II locations than it is in Class I locations, because the safety factors associated with ignition temperature as determined for gases and vapors do not exist, at least to the same extent, for Class II locations.

The reason that sealing is not required when using a conduit of a prescribed length is the intent of Class II locations is to prevent the passage of **dust**. The passage of vapors in a Class I location requires more stringent sealing.

502.25. Uninsulated exposed parts, Class II, Division 1 and 2. There shall be no uninsulated exposed parts, such as conductors, buses, terminals, or components that operate at more than 30 volts (15 volts in wet locations).

30 VOLTS
•15 VOLTS wet locations

502.30. Wiring and equipment in Class II, Divisions 1 and 2 must be grounded as required by Article 250.

502.30(A). Because of the importance of preventing ignition from **dust**, additional grounding requirements are required. Bonding jumpers with proper fittings, or other approved means of bonding, must be used. The Code does not permit double locknuts and locknut-and-bushing combinations. Proper bonding must be applied between the Class II location and the point of grounding for service equipment or point of grounding of a separately-derived system.

Exception: This relieves the necessity for using service bonding techniques ahead of the "point of grounding" for a building disconnect in a multi-building facility where the service equipment is in a different location than the building containing the hazardous location. Ground continuity only needs to be maintained to the building disconnect.

502.30(B). Where flexible conduit is used, it shall be installed with internal or external equipment bonding jumpers in parallel with each conduit and complying with 250.102.

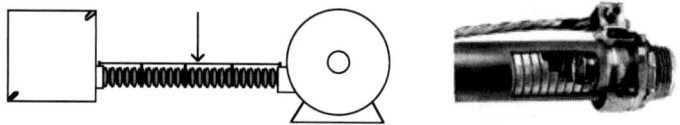

Exception: In Class II, Division 2 locations, the bonding jumper can be omitted where all of the following are met:

(1) Listed liquidtight flexible metal conduit 6' or less in length with listed grounding fittings.

(2) Overcurrent protection in the circuit is 10 amps or less.

(3) The load is **not** a power utilization load.

502.35. Surge protection is found in grain elevators in areas where severe lightning storms are common. The surge-protective equipment consists of primary lightning arresters at the transformers and surge-protective capacitors connected to the supply side of the service equipment.

Part III. Equipment

502.100(A)(1). Transformers or capacitors containing a liquid that will burn shall be installed only in vaults that comply with section 450.41 through 450.48, and, in addition (1), (2) and (3) shall apply.

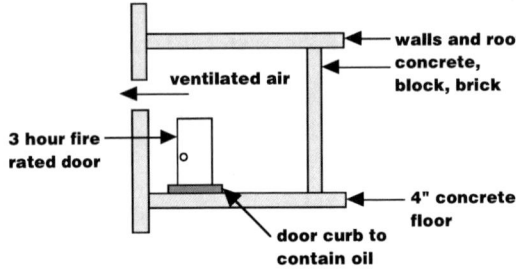

(1) Doors or other openings shall have self closing fire doors on both sides of the wall, and the doors shall be carefully fitted and provided with suitable seals.

(2) Vent openings and ducts shall communicate only with the outside air.

(3) Suitable pressure relief openings communicating with the outside air shall be provided.

502.100(A)(2). If the liquid contained will not burn, the transformer either must be installed in a vault, or must be approved for Class I locations.

502.100(A)(3). No transformer or capacitor shall be installed in a Class II, Division 1, Group E location.

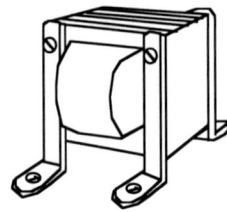

502.100(B)(1). Class II, Division 2 transformers and capacitors, if they contain liquids that will burn, they must also be installed in a vault.

502.100(B)(3). Dry-type transformers operating at not over 600 volts do not have to be installed within a vault as long as their windings and terminal connections are enclosed in tight metal housings that do not have ventilating or other openings.

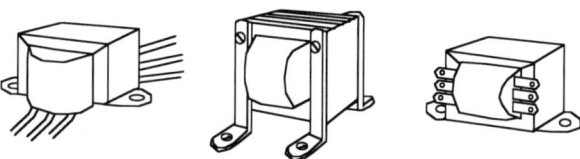

502.115(A). Class II, Division 1 locations, switches, breakers, fuses, motor controllers, pushbuttons, relays and similar devices that interrupt current during normal operation or that are installed where combustible dusts of an electrically conductive nature may be present shall be provided with *enclosures* identified for the location.

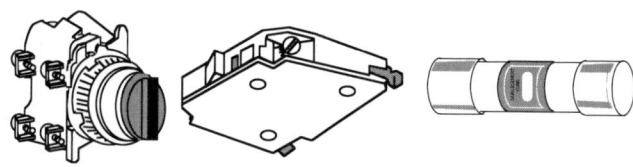

502.115(B). In Class II, Division 2 locations, enclosures for fuses, switches, breakers, and motor controllers, including pushbuttons, relays, and similar devices shall be dusttight or otherwise identified for the location.

502.120(A). In Class II, Division 1 locations, control transformers, resistors, impedance coils, or any overcurrent devices or switching mechanisms associated with them shall be provided with enclosures identified for the location.

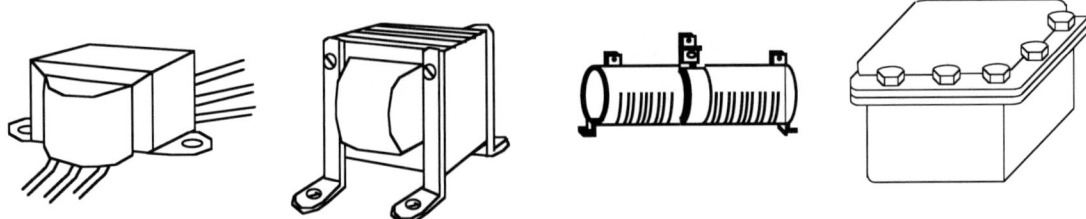

502.120(B)(1). Class II, Division 2 switching mechanisms associated with this type of equipment must be provided with dusttight enclosures or otherwise identified for the location.

(B)(2). Where coils and windings are not located in the same enclosure with switching mechanisms, solenoids, etc., the enclosure shall be a dusttight, or otherwise identified for the location.

.

(B)(3). Resistors and resistance devices must have dust-ignitionproof enclosures that are dusttight or otherwise approved for the location.

502.125(A)(1). In Class II, Division 1 locations, motors, generators, and other rotating electric machinery shall be one of the following:

(1) Identified (not just approved) for Class II, Division 1 locations.

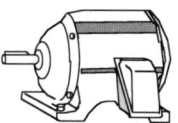 **IDENTIFIED CLASS II DIVISION 1**

(2) Totally enclosed pipe-ventilated.

502.125(B). Class II, Division 2 motors and other rotating equipment that can be installed in these areas are totally enclosed nonventilated (TENV), totally enclosed fan cooled (TEFC), totally enclosed pipe-ventilated or dust-ignitionproof with a maximum full-load external surface temperature not in excess of the ignition temperature of the specific dust to be encountered, when operating under normal conditions in **free air** (not dust blanketed). It must have no external openings.

Exception: Standard open-type machines (with restrictions on construction) and squirrel-cage-type textile motors can be installed if the authority having jurisdiction believes accumulations of non-conductive nonabrasive dust will be moderate, and the machines can be easily reached for routine cleaning and maintenance.

SQUIRREL CAGE

502.128. In locations where dust will collect on or in motors and interfere with the ventilation or cooling of the motor, it may be necessary to use an enclosed pipe-ventilated motor.

Ventilating pipes installed for rotating electrical machinery or enclosures for electrical equipment must be of metal not less than 0.021 inch thick, or of equally substantial noncombustible material.

(1) They must be installed to lead directly to a source of clean air outside the building.

(2) Be screened at the outer end to prevent the entrance of small animals or birds.

(3) Be protected against physical damage and against rusting or other corrosive influences.

Class II, Division 1 requires ventilating pipes and their connections to equipment to be dusttight throughout their length.

502.128(B). Class II, Division 2 requires ventilating pipes must be sufficiently tight to prevent the entrance of appreciable quantities of dust into the ventilated equipment, and to prevent the escape of sparks, flame, or burning material that might ignite dust accumulations or combustible material in the area. Metal pipes can have lock seams, riveted or welded joints, and tight-fitting slip joints where flexibility is necessary, such as connecting to the motor.

 **Author's note**: In most installations of pipe-ventilating systems, the persons fabricating and installing the ventilating piping system will not be electricians. Pressurized equipment is usually custom-built equipment. The Code has set the rules for installation because ordinary sheet-metal ducts are not satisfactory for cooling electrical equipment in a Class II location. The electrician still has the responsibility for assuring that the installation meets the Code requirements.

502.130(A)(1). Class II, Division 1 luminaires must be identified for Class II locations. The maximum wattage of lamps installed must not exceed the wattage for which it is designed. Where metal dust from magnesium, aluminum, aluminum bronze powder, or other metals of similarly hazardous characteristics might be present, fixtures for fixed or portable, and all auxiliary equipment must be identified for the specific location.

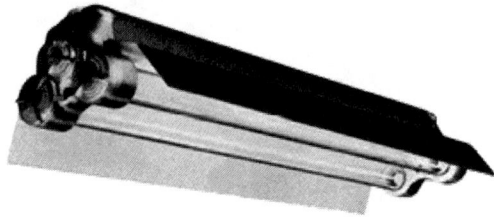 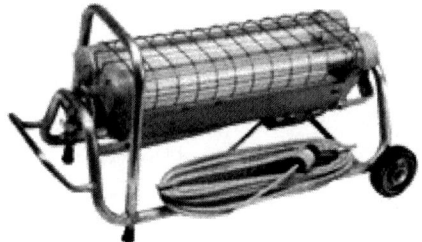

502.130(A)(2). Each luminaire shall be protected against physical damage by a suitable guard or by location.

502.130(A)(3). Pendant luminaires are subject to specific rules in mounting. Either threaded rigid metal conduit or threaded IMC stems or by chains with approved fittings must be used to support the luminaires. Threaded joints must be provided with set screws or other effective means to prevent loosening. Stems over 12" long must have permanent and effective bracing against lateral displacement that must be provided at a level not more than 12" above the lower end of the stem or a fitting or flexible connector must be provided not more than 12" from the point of attachment to its supporting box or fitting.

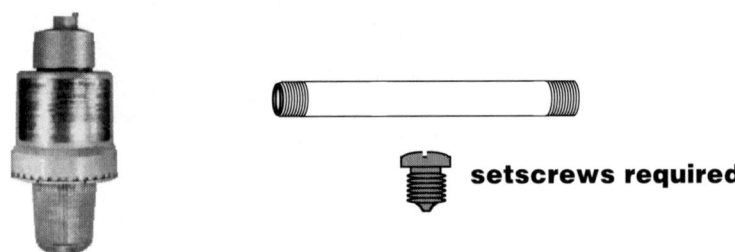

setscrews required

Where wiring between an outlet box or fitting and a pendant luminaire is not enclosed in conduit, flexible cord listed for hard usage must be used, and suitable seals provided where the cord enters the luminaire and the outlet box or fitting. The flexible cord must not act as the support for the luminaire.

502.130(A)(4). Boxes, box assemblies, or fittings used for the support of luminaires shall be identified for Class II locations.

502.130(B)(1). Class II, Division 2 portable lighting equipment shall be identified for Class II locations. They shall be clearly marked to indicate the maximum wattage of lamps for which they are designed.

502.130(B)(2). Class II, Division 2 luminaires for fixed lighting shall be provided with enclosures that are dusttight or otherwise identified for the location. Each luminaire shall be clearly marked to indicate the maximum wattage of the lamp that shall be permitted without exceeding an exposed surface temperature under normal conditions of use.

502.130(B)(3). Class II, Division 2 luminaires for fixed light fixtures shall be protected against physical damage by a suitable guard or by location.

502.130(B)(4). Class II, Division 2 pendant luminaires follow the same rules as Class II, Division 1 locations except that setscrews are not required for threaded joints.

setscrews **NOT** required

502.130(B)(5). Class II, Division 2 starting and control equipment for electric-discharge lamps must comply with the requirements for control transformers and resistors which requires dusttight enclosures.

502.135(A). Class II, Division 1 locations all utilization equipment must be identified for Class II locations.

502.135(B). Class II, Division 2 locations utilization equipment must comply with the following: (1) Electrically heated items must be identified for Class II locations, except for metal-enclosed radiant heating panels, which must be dusttight and marked to show the class, group, and temperature identification numbers.

(2) Motors of motor-driven utilization equipment shall comply with 502.125(B).

(3) Enclosures for switches, breakers, and fuses must be dusttight or otherwise identified for the location.

 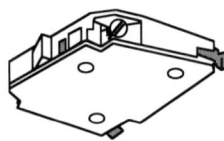 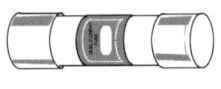

(4) Transformers, solenoids, impedance coils, and resistors shall comply with 502.120(B).

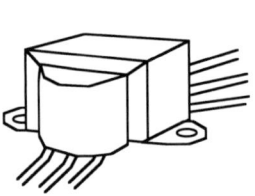 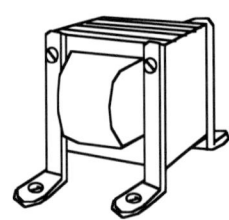 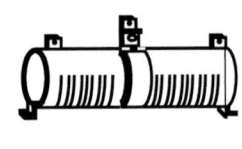 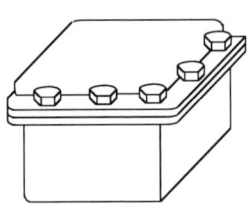

502.140(B). Class II, Division 1 and 2 flexible cords shall comply with:

(1) Be of a type listed for extra-hard usage.

Exception: Flexible cord listed for *hard usage* as permitted by 502.130(A)(3) and (B)(4).

(2) In addition to the circuit conductors, contain an equipment grounding conductor complying with 400.23.

(3) Be supported so there is no tension on terminal connections.

 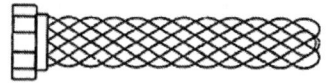

(4) The cord shall be terminated with a cord connector listed for the location or a listed cord connector installed with a seal listed for the location. In Division 2 locations, the cord shall be terminated with a listed dusttight cord connector.

(5) Be of continuous length.

502.145(A). Class II, Division 1 location receptacles and attachment plugs shall be of the type providing for connection to the grounding conductor of the flexible cord and shall be identified for Class II locations.

502.145(B)(2). Class II, Division 2 location receptacles and attachment plugs shall be of the type providing for connection to the grounding conductor of the flexible cord.

502.150(A). In Class II, Division 1 locations, signaling, alarm, remote-control, and communications systems; and meters, instruments, and relays shall comply with:

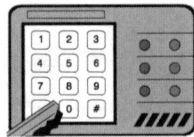

(A) The wiring methods shall comply with 502.150(A)(1) through (A)(3).

(1) Switches, breakers, relays, contactors, fuses and current-breaking contacts for bells, horns, howlers, sirens, and other devices in which sparks or arcs may be produced shall be provided with enclosures identified for a Class II location.

Exception: Current-breaking contacts that are immersed in oil or in a sealed chamber can have a general-purpose enclosure.

(2) Resistors, transformers, and other heat-generating equipment must be provided with enclosures identified for Class II locations. Resistors and similar equipment that are immersed in oil or in a sealed chamber can have a general-purpose enclosure per the exception.

(3) Motors and other rotating electric machinery must either be identified for use in Class II, Division 1 locations or be totally enclosed pipe ventilated, meeting the temperature rules as to not dry out dust too much to ignite it.

502.150(B). In Class II, Division 2 locations, signaling, alarm, remote-control, and communications systems; and meters, instruments, and relays shall comply with 502.150(B)(1) through (B)(4):

(1) Contacts that may produce arc and sparks shall comply with 502.150(A)(1) or shall be installed in enclosures that are dusttight or otherwise identified for the location.

Exception: In nonincendive circuits, enclosures are permitted to be the general-purpose type.

(2) Windings of transformers, choke coils, etc. must be provided with tight metal enclosures that are dusttight or otherwise identified for the location.

(3) Resistors, transformers, and other heat-generating equipment must be provided with enclosures identified for Class II locations. Resistors and similar equipment that are immersed in oil or in a sealed chamber can have a general-purpose enclosure.

(4) Motors and other rotating electric machinery must comply with 502.125(B).

ARTICLE 503

Class III
Locations

Part I. General

503.1. A Class III location is one that is hazardous because of **easily ignitible fibers or flyings**, but in which such fibers or flyings are not likely to be in suspension in the air in quantities sufficient to produce ignitible mixtures.

The major hazard from Class III materials is not an explosion hazard, but a fire hazard. Boxes and fittings are required to be dusttight. There are no requirements for seals.

A house that has an electric clothes dryer is an example of ignitible fibers as the lint from the clothes has caused fires, but yet the amount of material present is insufficient to result in classification of the area as a Class III location. In fabric mills, essentially the same material is present but in larger quantities so it is classified as a hazard.

Dryer lint

There are no groups in Class III hazardous locations.

A Class III, Division 1 location is a location in which the easily ignitible fibers or materials producing combustible flyings are handled, manufactured, or used. A cotton mill with small fibers of cotton in the air or the sawdust and wood shavings around planers in woodworking plants are common examples of a Division 1 location. Sawdust, where it can accumulate quickly in large quantities and dry out presents a severe fire hazard.

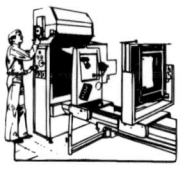 **Manufacturing**

A Class III, Division 2 location is a location where easily ignitible fibers are stored or handled except in the process of manufacture, where then it would be a Division 1 location. A cotton warehouse is a common example of a Division 2 location.

 **Warehouse**

Compared to classifying a Class I, Division 1 or 2 location or a Class II, Division 1 or 2 location, it is much simpler to determine a Class III, Division 1 or 2 location. It depends on the use of the area rather than the amount of material present or likely to be present.

Division 1

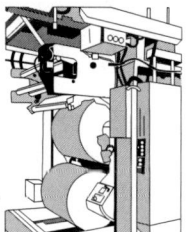

Division 2

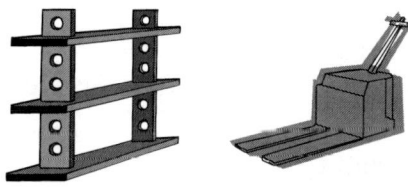

503.5. Class III hazards concentrate on the selection of equipment that will function at full rating without developing surface temperatures high enough to cause excessive dehydration or gradual carbonization of the accumulated material or flyings. To reduce the danger of spontaneous combustion, the Code limits the surface temperature of electrical equipment used in these locations to 165°C (329°F) for equipment that is not subject to overloading, such as light fixtures. The temperature for motors, transformers, etc. that can operate while overloaded is 120°C (248°F).

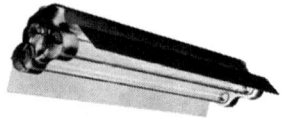 **165°C (329°F)**  **120°C (248°F)**

503.6. Equipment listed and marked for installation in combustible dust environments under the zone classifications system per 506.9(C)(2) as suitable for Zone 20 can be used in Class III, Division 1 locations provided it does not operate at a high temperature.

Part II. Wiring

503.10(A)(1). Class III, Division 1 wiring method must be rigid metal conduit, rigid nonmetallic conduit, IMC, EMT, dusttight wireways, MI, MC, PLTC, PLTC-ER, ITC, ITC-ER, and TC cable with listed termination fittings.

503.10(A)(2). All boxes and fittings shall be dusttight.

503.10(A)(3). Where it is necessary to employ flexible connections, dusttight flexible connectors, liquidtight flexible metal conduit with listed fittings, liquidtight flexible nonmetallic conduit with listed fittings, interlocked armor Type MC cable with an overall jacket of suitable polymeric material and listed dusttight termination fittings, or flexible cord in conformance with 503.140 shall be used.

503.10(A)(4). Separate nonincendive field wiring circuits shall be installed in accordance with one of the following:
(1) In separate cables.
(2) In multiconductor cables where the conductors of each circuit are within a grounded metal shield.
(3) In multiconductor cables where the conductors of each circuit have insulation with a minimum thickness of 0.01 inch.

503.10(B). Class III, Division 2 wiring methods is the same as Class III, Division 1 methods.

Exception: Open wiring on insulators shall be permitted in accordance with Article 398 in sections, compartments, or areas used solely for storage and containing no machinery, provided conductors are not run in roof spaces and are well out of reach of sources of physical damage.

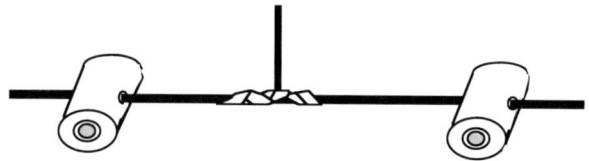

Seals are not required in Class III locations.

503.25. **Uninsulated exposed parts, Class III, Division 1 and 2**. There shall be no uninsulated exposed parts, such as conductors, buses, terminals, or components that operate at more than 30 volts (15 volts in wet locations).

 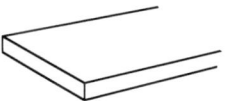 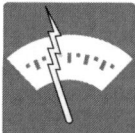

30 VOLTS
•15 VOLTS wet locations

503.30. Wiring and equipment in Class III, Divisions 1 and 2 must be grounded as required by Article 250.

503.30(A). Because of the importance of preventing ignition from easily ignitible fibers, additional grounding requirements are required. Bonding jumpers with proper fittings, or other approved means of bonding, must be used. The Code does not permit double locknuts and locknut-and-bushing combinations. Proper bonding must be applied between the Class III location and the point of grounding for service equipment or point of grounding of a separately-derived system.

Exception: This relieves the necessity for using service bonding techniques ahead of the "point of grounding" for a building disconnect in a multi-building facility where the service equipment is in a different location than the building containing the hazardous location. Ground continuity only needs to be maintained to the building disconnect.

503.30(B). Where flexible conduit is used, it shall be installed with internal or external equipment bonding jumper complying with 250.102.

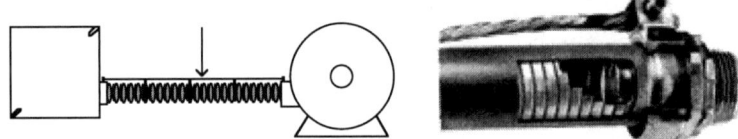

Exception: In Class III, Division 1 and 2 locations, the bonding jumper can be omitted where all of the following are met:

(1) Listed liquidtight flexible metal conduit 6' or less in length with listed grounding fittings.

(2) Overcurrent protection in the circuit is 10 amps or less.

(3) The load is not a power utilization load.

Part III. Equipment

503.100. Class III, Division 1 and 2 transformers and capacitors, if they contain liquids that will burn, they must be installed in a vault.

503.115. Class III, Division 1 and 2 locations, switches, breakers, fuses, motor controllers, pushbuttons, relays and similar devices shall be provided with dusttight enclosures.

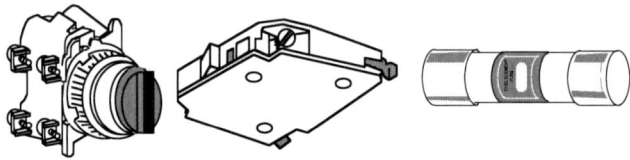

503.120. In Class III, Division 1 and 2 locations, control transformers, resistors, impedance coils, etc., are often in control circuitry shall be provided with dusttight enclosures and comply with temperature limitations of 503.5.

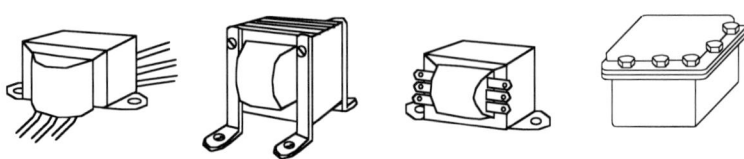

503.125. Class III, Division 1 and 2 motors and other rotating equipment that can be installed in these areas are totally enclosed nonventilated (TENV), totally enclosed fan cooled (TEFC), totally enclosed pipe-ventilated.

Exception: Standard open-type machines (with restrictions on construction) and squirrel-cage-type textile motors can be installed if the authority having jurisdiction believes accumulations of lint or flyings will be moderate, and the machines can be easily reached for routine cleaning and maintenance.

503.128. Ventilating pipes installed for rotating electrical machinery or enclosures for electrical equipment must be of metal not less than 0.021 inch thick, or of equally substantial noncombustible material.

(1) They must be installed to lead directly to a source of clean air outside the building.

(2) Be screened at the outer end to prevent the entrance of small animals or birds.

(3) Be protected against physical damage and against rusting or other corrosive influences.

503.130(A). Class III, Division 1 and 2 luminaires must be clearly marked to show the maximum size lamp that can be installed without exceeding a 165°C (329°F) limitation. Fixed luminaires are required to be of a type that will minimize the entrance of fibers or flyings and prevent the escape of sparks, burning material or hot metal.

503.130(B). When a luminaire is installed in a location where it may be subject to physical damage, it must be provided with a guard.

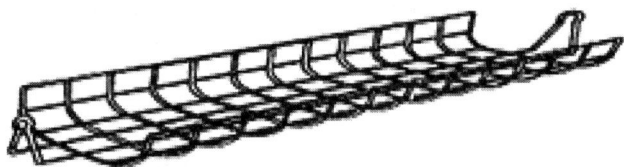

503.130(C). Pendant luminaires can be suspended from threaded stems made of rigid metal conduit, IMC, or metal tubing. Chains with approved fittings are an alternative method. Where the stems are longer than 12", permanent bracing to prevent lateral movement must be provided at a point not more than 12" above the top of the fixture. Flexibility can be employed in place of bracing.

503.130(D). Portable lighting must follow the same rules, and in addition, must be provided with handles and be protected with substantial guards. Lampholders must be unswitched and contain no provision for accepting an attachment plug. No current-carrying parts are allowed to be exposed, and all noncurrent-carrying metal parts are to be grounded.

503.135(A). Electrically heated utilization equipment shall be identified for Class III locations.

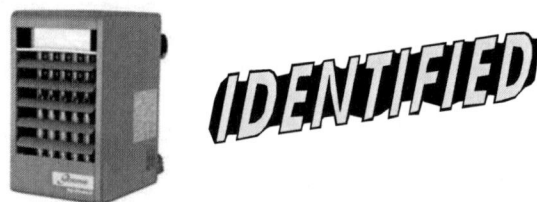

503.135(B). Motors of motor-driven utilization equipment shall comply with 503.125.

503.135(C). Switches, breakers, motor controllers, and fuses shall comply with 503.115.

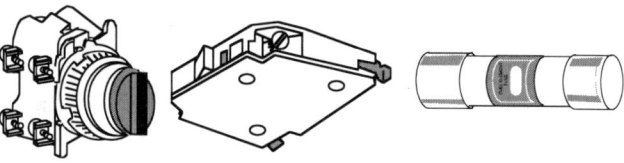

503.140. Class III, Division 1 and 2 flexible cords shall comply with:

(1) Listed for extra-hard usage.

(2) In addition to the circuit conductors, contain an equipment grounding conductor complying with 400.23.

(3) Be supported so there is no tension on terminal connections.

(4) Be terminated with a listed dusttight cord connector.

503.145. Receptacles and attachment plugs in Class III, Division 1 and 2 locations shall be of the grounding type and shall be designed to minimize the accumulation or the entry of fibers or flyings, and shall prevent the escape of sparks or molten particles.

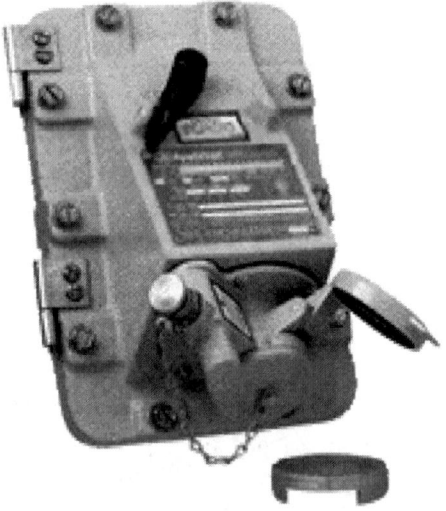

Exception: In locations where, in the judgement of the authority having jurisdiction, only moderate accumulations of lint or flyings will be likely to collect in the vicinity of a receptacle, and where such receptacle is readily accessible for routine cleaning, general-purpose grounding-type receptacles mounted to minimize the entry of fibers or flyings shall be permitted.

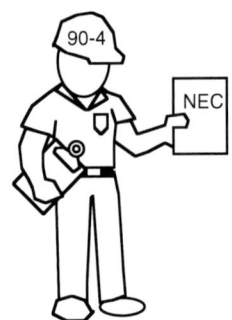

Definition of readily accessible: Capable of being reached quickly for operation, renewal, or inspections without requiring those to whom ready access is requisite to climb over or remove obstacles or to resort to portable ladders, and so forth.

503.150. Signaling, alarm, remote-control, and local loudspeaker intercommunications systems in Class III, Division 1 and 2 locations shall comply with the wiring methods of Article 503.

 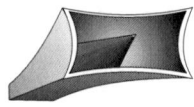

503.155(A). Electric cranes, hoists, and similar equipment where installed in Class III, Division 1 and 2 locations, the power supply to contact conductors shall be electrically isolated from all other systems, ungrounded, and shall be equipped with an acceptable ground detector that gives an alarm and automatically de-energizes the contact conductors in case of a fault to ground or gives a visual and audible alarm as long as power is supplied to the contact conductors and the ground fault remains.

503.155(B). Contact conductors shall be located or guarded so as to be inaccessible to other than authorized persons and shall be protected against accidental contact with foreign objects.

503.155(C). Current collectors shall be arranged or guarded so as to confine normal sparking and prevent escape of sparks or hot particles. To reduce sparking, two or more separate surfaces of contact shall be provided for each contact conductor.

503.155(D). Control equipment shall comply with 503.115 and 503.120.

503.160. Storage battery charging equipment in Class III, Divisions 1 and 2 must be located in a separate room built of, or lined with, substantial noncombustible materials. The construction of the room must minimize the entrance of lint or flyings and must be adequately ventilated.

Author's note: The exception to section 503.145 gives the inspector the authority to allow a general-purpose receptacle based on expected cleanliness of the site and the accessibility of the items for routine cleaning.

Will the inspector follow up periodically to see if the area is kept clean??? I doubt it!

ARTICLE 504

Intrinsically Safe Systems

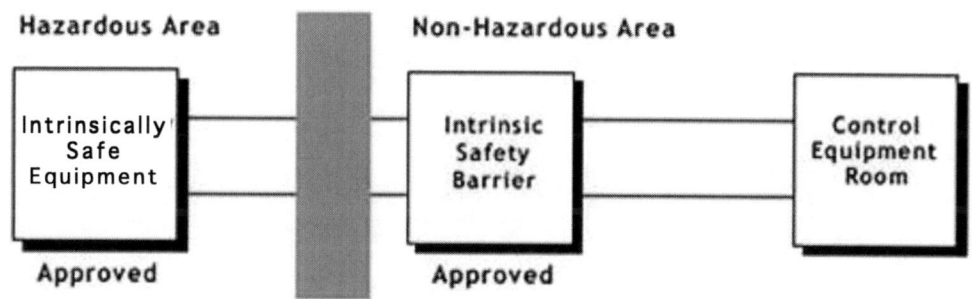

Author's note: The Code is a little more relaxed on the rules in hazardous locations since intrinsically safe systems cannot produce an arc with sufficient energy to ignite combustion.

Much of the early development and application of intrinsically safe equipment took place in Europe to answer the need for electrical equipment in the coal mines.

Article 100 Part III. Definition of **intrinsic**: (1a) belonging to the essential of nature or constitution of a thing (b) being or related to a semiconductor in which the concentration of charge carriers is characteristic of the material itself instead of the content of any impurities it contains (2) originating or situated within the body or part acted on.

Wiring a hazardous location can become very expensive because many of the devices installed are current interrupting devices, or part of a circuit that can release significant energy under fault conditions. This requires the use of explosionproof devices and wiring methods suitable for the hazard involved.

The introduction of intrinsically safe systems has significantly reduced these costs.

Definitions.

Article 100 Part III. Associated apparatus contains circuits that are not necessarily intrinsically safe, but affect the energy in the intrinsically safe circuits and are relied upon to maintain intrinsic safety. An example is an *intrinsic safety barrier*, which is a network that limits the voltage and current (and thus the energy) available to the protected circuit in the hazardous location under specified fault conditions.

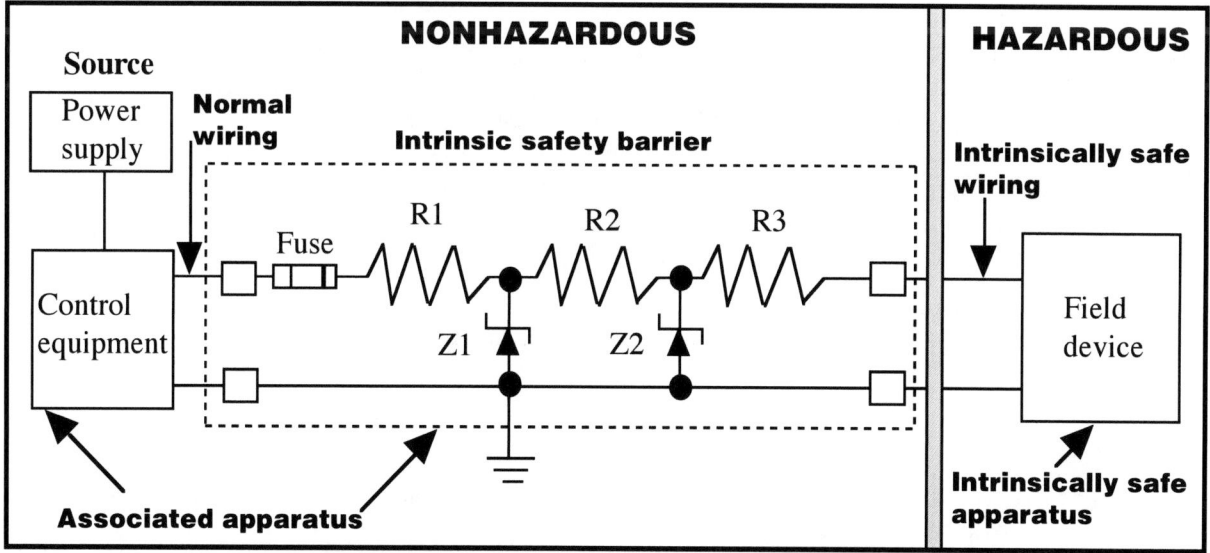

The *intrinsic safety barrier* is a passive electronic device that requires no power source. Inside are precision resistors to limit current and zener diodes for limiting the voltage. Under normal conditions, the barrier allows signals to pass between the field and the control equipment in the nonhazardous location. When a fault occurs and the voltage rises to a high enough level at the nonhazardous-side terminals, the Z1 diode will conduct and the resulting current increase will cause the fuse to blow. Redundant components are used to protect against failure of individual items. The excess current is diverted to ground, thus never reaching the hazardous location.

Article 100 Part III. Control drawing is a drawing or other document provided by the manufacturer of the intrinsically safe or associated apparatus, or of the nonincendive field wiring apparatus or associated nonincendive field wiring apparatus, that details the allowed interconnections between the intrinsically safe and associated apparatus or between the nonincendive field wiring apparatus or associated nonincendive field wiring apparatus.

Different intrinsically safe circuits are intrinsically safe circuits in which the possible interconnections have not been evaluated and identified as intrinsically safe.

Article 100 Part III. Intrinsically safe apparatus is an apparatus in which all of the circuits are intrinsically safe.

Intrinsically safe circuit is one in which any spark or thermal effect is incapable of causing ignition of a mixture of flammable or combustible material in air under prescribed test conditions. These circuits are permitted to be installed in any classified location for which they have been identified.

Article 100 Part III. Intrinsically safe system is an assembly of interconnected intrinsically safe apparatus, associated apparatus, and interconnecting cables. Those parts of the system that are installed in a hazardous (classified) location consist of one or more intrinsically safe circuits.

Article 100 Part III. Simple apparatus is an electrical component or combination of components of simple construction with well defined electrical parameters that does not generate more than 1.5 volts, 100 milliamps, and 25 milliwatts, or a passive component that does not dissipate more than 1.3 watts and is compatible with the intrinsic safety of the circuit which it is used.

504.3. Except as modified by this article, all applicable articles of the Code shall apply.

504.4 All intrinsically safe apparatus and associated apparatus shall be listed.

Exception: Simple apparatus that does not interconnect intrinsically safe circuits.

504.10. Intrinsically safe apparatus, associated apparatus, and other equipment shall be installed in accordance with the control drawing(s).

Simple apparatus, whether or not shown on the control drawing(s), shall be permitted to be installed provided the simple apparatus does not interconnect intrinsically safe circuits.

504.10(B). Intrinsically safe apparatus shall be permitted to be installed in any hazardous (classified) location for which it has been identified.

   Associated apparatus shall be permitted to be installed in any hazardous (classified) location for which it has been identified.

   Simple apparatus shall be permitted to be installed in any hazardous (classified) location in hazardous (classified) location in accordance with 504.10(D).

504.20. This section makes it clear that any of the wiring methods suitable for use in nonhazardous (unclassified) locations are permitted to be used for the installation of intrinsically safe apparatus and wiring.

504.30(A)(1). Conductors and cables of intrinsically safe circuits not installed in a raceway must be separated from conductors and cables of nonintrinsically safe circuits by at least 2". This separation is not required if either all the intrinsically safe circuits or all the nonintrinsically safe circuits are in metal raceways or in Type MI or MC cables that have sheaths or cladding capable of carrying fault current to ground.

Intrinsically safe circuits  **2"** **Nonintrinsically safe circuits**

504.30(A)(2)(1). Within an enclosure, conductors of intrinsically safe circuits must be separated from other nonintrinsically safe conductors by at least 2".

504.30(A)(2)(2). All conductors within the enclosure must be secured so that any conductor that might come loose from a terminal cannot come in contact with another terminal.

Informational Note 1:   Cables meeting the requirements of Articles 330 and 332 are typical of those considered acceptable (MI or MC cable).

Informational Note 2:   The use of separate wiring compartments for the intrinsically safe and nonintrinsically safe terminals is the preferred method of complying with this requirement.

Informational Note 3:   Physical barriers such as grounded metal partitions or approved insulating partitions or approved restricted access wiring ducts separated from other such ducts by at least 3/4" can be used to help ensure required separation of the wiring.

504.30(A)(3). Conductors and cables of intrinsically safe circuits run in other than raceway or cable tray systems shall be separated by at least 2" and secured from conductors and cables of any nonintrinsically safe circuits.

Intrinsically safe circuits   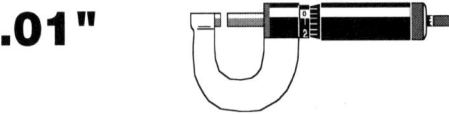 **2"**   **Nonintrinsically safe circuits**

Exception: Where either (1) all the intrinsically safe circuits are in Type MI, or MC cables or (2) all the nonintrinsically safe circuits are in raceways or Type MI, MC cables where the sheaths or cladding are capable of carrying fault current to ground.

504.30(B). The clearance between two terminals for connection of field wiring of different intrinsically safe circuits shall be at least 0.25 inches unless this clearance is permitted to be reduced by the control drawing.

Different intrinsically safe circuits shall be in separate cables or shall be separated from each other by one of the following:
(1) The conductors of each circuit are within a grounded metal shield.

(2) The conductors of each circuit have insulation with a minimum thickness of 0.01".

.01"

Exception: Unless otherwise identified.

504.50(A). Intrinsically safe apparatus, associated apparatus, cable shields, enclosures, and raceways, if of metal shall be grounded.

504.50(B). Where shielded conductors or cables are used, shields shall be grounded.

504.50(C). Where connection to a grounding electrode, a made electrode shall not be used if 250.52 (A)(1), (A)(2), (A)(3) or (A)(4) are available.

METAL UNDER GROUND WATER PIPE   METAL BUILDING FRAME   CONCRETE-ENCASED ELECTRODE   GROUND RING   ROD ELECTRODE

250.52(A1)   **250.52(A2)**   **250.52(A3)**   **250.52(A4)**

504.60(A). Intrinsically safe apparatus, if of metal, shall be bonded in the hazardous (classified) location in accordance with 501.30(A), 502.30(A), 505.25, or 506.25, as applicable.

504.60(B). Where metal raceways are used for intrinsically safe system wiring, bonding at all ends of the raceways, regardless of the location, shall in accordance with 501.30(A), 502.30(A), 503.30(A),505.25, or 506.25 as applicable.

 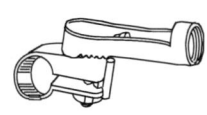 

504.70. Conduits and cables containing intrinsically safe wiring must be sealed where required by Articles 501.15, 502.15, 505.16, and 506.16. This includes where the transistion is from a Division 1 to an unclassified location, from a Division 1 to a Division 2 location, etc. These seals are **not** required to be explosionproof.

An exception to this nonexplosionproof requirement is for the association apparatus to be installed in a Class I hazardous location within an explosionproof enclosure. Also, where the intrinsically safe apparatus depends upon a single compression seal, diaphragm, or tube to prevent flammable or combustible fluids from entering the raceway or cable, an explosionproof seal is required.

504.80. Labels required must be suitable for the environment where they are installed. Their exposure to **chemicals and sunlight** must be considered. Since methods used in nonhazardous locations can be used for intrinsically safe systems in hazardous locations, without the labels the authority having jurisdiction could experience difficulty in determining Code compliance. In nonhazardous locations, the identification is necessary to ensure that nonintrinsically safe wire will not be added to existing raceways at a later date.

504.80(A). Intrinsically safe circuits must be identified at terminal and junction locations in a manner that is intended to prevent unintentional interference with the circuits while testing and servicing.

504.80(B). Raceways, cable trays, and open wiring for intrinsically safe system wiring must be identified with permanently affixed labels. The labels must contain the wording "INTRINSIC SAFETY WIRING." The labels must be located where they are visible after installation. The labels must be placed so they can be readily traced through the entire length of the installation. Spacing between labels must not exceed 25 feet.

Not exceeding 25 feet

Exception: Circuits run underground shall be permitted to be identified where they become accessible after emergence from the ground.

504.80(C). Color coding is permitted as a method of identifying intrinsically safe conductors, raceways, cable trays, and junction boxes containing only intrinsically safe wiring. The color is to be light blue.

LIGHT BLUE

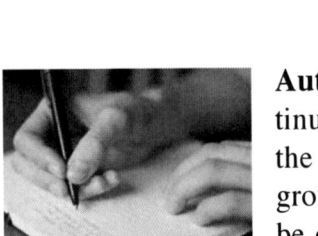

Author's note: Intrinsically safe systems need maintenance to ensure continued safety. The first priority is to check to see that all safety components of the system are intact, including both diodes in a zener diode barrier. The grounding system is also essential in maintaining intrinsic safety and should be checked regularly. Terminals and connections should be checked to see that they are tight and that there are no stray strands of wire that could short-circuit the terminals.

Intrinsically safe equipment and wiring is a system concept. Any piece of equipment connected to the system or that can be connected to the system is part of the system. The only exception is self-contained battery-operated equipment that is not connected to any other equipment or apparatus.

The concept of the intrinsically safe protection system is to maintain the available energy below that required to cause ignition, even under fault conditions.

Battery-operated flashlights using small dry-cell batteries can cause a spark which may result in ignition. Tests have shown that if a flashlight bulb is broken in a flammable atmosphere without simultaneously breaking the lamp filament, the combination of high temperature and the spark created when the filament burns open as a result of exposure to the oxygen in the air can result in ignition. There are Listed flashlights and lanterns for use in hazardous locations.

Intrinsically safe systems are designed to always fail in the *safe* position. Should a wire or cable be cut accidentally, the operation of the equipment must be *fail-safe* in every instance. No arcing or sparking will occur because of the design and nature of intrinsically safe systems.

ARTICLE 505

Class I,
Zone 0, 1, and 2 Locations

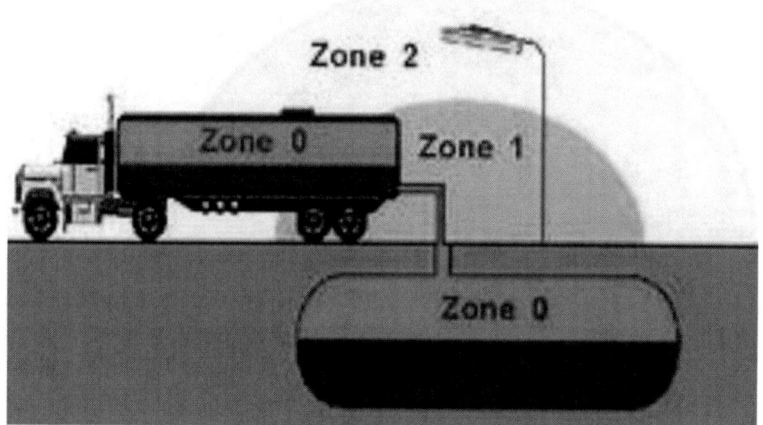

Class I
Flammable gases,
liquids, or vapors.

Zone 0
Ignitible concentrations
of flammable gases or
vapors are continuously
present or present for
long periods.

Zone 1
Ignitible concentrations
of flammable gases or
vapors are likely to exist
during normal operations.

Zone 2
Ignitible concentrations
of flammable gases or
vapors are NOT likely to
occur during normal
operations.

Group IIC: Atmospheres containing acetylene, hydrogen, or flammable gas, flammable liquid produced vapor, or combustible liquid produced vapor mixed with air that may burn or explode.
Note: This grouping is equivalent to Class I, Groups A and B.

Group IIB: Atmospheres containing acetaldehyde, ethylene, or flammable gas, flammable liquid produced vapor, or combustible liquid produced vapor mixed with air that may burn or explode.
Note: This grouping is equivalent to Class I, Group C.

Group IIA: Atmospheres containing acetone, ammonia, ethyl alcohol, gasoline, methane, propane, or flammable gas, flammable liquid produced vapor, or combustible liquid produced vapor mixed with air that may burn or explode.
Note: This grouping is equivalent to Class I, Group D.

Article 505 is for hazardous (classified) locations where fire or explosion hazards may exist due to flammable gases, vapors, or liquids.

Article 100 Definitions Part III.

Article 100 Part III. Combustible Gas Detection System. This protection utilizes stationary gas detectors in industrial establishments. Normally, when a certain gas is sensed by one or more detectors, an alarm is sent to plant workmen, and in some cases the alarm initiates a plant emergency shutdown system.

Article 100 Part III. Electrical and Electronic Equipment. Materials, fittings, devices, appliances, and the like that are part of, or in connection with, an electrical installation.

Note: Portable or transportable equipment having self-contained power supplies, such as battery-operated equipment, could potentially become an ignition source in hazardous locations.

Article 100 Part III. Encapsulation "m." Protection is provided by embedding the sparking or potentially dangerous electrical parts in a potting compound so that any explosive atmosphere will not come in contact with these parts.

Article 100 Part III. Flameproof "d." This protection is the closest equivalent to the NEC explosionproof enclosures.

Article 100 Part III. Increased Safety "e." This protection includes increased measures to prevent the possibility of excess heat, arcs, or sparks from occurring on internal or external parts of equipment, which normally do not produce such sources. The methods include: terminals that are protected against self loosening, and must provide an adequate contact pressure when the cable is cold; air gaps and creep path specific to the voltage of the circuit; resistance to temperatures at least 20°C above the usual working temperature; specification of minimum wire thickness and csa; and others.

HOT!

Article 100 Part III. Intrinsic Safety "i." This protection involves intrinsically safe circuits in which no spark and no thermal effect can rise under normal working conditions, or some types of failures, can lead to an explosion in a specific potentially hazardous atmosphere.

Article 100 Part III. Oil Immersion "o." In this type of protection, the arcing parts are immersed in a volume of oil, so the flammable vapor or gas cannot come into contact with the arc.

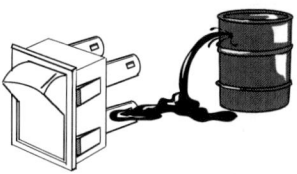

Article 100 Part III. Powder Filling "q." This protection assures that an arc occurring within the enclosure will be cooled and extinguished by the finely granulated quartz sand that fills the enclosure. The enclosure has an inspection glass to monitor the settling of the sand.

Article 100 Part III. Pressurization "p." This type of protection uses the technique of guarding against the ingress of the external atmosphere, which may be explosive, into an enclosure by maintaining a protective gas therein at a pressure above that of the external atmosphere.

Article 100 Part III. Type of Protection "n." This type of protection is where electrical equipment, in normal operation, is not capable of igniting a surrounding gas atmosphere and a fault capable of causing ignition is not likely to occur.

505.3. All other applicable rules contained in the Code shall apply to electrical equipment and wiring installed in hazardous (classified) locations.

Exception: As modified by Articles 504.

505.4(A). All areas in industrial occupancies designated as hazardous (classified) locations shall be properly documented. This documentation shall be available to those authorized to design, install, inspect, maintain, or operate electrical equipment at the location.

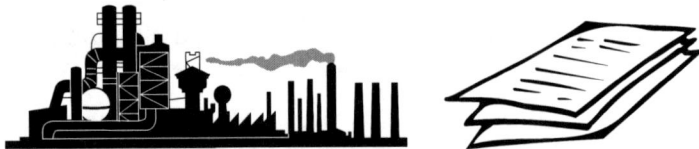

Important information relating to topics covered in Chapter 5 may be found in other publications.

505.5(A). Locations shall be classified depending on the properties of the flammable vapors, liquids, or gases that may be present and the likelihood that a flammable or combustible concentration or quantity is present. Where pyrophoric materials (emitting sparks when scratched or struck with steel) are the only materials used or handled, these locations shall not be classified. Each room, section, or area shall be considered individually in determining its classification.

Rooms and areas containing ammonia refrigeration systems that are equipped with adequate mechanical ventilation may be classified as "unclassified" locations.

505.5(B). Class I, Zone 0, 1 and 2 locations are those in which flammable vapors or gases are or may be present in the air in quantities sufficient to produce explosive or ignitible mixtures.

505.5(B)(1). Zone 0 is defined as being where ignitible concentrations of flammable gases or vapors are present *continuously* or for long periods of time. This includes the interior of vented vessels holding volatile flammable liquids; the space between the inner and outer roof sections of a floating-roof tank containing volatile flammable liquids; the inside ducts of exhausting ignitible concentrations of flammable vapors; and similar installations.

505.5(B)(2). Class I, Zone 1 locations are those in which:

(1) Ignitible concentrations of flammable gases or vapor are likely to exist under normal operating conditions.

 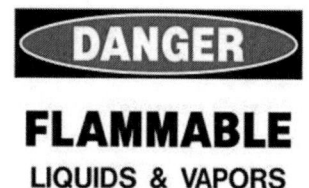

(2) They may exist frequently because of repair or maintenance operations or because of leakage.

(3) Equipment or processes exist of such a nature that equipment breakdown or faulty operation could result in the release of ignitible concentrations of flammable gases or vapors, and also cause simultaneous failure of electrical equipment in a manner that makes it become a source of ignition.

(4) That is adjacent to a Class I, Zone 0 location from which ignitible concentrations of vapors could be communicated. This classification can be reduced if communication is prevented by adequate positive-pressure ventilation from a source of clean air and effective safeguards against ventilation failure is provided.

505.5(B)(2).

Informational Note 1: Normal operation as used in the definition of Zone 1 is considered to be the situation when plant equipment is operating with its design parameters. Minor releases from seals and accidental spillages are not considered part of normal operations, locations where they might occur merit a Zone 1, instead of a Zone 0 classification.

Informational Note 2: A Zone 1 classification is required for a location where: volatile flammable liquids or liquefied flammable gases are transferred from one container to another; in areas in the vicinity of spraying and painting operations where flammable solvents are used; adequately ventilated drying rooms or compartments for the evaporation of flammable solvents; adequately ventilated locations containing fat and oil extraction equipment using volatile (explosive) flammable solvents; portions of cleaning and dyeing plants where volatile flammable liquids are used; adequately ventilated gas generator rooms and other portions of gas manufacturing plants where flammable gas may escape; inadequately ventilated pump rooms for flammable gas or for volatile flammable liquids; the interiors of refrigerators and freezers in which volatile flammable materials are stored in the open or in lightly stoppered or easily ruptured containers; and other locations where ignitible concentrations of flammable vapors and gases are likely to occur in the course of normal operation, but not classified as Zone 0.

505.5(B)(3). Class I, Zone 2 location includes locations where:
(1) Ignitible concentrations of flammable gases or vapors are not likely to occur in normal operation, and if they do, it's only for a short period of time.

(2) Where volatile flammable liquids, flammable gases, or flammable vapors are handled, processed, or used, but in which these items normally are confined within closed containers or closed systems from which they can escape only as a result of accidental rupture or breakdown of the containers or system, or as the result of the abnormal operation of the equipment with which the liquids or gases are handled, processed or used.

505.5(B)(3).

(3) Where ignitible concentrations of flammable gases or vapors normally are prevented by positive mechanical ventilation, but which may become hazardous as a result of failure or abnormal operation of the ventilation equipment.

(4) It is adjacent to a Class I, Zone 1 location from which ignitible concentrations of flammable gases or vapors could be communicated, unless such communication is prevented by adequate positive-pressure ventilation from a source of clean air, and effective safeguards against ventilation failure are provided.

The definition of Zone 2 is functionally identical to NEC Division 2 location, where hazardous concentrations occur only under accidental or unusual operating conditions.

505.6. For purposes of testing, approval, and area classification, various air mixtures (not oxygen enriched) shall be grouped as required in 505.6(A), (B), and (C).

Informational Note: Group I is intended for use in describing atmospheres that contain firedamp (a mixture of gases, composed mostly of methane, found underground in mines). Section 90.2(B)(2) states this Code does NOT apply to mines.

There are two principal groups of mines: underground and surface mines. The Code does **not** cover underground mines, but surface mines and other facilities that handle coal products are usually governed by the requirements of the Code.

505.6(A). Group IIC atmospheres containing acetylene, hydrogen, or flammable gas, flammable liquid-produced vapor, or combustible liquid-produced vapor mixed with air that may burn or explode, having either a maximum experimental safe gap (MESG) value less than or equal to 0.50 mm or minimum igniting current ratio (MIC ratio) less than or equal to 0.45.

Flammable
gas

505.6(B). Group IIB atmospheres containing acetaldehyde, ethylene, or flammable gas, flammable liquid-produced vapor, or combustible liquid-produced vapor mixed with air that may burn or explode, having either a maximum experimental safe gap (MESG) value greater than 0.50 mm and less than or equal to 0.90 mm or minimum igniting current ratio (MIC ratio) greater than 0.45 and less than or equal to 0.80.

505.6(C). Group IIA atmospheres containing acetone, ammonia, ethyl alcohol, gasoline, methane, propane, or flammable gas, flammable liquid-produced vapor, or combustible liquid-produced vapor mixed with air that may burn or explode, having either a maximum experimental safe gap (MESG) value greater than 0.90 mm or minimum igniting current ratio (MIC ratio) greater than 0.80.

Informational Note: Group IIA is equivalent to Class I, Group D per 500.6(A)(4).

505.7. Article 505 requires equipment construction and installation that ensures safe performance under conditions of proper use and maintenance.

Informational Note 1: It is important that inspection authorities and users exercise more than ordinary care with regard to the installation and maintenance of electrical equipment in hazardous (classified) locations.

Informational Note 2. Low ambient temperatures require special consideration.

505.7(A). Classification of areas and selection of equipment and wiring methods, installation, and inspection, shall be performed by qualified persons.

Author's note: In reference to the word *qualified*, it appears the local inspector must decide who is, and who is not, *qualified*.

Construction and maintenance activities have little to do with each other from a job task standpoint. Most construction electricians rarely, if ever get involved in maintenance or trouble shooting. Looking at the definition of qualified person from both OSHA and NFPA 70E makes it clear just because we have a license and years of experience, it does not mean we are qualified to do all electrical work.

OSHA You can't train an employee and then wait five years and expect them to remember what was learned. OSHA 29CFR1910.269(a)(2) (iv) (C) Note states, *"OSHA would consider tasks that are performed **less often than once per year** to necessitate **retraining** before the performance of the work practices involved."*

505.7(B). Division 1 areas are NOT permitted to be adjacent to Zone-classified areas, even if these are in the same facility. A Class 2 location can be adjacent to a Zone 2 location.

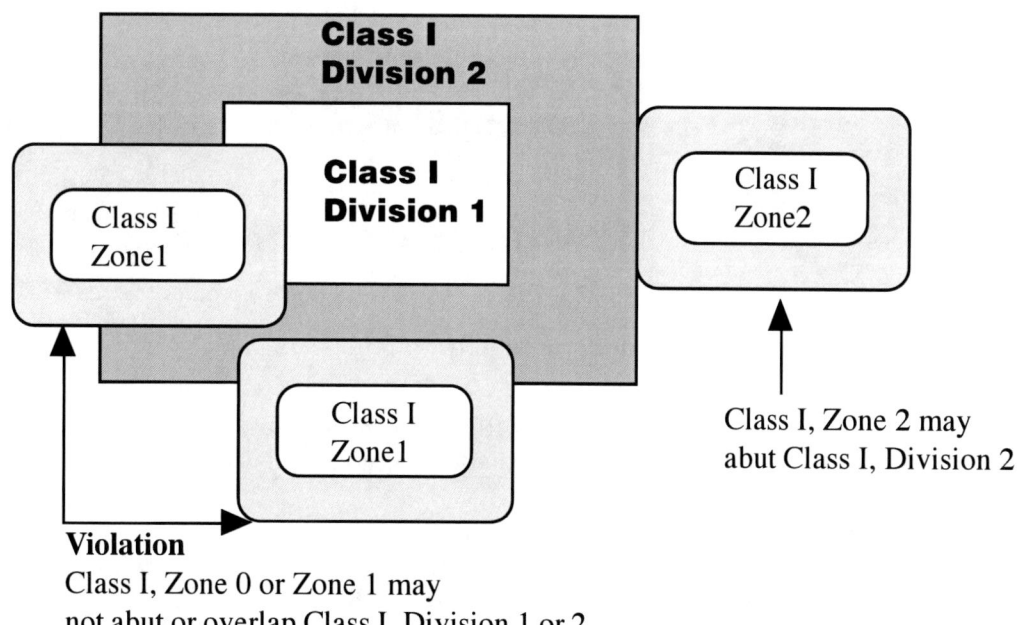

Violation
Class I, Zone 0 or Zone 1 may
not abut or overlap Class I, Division 1 or 2

Class I, Zone 2 may
abut Class I, Division 2

505.7(C). A Class I, Division 1 or 2 location shall be permitted to be reclassified as a Class I, Zone 0, Zone 1, or Zone 2 location, provided all of the space that is classified because of a single flammable gas or vapor source is reclassified under the requirements of this Article.

505.7(D). This section requires equipment having flanged openings be placed a certain minimum distance away from steel, walls, weather guards, mounting brackets, pipes, etc. unless the equipment is listed for a smaller distance of separation. This distance provides for the expanding gases flowing out through the flanged opening. The minimum distances for each gas group are shown in Table 505.7(D).

	Minimum Distance
Gas Group	Inches
IIC	1 37/64
IIB	1 3/16
IIA	25/64

505.7(E). Where flammable gases, combustible dusts, or fibers/flyings are or may be present at the same time, the simultaneous presence shall be considered during the selection and installation of the electrical equipment and the wiring methods, including the determination of the safe operating temperature of the electrical equipment.

  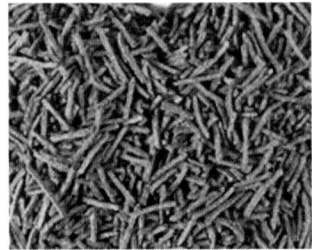

505.8. Acceptable protection techniques shall be:

505.8(A). Flameproof "d" protection technique shall be permitted for equipment in Class I, Zone 1 or 2 locations. This protection is the closest equivalent to the NEC explosionproof enclosures.

505.8(B). Purged and Pressurized protection technique shall be permitted for equipment in those Class I, Zone 1 or 2 locations for which it is identified. This type of protection uses the technique of guarding against the ingress of the external atmosphere, which may be explosive, into an enclosure by maintaining a protective gas therein at a pressure above that of the external atmosphere.

505.8(C). Intrinsic safety protection technique shall be permitted for apparatus and associated apparatus in Class I, Zone 1 or 2 locations for which it is listed. This protection involves intrinsically safe circuits in which no spark and no thermal effect can rise under normal working conditions, or some types of failures, can lead to an explosion in a specific potentially hazardous atmosphere.

505.8(D). Protection "n" technique shall be permitted for equipment in Class I, Zone 2 locations. This type of protection is where electrical equipment, in normal operation, is not capable of igniting a surrounding gas atmosphere and a fault capable of causing ignition is not likely to occur.

505.8(E). Oil immersion protection technique shall be permitted for equipment in Class I, Zone 1 or 2 locations. In this type of protection, the arcing parts are immersed in a volume of oil, so the flammable vapor or gas cannot come into contact with the arc.

505.8(F). Increased safety "e" protection technique shall be permitted for equipment in Class I, Zone 1 or 2 locations. This protection includes increased measures to prevent the possibility of excess heat, arcs, or sparks from occurring on internal or external parts of equipment, which normally do not produce such sources. The methods include: terminals that are protected against self loosening, and must provide an adequate contact pressure when the cable is cold; air gaps and creep path specific to the voltage of the circuit; resistance to temperatures at least 20°C above the usual working temperature; specification of minimum wire thickness and csa; and others.

505.8(G). Encapsulation "m" protection technique shall be permitted for equipment in Class I, Zone 0, 1, or 2 locations for which it is identified. Protection is provided by embedding the sparking or potentially dangerous electrical parts in a potting compound so that any explosive atmosphere will not come in contact with these parts.

505.8(H). Powder filling "q" protection technique shall be permitted for equipment in Class I, Zone 1 or 2 locations. This protection assures that an arc occurring within the enclosure will be cooled and extinguished by the finely granulated quartz sand that fills the enclosure. The enclosure has an inspection glass to monitor the settling of the sand.

505.8(I). Combustible Gas Detection System. This protection utilizes stationary gas detectors in industrial establishments. Normally, when a certain gas is sensed by one or more detectors, an alarm is sent to plant workmen, and in some cases the alarm initiates a plant emergency shutdown system.

505.8(B)(2) Inadequate Ventilation. A location, enclosed space, or building that is classified as a Zone 1 location due to inadequate ventilation, that is provided with a combustible gas detection systemwill be allowed to utilize electrical equipment, installation methods, and wiring suitable for Zone 2 installations.

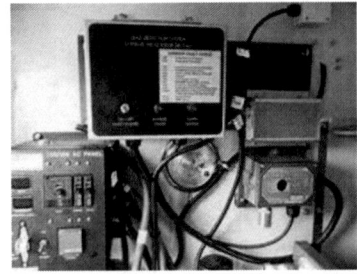

505.9(A). The suitability of equipment can be determined by any one of the following:
(1) Equipment listing or labeling.
(2) Evidence of equipment evaluation from a qualified testing laboratory or inspection agency concerned with product evaluation.
(3) Evidence acceptable to the authority having jurisdiction such as a manufacturer's self-evaluation or an owner's engineering judgement.

505.9(B). Equipment that is listed for a Zone 0 location is also permitted to be used in a Zone 1 or 2 location. Equipment that is listed for a Zone 1 location is also permitted to be used in a Zone 2 location.

Equipment can be listed for a specific gas or vapor, specific mixtures of gases or vapors, or any specific combination of gases or vapors.

505.9(C)(1). Equipment identified for Class I, Division 1 or Division 2 shall, in addition to being marked in accordance with 500.8(C), be permitted to be marked with all of the following;
(1) Class I, Zone 1 or 2 (as applicable)
(2) Applicable gas classification group(s) in accordance with Table 505.9(C)(1)(2)
(3) Temperature classification in accordance with 505.9(D)(1)

Table 505.9(C)(1)(2) Material Groups

Gas Group	Comment
IIC	Group IIC atmospheres containing acetylene, hydrogen, or flammable gas, flammable liquid-produced vapor, or combustible liquid-produced vapor mixed with air that may burn or explode, having either a maximum experimental safe gap (MESG) value less than or equal to 0.50 mm or minimum igniting current ratio (MIC ratio) less than or equal to 0.45.
IIB	Group IIB atmospheres containing acetaldehyde, ethylene, or flammable gas, flammable liquid-produced vapor, or combustible liquid-produced vapor mixed with air that may burn or explode, having either a maximum experimental safe gap (MESG) value greater than 0.50 mm and less than or equal to 0.90 mm or minimum igniting current ratio (MIC ratio) greater than 0.45 and less than or equal to 0.80.
IIA	Group IIA atmospheres containing acetone, ammonia, ethyl alcohol, gasoline, methane, propane, or flammable gas, flammable liquid-produced vapor, or combustible liquid-produced vapor mixed with air that may burn or explode, having either a maximum experimental safe gap (MESG) value greater than 0.90 mm or minimum igniting current ratio (MIC ratio) greater than 0.80.

505.9(C)(2). Equipment meeting one or more of the protection techniques described in 505.8 shall be marked with all of the following in the order shown;

(1) Class I (equipment shall be permitted to omit the Class I marking)

(2) Zone [in accordance with Table 505.9(C)(2)(4)]

(3) Symbol "AEx"

(4) Protection technique(s) in accordance with Table 505.9(C)(2)(4)

(5) Applicable gas classification group(s) in accordance with Table 505.9(C)(1)(2)

(6) Temperature classification in accordance with 505.9(D)(1)

(7) Equipment protection level (EPL)

Exception 1: Associated apparatus NOT suitable for installation in a hazardous location shall be required to be marked only with (3), (4), and (5), but BOTH the symbol AEx (3) and the symbol for the type of protection (4) shall be enclosed within the same square brackets, for example, [AEx ia] IIC.

Exception 2: Simple apparatus as defined in Article 100 Part III shall not be required to have a marked operating temperature or temperature class.

Table 505.9(C)(2)(4) Equipment Suitability

Type of Protection	Marking	Permitted Location
Associated apparatus for Zone 0	[ia]	Unclassified[1]
Associated apparatus for Zone 1	[ib]	Unclassified[1]
Associated apparatus for Zone 2	[ic]	Unclassified[1]
Associated pressurization equipment	[p]	Unclassified[1]
Intrinsic safety	ia; Class I, Division 1 Intrinsic Safety	Zone 0
Encapsulation	ma	
Optical radiation, inherently safe	op is, with EPL Ga[2]	
Optical radiation, with interlock	op sh, with EPL Ga[2]	
EPL Ga, with suitable type of protection[3]		
Equipment Suitable for Use in Zone 0		
Equipment Suitable for Use in Class I, Division 1		
Flameproof enclosure	d; db	
Intrinsic safety	ib	
Increased safety	e; eb	
Pressurized enclosure	p; px, pxb; py; pyb	
Encapsulation	m; mb	
Powder filling	q; qb	Zone 1
Liquid immersion	o; ob	
Electrical resistance trace heating	60079-30-1, with EPL Gb[2] Skin effect trace heating	
IEEE 844.1, with EPL Gb[2]	Optical radiation, inherently safe	
op is, with EPL Gb[2]		
Optical radiation, with interlock	op sh, with EPL Gb[2]	
Optical radiation, protected	op pr, with EPL Gb[2]	
EPL Gb, with suitable type of protection[3]		

(continued on next page)

Table 505.9(C)(2)(4) Equipment Suitability (continued)

Type of Protection	Marking	Permitted Location
Equipment Suitable for Use in Zone 1		
Equipment Suitable for Use in Class I, Division 2		
Type of protection "n"	nA; nC; nR	
Pressurized enclosure	pz, pzc	
Intrinsic safety	ic	
Flameproof enclosure	dc	
Increased safety	ec	
Liquid immersion	oc	Zone 2
Encapsulation	mc	
Electrical resistance trace heating	60079-30-1, *with EPL Gc*[2]	
Skin effect trace heating	IEEE 844.1, with EPL Gc[2]	
Optical radiation, inherently safe	op is, *with EPL Gc*[2]	
Optical radiation, with interlock	op sh, *with EPL Gc*[2]	
Optical radiation, protected	op pr, *with EPL Gc*[2]	
EPL Gc, with suitable type of protection[3]		

[1]Permitted to be installed in a hazardous (classified) location if suitably protected using another type of protection.

[2]Equipment marked with these types of protection is available in multiple levels of protection that are not specifically identified within the AEx marking.

[3]The EPL takes precedence over the types of protection. For example, "ia Gb" is suitable for Zone 1 (not Zone 0). "60079-30-1 Gc" is suitable for Zone 2 (not Zone 1). Selection according to the marked EPL is critical to the safe application of this equipment.

[4]"Other electrical equipment — general purpose motors" refers to motors in accordance with Exception No. 4 to 505.20(C).

505.9(D). Class I Temperature. The temperature marking specified below shall not exceed the ignition temperature of the specific gas or vapor to be encountered.

505.9(D)(1). Identified equipment must be marked to show the operating temperature or temperature range referenced to a 40°C (104°F) ambient, or at the higher ambient temperature if the equipment is rated and marked for an ambient temperature greater than 40° C (104° F). The temperature range, if provided, must be indicated in identification numbers, as shown in Table 505.9(D1).

Table 505.9(D)(1).

Temperature Class (T Code)	Maximum Surface Temperature	
	Degree C	Degree F
T1	≤450	842
T2	≤300	572
T3	≤200	392
T4	≤135	275
T5	≤100	212
T6	≤ 85	185

Equipment that is designed for use in a range of ambient temperatures other than -20°C and +40°C must have the ambient temperature range marked on the equipment, including either the symbol "Ta" or "Tamb" together with the special range of ambient temperatures, in degrees Celsius.

505.9(E). All threaded conduit must be threaded with NPT, made up wrenchtight to prevent sparking when fault current flows through the conduit, and to ensure the explosionproof integrity of the conduit system. Threaded joints must be made up with at least five full threads engaged for entries into flameproof or explosionproof equipment.

Equipment with metric threads must be identified as such or listed adapters to NPT threads must be provided.

505.15(A). In Class I, Zone 0 locations, only intrinsically safe wiring methods in accordance with Article 504 shall be permitted.

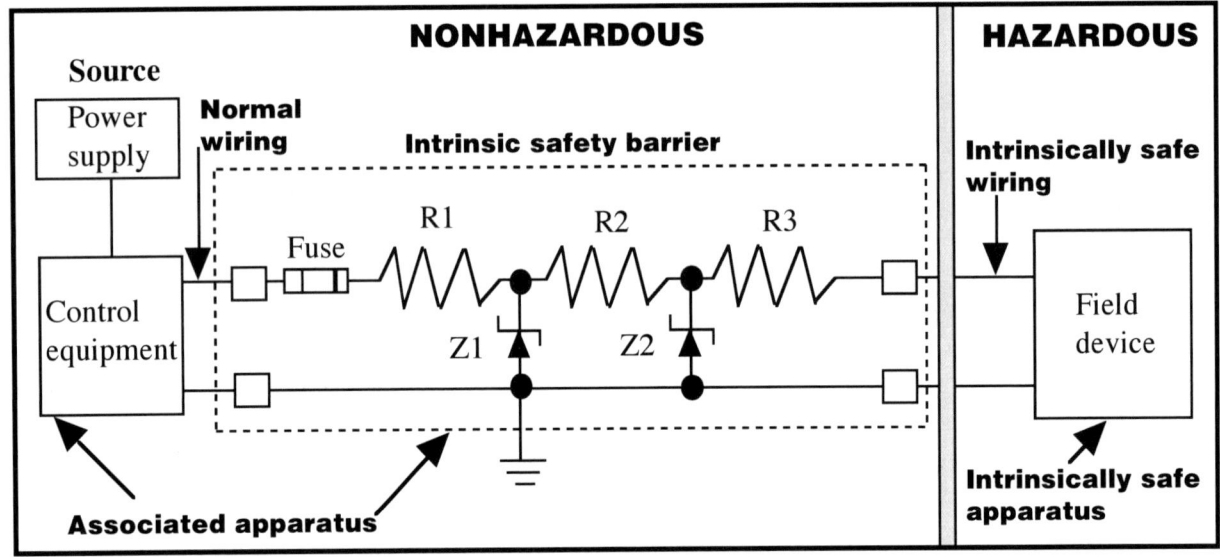

505.15(B)(1). In Class I, Zone 1 locations, the following wiring methods shall be permitted:

(1) All wiring methods permitted by 505.15(A).

(2) In industrial establishments only, where restricted public access and qualified maintenance personnel and supervision exist, and where the cable is not subject to physical damage, Type MC-HL Cable listed for use in Class I, Zone 1 or Division 1 locations having a gas/vaportight continuous corrugated metallic sheath, an overall jacket of suitable polymeric material, separate grounding conductors in accordance with 250.122, and with termination fittings that are listed for the application. Type MC-HL cable shall be installed per Article 330, Part II.

(3) Type ITC-HL Cable listed for Class I, Zone 1 or Division 1 locations having a gas/vaportight continuous corrugated metallic sheath, an overall jacket of suitable polymeric material, and with termination fittings that are listed for the application. Type ITC-HL cable shall be installed per 727.4.

(4) Type MI Cable with termination fittings listed for Class I, Division 1 locations.

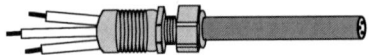

(5) Threaded rigid metal conduit, or threaded steel IMC.

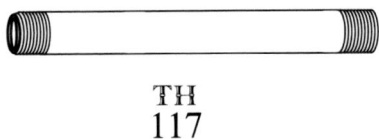

(6) Rigid nonmetallic conduit where encased in 2" of concrete and 24" of cover, measured from the top of the conduit to grade. The stub-up must be rigid steel or IMC with an equipment grounding conductor.

(7) Intrinsic safety type protection "ib."

(8) Optical fiber cable.

(9) Type TC-ER-HL cable in industrial establishments with maintenance and supervision.

(10) In industrial establishments listed Type P cable with metal braid of armor.

505.15(B)(2). Flexible fittings (such as explosionproof flex) listed for Class I, Zone 1 or Division 1 locations or flexible cord in accordance with 505.17 terminated with a listed cord connector that maintains the type of protection of the terminal compartment shall be permitted.

505.15(C)(1). In Class I, Zone 2 locations, the following wiring methods are permitted:
(1) All wiring methods permitted for Zone 1.
(2) Types MI, MC, MV, or TC cable with termination fittings, or in cable tray systems and installed in a manner to avoid tensile stress at the termination fittings. Single conductor Type MV cables shall be shielded or metallic-armored.

(3) ITC and ITC-ER cable.
(4) PLTC and PLTC-ER cable.
(5) Enclosed gasketed busways, enclosed gasketed wireways.

(6) Threaded rigid metal conduit, threaded IMC, RTRC marked with suffix-XW and Schedule 80 PVC conduit.
(7) Intrinsic safety type protection "ic" field wiring shall be permitted using any of the wiring methods for unclassified locations.
(8) Optical fiber cable.
(9) Cablebus.
(10) In industrial establishments listed Type P cable with metal braid of armor.

505.15(C)(2). Flexible metal fittings, flexible metal conduit with listed fittings, liquidtight flexible metal conduit with listed fittings, liquidtight flexible nonmetallic conduit with listed fitting, or flexible cord in accordance with 505.15 shall be permitted as wiring methods in Zone 2.

505.16(A)(1). In Class I, Zone 0 locations, seals shall be provided within 10' of where a conduit leaves a Zone 0 location. There shall be no unions, couplings, boxes, or fittings, except listed reducers at the seal, in the conduit run between the seal and the point at which the conduit leaves the location.

Exception: A rigid unbroken conduit that passes completely through the Zone 0 location with no fittings less than 12" beyond each boundary shall not be required to be sealed if the termination points of the unbroken conduit are in unclassified locations.

505.16(A)(2). Seals shall be provided on cables at the first point of termination after entry into the Zone 0 location.

505.16(A)(3). Seals shall **not** be required to be explosionproof or flameproof.

505.16(B)(1). Conduit seals shall be provided within 2" for each conduit entering enclosures having type "d", "db", "e" or "eb" protection, unless the enclosure is marked to indicate that a seal is not required.

505.16(B)(2). Conduit seals shall be provided for each conduit entering explosionproof equipment that contains arcing or heating (at 80% of the ignition temperature of the gas) equipment, or has an entry of 2" or larger and the enclosure contains wire joints.

These seals must be located close to the enclosure to minimize the volume of explosive gas and to prevent pressure piling in the conduit. The seals are required to be installed 18" from the enclosure with only explosionproof fittings permitted between the sealing fitting and the explosionproof enclosure. These explosionproof fittings between the enclosure and the sealing fitting are not to be larger than the trade size of the conduit. Where two explosionproof enclosures are located not more than 36" apart, the 18" rule permits the use of only one sealing fitting, but it must not be more than 18" from either enclosure.

505.16(B)(3). Conduit seals shall be provided in each conduit entry into a pressurized enclosure where the conduit is not pressurized as part of the protection system. Conduit seals shall be installed within 18" from the pressurized enclosure.

505.16(B)(4). Conduit seals shall be provided in each conduit leaving a Class I, Zone 1 location. The sealing fitting shall be permitted on either side of the boundary, within 10' of the boundary. Except for listed explosionproof reducers at the seal, there shall be no other fittings between the seal and the point where it leaves the Zone 1 location. As with Zone 0, metal conduit that is unbroken does not require a seal.

505.16(B)(5). Conduits containing cables with a gas/vaportight continuous sheath capable of transmitting gases or vapors through the cable core shall be sealed in the Zone 1 location after removing the jacket and any other coverings so that the sealing compound surrounds each individual insulated conductor and the outer jacket.

505.16(B)(6). Each multiconductor cable in conduit shall be considered as a single conductor if the cable is incapable of transmitting gases or vapors through the cable core. These cables shall be sealed per 505.16(D).

505.16(B)(7). Cable seals shall be provided for each cable entering flameproof or explosionproof enclosures. The seal shall comply with 505.16(D).

505.16(B)(8). Cables shall be sealed at the point at which they leave the Zone 1 location.

505.16(C)(1). Zone 2 conduit seals for connections to enclosures that are required to be flameproof or explosionproof shall be provided in accordance with 505.16(C)(1)(a) & (C)(1)(b). In each conduit run passing from a Zone 2 location into an unclassified location, the sealing fitting shall be permitted on either side of the boundary.

505.16(C)(2). Where a cable enters a flameproof or explosionproof enclosure, the cable must be terminated in a sealing fitting. The overall gas/vaportight continuous sheath and/or the jacket of multiconductor cables within the sealing fitting must be removed so the sealing compound can fully surround each individual insulated conductor and the outer jacket. The removal of shielding or breaking open twisted pairs is not required.

505.16(D). Seals can either be integral to enclosures or thay can be individual fittings specifically designed for the application. Sealing fittings must be listed for use with one or more sealing compounds, and must be accessible.

Sealing compounds must provide a seal against the passage of fluids through the sealing fitting, and not be affected by the surrounding atmosphere or process fluids, and must not have a melting point of less than 200°F. When poured, the thickness of the sealing compound shall not be less than the trade size of the sealing fitting, and not less than 5/8".

Splices and taps are not permitted in the fitting. The conductor fill shall not exceed 25% of the csa of a rigid conduit.

200°F  **5/8"**

505.16(E)(1). Drain fittings are intended to allow accumulated moisture or other fluid trapped within enclosures or conduits to escape. Drains and vents also serve the purpose of making evident the leakage of hazardous materials past seals.

505.16(E)(2). Where the inspector thinks there is a probability that liquid or condensed vapor may accumulate within motors or generators, joints and conduit systems must be arranged to minimize its entrance.

505.17. The Code permits flexible cords in Zone 1 and 2 locations for:
•Connection to portable lighting equipment

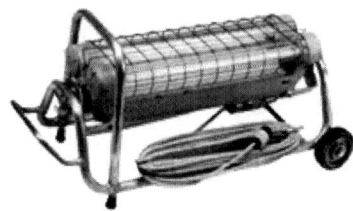

•Connection to portable appliances
•For flexibility for fixed appliances where limited to industrial establishments where maintenance and engineering supervision ensure that only qualified persons install the cord.

The Code requires that flexible cords be:
(1) Listed for extra-hard usuage

(2) Contain an equipment grounding conductor

(3) Connected in an approved manner

(4) Be supported so there is no tension on the terminals

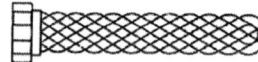

(5) Be terminated with a listed cord connector that maintains the type of protection, explosionproof or flameproof

(6) Cord entering an increased safety "e" enclosure shall be terminated with a listed increased safety "e" cord connector.

   Although the Code in Chapter 4 prohibits flexible cords installed in conduit, this section permits this where the cord supplies a submersible sump pump.

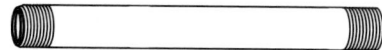

505.18(A). Requires that conductors used for type of protection "e" be made of copper.

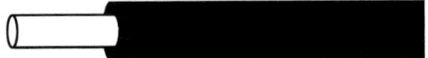

505.18(B). Where process fluids may come into contact with the conductor insulation, the insulation must be of a type identified for use under such conditions, or the insulation must be protected by a sheath of lead or other approved means.

505.19. There shall be no uninsulated live parts that operate at more than 30 volts (15 volts in wet locations).

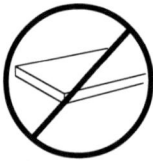

505.20(A). In Class I, Zone 0 locations, only equipment specifically listed and marked suitable for the location shall be permitted.
Exception: Intrinsically safe apparatus listed for use in Class I, Division 1 locations for the same gas, or as permitted by 505.9(B)(2), and with a suitable temperature class.

505.20(B). In Class I, Zone 1 locations, only equipment specifically listed and marked suitable for the location shall be permitted.

Exception 1: Equipment identified for use in Class I, Division 1 locations or listed for use in Class I, Zone 0 locations for the same gas, or as permitted by 505.9(B2), and with a suitable temperature class.

Exception 2: Equipment identified for Class I, Zone 1, or Zone 2 type of protection "p".

505.20(C). In Class I, Zone 2 locations, only equipment specifically listed and marked suitable for the location shall be permitted.

Exception 1: Equipment listed for use in Class I, Zone 0 or 1 locations for the same gas and suitable temperature.

Exception 2: Equipment identified for use in Class I, Zone 1 or 2 locations, protection type "p".

Exception 3: Equipment identified for use in Class I, Division 1 or 2 locations for the same gas and suitable temperature.

Exception 4: Open or nonexplosionproof or nonflameproof motors that do not contain arc-producing devices such as brushes.

505.20(D). Electrical equipment installed in hazardous locations shall be installed in accordance with the instructions (if any) provided by the manufacturer.

505.22. This section lists the rules in Class I, Zone 1 locations for Increased Safety "e" motors and generators.

505.25. Grounding and bonding shall comply with Article 250.

505.25(A). The locknut-bushing and double-locknut types of contact shall not be depended on for bonding purposes, but bonding jumpers with proper fittings or other approved means of bonding shall be used.

505.25(B). Where flexible metal conduit or liquidtight flexible metal conduit is used and is relied on to complete a sole equipment grounding path, it shall be installed with internal or external equipment bonding jumpers complying with 250.102.

ARTICLE 506

Zone 20, 21, and 22 Locations for Combustible Dusts, Fibers, and Flyings

506.1. This article covers the requirements for the Zone classification system as an alternative to the Division classification system covered in Article 500, Article 502 and Article 503 for electrical and electronic equipment and wiring for all voltages in Zone 20, Zone 21 and Zone 22 hazardous (classified) locations where fire and explosion hazards may exist due to combustible dusts, or ignitible fibers, or flyings.

Combustible metallic dusts **are not** covered by the requirements of this article.

506.5(B). The three Zones defined as follows:

(1) **Zone 20** is a location in which:

(1) Ignitible concentrations of combustible dust, ignitible fibers or flyings are present continuously, or

(2) Ignitible concentrations of combustible dust, or ignitible fibers or flyings are present for long periods of time.

(2) **Zone 21** is a location:

(1) In which ignitible concentrations of combustible dust, or ignitible fibers or flyings are likely to exist occasionally under normal operating conditions; or

(2) In which ignitible concentrations of combustible dust, or ignitible fibers or flyings may exist frequently because of repair, maintenance operations or because of leakage; or

(3) In which equipment is operated or processes are carried on, of such nature that equipment breakdown or faulty operations could result in the release of ignitible concentrations of combustible dust, or ignitible fibers or flyings and also cause simultaneous failure of electrical equipment in a mode to cause the electrical equipment to become a source of ignition; or

(4) That is adjacent to a Zone 20 location from which ignitible concentrations of combustible dust, ignitible fibers or flyings could be communicated, unless communication is prevented by adequate positive pressure ventilation from a source of clean air and effective safeguards against ventilation failure are provided.

(5) Group IIIC combustible dusts are present in quantities sufficient to be hazardous occasionally; under normal or abnormal operating conditions; or frequently because of repair or maintenance operations or because of leakage.

(3) Zone 22 is a location:

(1) In which ignitible concentrations of combustible dust, or ignitible fibers or flyings are not likely to occur in normal operation, and if they do occur, will only persist for a short period; or

(2) In which combustible dust, or ignitible fibers or flyings are handled, processed or used but in which the dust, fibers, or flyings are normally confined within closed containers or closed systems from which they can escape only as a result of the abnormal operation of the equipment with which the dust, or fibers, or flyings are handled, processed or used; or

(3) That is adjacent to a Zone 21 location, from which ignitible concentrations of combustible dust, or ignitible fibers or flyings could be communicated, unless communication is prevented by adequate positive pressure ventilation from a source of clean air and effective safeguards against ventilation failure are provided.

ZONE SUMMARY

Author's note: Zone 0 locations are those where the atmosphere is within the flammable range *all or almost all the time* under normal conditions. The equipment design concept is that there must be at least two simultaneous faults in the protection system (three in intrinsically safe systems) before ignition can occur.

Explosionproof systems, even though acceptable for Division 1 locations, do not meet this criteria.

A single fault, such as a loose or missing enclosure bolt or a bad scratch on a flat joint surface, can render the protection useless.

DIFFERENCE BETWEEN ZONES and DIVISIONS

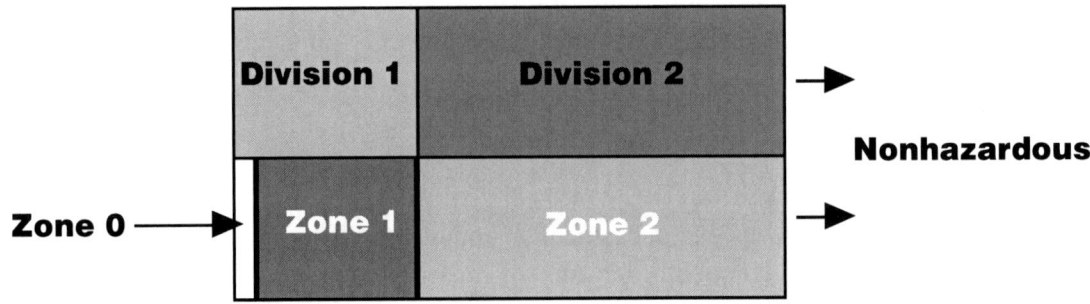

Articles 502 - 506   Quiz #1   -   Open Book

*•Circle your choice of answer and **write the Code section where it was found**.*

1. Which of the following statements is **false**?

(a) Intrinsically safe circuits must be identified at terminal and junction locations in a manner that will prevent unintentional interference with the circuits while testing and servicing.
(b) In hazardous (classified) locations, intrinsically safe apparatus shall be bonded in the hazardous (classified) location per 250.100.
(c) Intrinsically safe apparatus shall be permitted to be installed in any hazardous (classified) location for which it has been identified.
(d) Within an enclosure, conductors of intrinsically safe circuits must be separated from other nonintrinsically safe conductors by at least 3".

2. Where magnesium, aluminum or aluminum-bronze powders may be present, transformers _____.

(a) must be dust-tight   **(b) may be pipe-ventilated**
(c) must be approved for Class II, Division 1   **(d) are not allowed**

3. Class I, Zone 2 is defined as where _____.

(a) ignitible concentrations of flammable gases or vapor are likely to exist under normal operating conditions
(b) ignitible concentrations of flammable gases or vapors are not likely to occur in normal operation, and if they do, it's only for a short period of time
(c) ignitible concentrations of flammable gases or vapors are present continuously or for long periods of time
(d) ignitible concentrations of flammable gases or vapor may exist frequently because of repair or maintenance operations or because of leakage

4. Color coding shall be permitted to identify _____ conductors where they are colored light blue and where no other conductors colored light blue are used.

(a) fire alarm   (b) elevator   (c) intrinsically safe   (d) electrolytic cell

5. Switches, circuit breakers, motor controllers, and fuses, including push buttons, relays, and similar devices that are intended to interrupt current during normal operation or that are installed where combustible dusts of an electrically conductive nature may be present, they shall be provided with identified dust ignition proof _____ identified for the location.

(a) labels   (b) enclosure   (c) sign   (d) warnings

6. Switches, circuit breakers, relays, contactors, fuses and current-breaking contacts for bells, horns, sirens, and other devices in which sparks or arcs may be produced shall be provided with enclosures that are dusttight or otherwise identified for _____ location.

(a) Class I   (b) Class II   (c) Class III   (d) Class IV

7. A Zone 22 is a location in which _____.

(a) ignitible concentrations of combustible dust, or ignitible fibers or flyings are present continuously
(b) combustible dust, or ignitible fibers or flyings are handled, processed or used but in which the dust, fibers, or flyings are normally confined within closed containers or closed systems from which they can escape only as a result of the abnormal operation of the equipment with which the dust, or fibers, or flyings are handled, processed or used
(c) ignitible concentrations of combustible dust, or ignitible fibers or flyings are likely to exist occasionally under normal operating conditions
(d) ignitible concentrations of combustible dust, or ignitible fibers or flyings are present for long periods of time

8. Which of the following statements is **false**?

(a) A Class III, Division 2 location is a location where easily ignitible fibers are stored or handled except in the process of manufacture, where then it would be a Division 1 location.
(b) A Class III, Division 1 location is a location in which the easily ignitible fibers or materials producing combustible flyings are handled, manufactured, or used.
(c) Compared to classifying a Class I, Division 1 or 2 location or a Class II, Division 1 or 2 location, it is much simpler to determine a Class III, Division 1 or 2 location. It depends on the use of the area rather than the amount of material present or likely to be present.
(d) There are three Groups in Class III hazardous locations.

9. Powder Filling "q" _____.

(a) uses the technique of guarding against the ingress of the external atmosphere, which may be explosive, into an enclosure by maintaining a protective gas therein at a pressure above that of the external atmosphere
(b) the arcing parts are immersed in a volume of oil, so the flammable vapor or gas cannot come into contact with the arc
(c) is provided by embedding the sparking or potentially dangerous electrical parts in a potting compound so that any explosive atmosphere will not come in contact with these parts
(d) where electrical parts capable of igniting an explosive atmosphere are fixed in position and completely surrounded by filling material (glass or quartz) to prevent the ignition of an external explosive atmosphere.

10. Article 505 requires the classification of areas and selection of equipment and wiring methods to be performed by _____.

(a) **Certified Electrical Engineer**   (b) **State Building Official**
(c) **Qualified persons**   (d) **Registered Chemical Engineer**

11. Zone equipment is required to have flanged openings placed a certain minimum distance away from steel, walls, weather guards, mounting brackets, pipes, etc. unless the equipment is listed for a smaller distance of separation. This distance provides for the expanding gases flowing out through the flanged opening. The minimum distance for IIB gas group is _____.

(a) **5/8"**   (b) **25/64"**   (c) **1 3/16"**   (d) **1 1/2"**

12. All of the following motors are permitted in a Class III, Division 1 area except _____.

(a) **totally enclosed pipe ventilated**   (b) **non-ventilated**
(c) **totally enclosed fan cooled**   (d) **water cooled**

Articles 502 - 506   Quiz #2   -   Open Book

•*Circle your choice of answer and **write the Code section where it was found**.*

1. Where flexible metal conduit or liquidtight flexible metal conduit is used as permitted and is to be relied on to complete a single equipment grounding path, it shall be installed with internal or _____ equipment bonding jumpers in parallel with each conduit. Unless the conduit is six feet or less in length.

(a) factory installed   (b) external   (c) field soldered   (d) field welded

2. Where shielded conductors or cables are used, shields shall be _____ in accordance with the required control drawing.

(a) connected   (b) terminated   (c) grounded   (d) bonded

3. A Zone 20 is a location in which _____.

(a) is adjacent to a Zone 21 location from which ignitible concentrations of combustible dust, or ignitible fibers or flyings could be communicated, unless communication is prevented by adequate positive pressure ventilation from a source of clean air and effective safeguards against ventilation failure are provided
(b) ignitible concentrations of combustible dust, or ignitible fibers or flyings are not likely to occur in normal operation, and if they do occur, will only persist for a short period of time
(c) equipment is operated or processes are carried on, of such nature that equipment breakdown or faulty operations could result in the release of ignitible concentrations of combustible dust, or ignitible fibers or flyings and also cause simultaneous failure of electrical equipment in a mode to cause the electrical equipment to become a source of ignition
(d) ignitible concentrations of combustible dust, or ignitible fibers or flyings are present for long periods of time

4. In a Class II location, there shall be no uninsulated exposed part that operates at more than _____ volts.

(a) 10   (b) 12   (c) 24   (d) 30

5. Simple apparatus, as described on the control drawing, shall **not** be required to be _____.

(a) grounded   (b) identified   (c) listed   (d) separated

6. To reduce the danger of spontaneous combustion in Class III locations, the Code limits the surface temperature of electrical equipment used in these locations. The temperature for motors, transformers, etc. that can operate while overloaded is _____.

(a) 212°F   (b) 248°F   (c) 304°F   (d) 329°F

7. Conductors and cables of intrinsically safe circuits not in raceways or cable trays shall be separated at least _____ and secured from conductors and cables of any nonintrinsically safe circuits.

(a) 24"   (b) 12"   (c) 6"   (d) 2"

8. Boxes and fittings shall be _____ in a Class III, Division 1 location.

(a) sealed   (b) dustproof   (c) dusttight   (d) not allowed

9. Which of the following would **not** be approved in all Class II locations?

**(a) flexible connections   (b) threaded bosses
(c) dusttight boxes   (d) EMT**

10. A/an _____ circuit is a circuit in which any spark or thermal effect is incapable of causing ignition of a mixture of flammable or combustible material in air under prescribed test conditions.

(a) low voltage   (b) intrinsically safe   (c) hazardproof   (d) explosiveproof

11. Class I, Zone 1 is defined as where _____.

**(a) ignitible concentrations of flammable gases or vapors normally are prevented by positive mechanical ventilation, but which may become hazardous as a result of failure or abnormal operation of the ventilation equipment
(b) ignitible concentrations of flammable gases or vapors are not likely to occur in normal operation, and if they do, its only for a short period of time
(c) ignitible concentrations of flammable gases or vapors are present continuously or for long periods of time
(d) ignitible concentrations of flammable gases or vapor may exist frequently because of repair or maintenance operations or because of leakage**

12. Oil Immersion "o" _____.

**(a) is where electrical equipment, in normal operation, is not capable of igniting a surrounding gas atmosphere and a fault capable of causing ignition is not likely to occur
(b) involves intrinsically safe circuits in which no spark and no thermal effect can rise under normal working conditions, or some types of failures, can lead to an explosion in a specific potentially hazardous atmosphere
(c) is a type of protection where electrical equipment is immersed in a protective liquid in such a way that an explosive atmosphere that may be above the liquid or outside the enclosure can not be ignited
(d) is the closest equivalent to the NEC explosionproof enclosures**

Articles 502 - 506   Quiz #3   -   Open Book

•*Circle your choice of answer and **write the Code section where it was found**.*

1. In Class I, Zone 0 locations, only intrinsically safe wiring methods in accordance with _____ shall be permitted.

(a) UL   (b) NEMA   (c) Article 504   (d) Article 725

2. Where magnesium, aluminum or aluminum-bronze powders may be present, transformers _____.

(a) must be dusttight
(b) may be pipe-ventilated
(c) must be approved for Class II, Division 1
(d) are not allowed

3. Class I, Zone 0 is defined as where _____.

(a) ignitible concentrations of flammable gases or vapor are likely to exist under normal operating conditions
(b) ignitible concentrations of flammable gases or vapors are not likely to occur in normal operation, and if they do, it's only for a short period of time
(c) ignitible concentrations of flammable gases or vapors are present continuously or for long periods of time
(d) ignitible concentrations of flammable gases or vapor may exist frequently because of repair or maintenance operations or because of leakage

4. Explosionproof equipment shall not be required and shall not be acceptable in Class II locations unless also _____ for such locations.

(a) marked   (b) listed   (c) approved   (d) identified

5. In a Class III location, each luminaire shall be clearly marked to show the _____.

(a) ballast rating   (b) voltage   (c) maximum lamp wattage   (d) current

6. Which of the following statements is **false**?

(a) The definition of Zone 2 is functionally identical to NEC Division 2 location, where hazardous concentrations occur only under accidental or unusual operating conditions.
(b) The Code does not cover underground mines, but surface mines and other facilities that handle coal products are usually governed by the requirements of the Code.
(c) Splices and taps are not permitted in the fitting. The conductor fill shall not exceed 40% of the csa of a rigid conduit.
(d) Division 1 areas are NOT permitted to be adjacent to Zone-classified areas, even if these are in the same facility. A Class 2 location can be adjacent to a Zone 2 location.

7. Which wiring method is **not** permitted in a Class II, Division 1 location?

(a) MI cable   (b) cable tray   (c) IMC   (d) rigid metal conduit

8. All areas in industrial occupancies designated as hazardous (classified) locations shall be properly ____.

(a) guarded   (b) listed   (c) documented   (d) maintained

9. In a Class II, Division 2 location, all boxes and fittings shall be ____.

(a) dustproof   (b) explosionproof   (c) ignitionproof   (d) dusttight

10. A Zone 21 is a location in which ____.

(a) ignitible concentrations of combustible dust, or ignitible fibers or flyings may exist frequently because of repair or maintenance operations or because of leakage
(b) ignitible concentrations of combustible dust, or ignitible fibers or flyings are not likely to occur in normal operation, and if they do occur, will only persist for a short period
(c) ignitible concentrations of combustible dust, or ignitible fibers or flyings are present for long periods of time
(d) ignitible concentrations of combustible dust, or ignitible fibers or flyings are present continuously

11. To reduce the danger of spontaneous combustion in Class III locations, the Code limits the surface temperature of electrical equipment used in these locations to ____ for equipment that is not subject to overloading, such as light fixtures.

(a) 212°F   (b) 250°F   (c) 304°F   (d) 329°F

12. Rooms and areas containing ammonia refrigeration systems that are equipped with adequate mechanical ventilation may be classified as ____ locations.

(a) unclassified   (b) Group D   (c) Division 2   (d) Class III

ARTICLE 510

Hazardous (Classified) Locations - Specific

510.1. Articles 511 through 517 cover occupancies or parts of occupancies that are or may be hazardous because of atmospheric concentrations of flammable liquids, gases, or vapors, or because of deposits or accumulations of materials that may be readily ignitible.

Article 511
Commercial Garages

Article 513
Aircraft Hangars

Article 514
Motor Fuel Dispensing

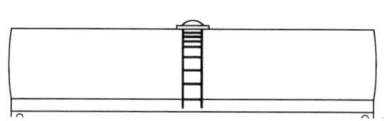

Article 515
Bulk Storage Plants

Article 516
Spray Application

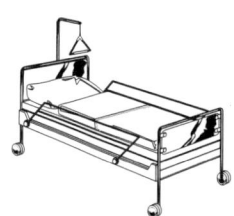

Article 517
Health Care Facilities

510.2. The general rules of the Code and the provisions of Articles 500 through 504 shall apply to electrical wiring and equipment in occupancies within the scope of Articles 511 through 517, except as such rules are modified in Articles 511 through 517. Where unusual conditions exist in a specific occupancy, the authority having jurisdiction shall judge with respect to the application of specific rules.

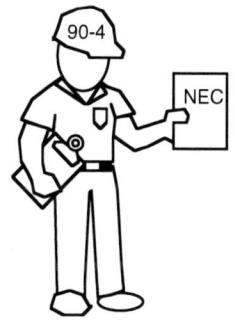

ARTICLE 511
Commercial Garages, Repair and Storage

511.1. This is a very important section to start the article as it defines the scope of a commerical garage. It includes locations used for service and repair operations in connection with self-propelled vehicles (including, but not limited to, passenger automobiles, buses, trucks, and tractors) in which volatile (explosive) flammable liquids or flammable gases are used for fuel or power.

Gasoline is a volatile flammable liquid

It is important to note that commerical repair shops for lawnmowers, boats, motor bikes, and other repair shops for volatile fuel-driven or propelled equipment are included in Article 511.

•Section 555.22 which states: *Electrical wiring and equipment located at facilities for the repair of marine craft containing flammable or combustible liquids or gases shall comply with Article 511.*

Article 100 Part III - Definitions.

Major Repair Garage. A building or portion of a building where major repairs, such as engine overhauls, painting, body and fender work, and repairs that require draining of the motor vehicle tank are performed on motor vehicles, including associated floor space used for offices, parking, or showrooms.

 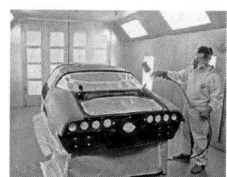 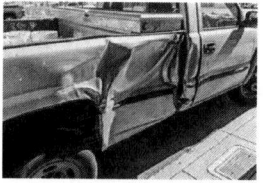

Minor Repair Garage. A building or portion of a building used for lubrication, inspection, and minor automotive maintenance work, such as engine tune-ups, replacement of parts, fluid changes (oil, antifreeze, transmission fluid, brake fluid, air-conditioning refrigerants), brake system repairs, tire rotation, and similar routine maintenance work, including associated floor space used for offices, parking, or showrooms.

    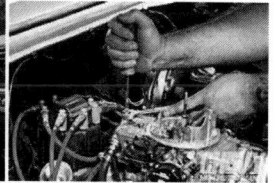

511.3(A). Parking garages used for parking or storage shall be permitted to be unclassified.

Where the term "Class I" is used with respect to Zone classification within this article of the Code, it shall apply to Zone 0, Zone 1, and Zone 2 designations.

511.3(B). Areas in which flammable fuel is dispensed into vehicle fuel tanks, it shall have the dispensing functions and components classified in accordance with Table 514.3(B)(1).

Article 514
Motor Fuel Dispensing

Dispenser for Class I liquids, **other than fuels**. Within 3' of any fill or dispensing point, extending in all directions shall be a Class I, Division 2 location.

511.3(C). Repair Garages, Major and Minor. Where vehicles using Class I liquids or heavier-than-air gaseous fuels (such as LPG) are repaired, hazardous area classification guidance is found in **Table 511.3(C)**.

Alternative Fuel Vehicles
•Liquefied propane gas (LPG)
-Cylinders similar to those in heating/cooking
-Heavier than air vapors will pool or collect in low areas

Table 511.3(C) Extent of Classified Locations for Major and Minor Repair Garages with Heavier - Than- Air Fuel

Location	Class I		Extent of Classified Location
	Division (Group D)	**Zone (Group IIA)**	
Repair garage, **major** (where Class I liquids or gaseous fuels are transferred or dispensed*)	1	1	Entire space within any pit, belowgrade work area, or subfloor work area that is **not ventilated**
	2	2	Entire space within any pit, belowgrade work area, or subfloor work area that is provided with ventilation of at least $(1\ ft^3/min./ft^2)$ of floor area, with suction taken from a point within 12 inches of floor level
	2	2	Up to 18 inches above floor level of the room, except as noted below, for entire floor area
	Unclassified	Unclassified	Up to 18 inches above floor level of the room where room is provided with ventilation of at least $(1\ ft^3/min./ft^2)$ of floor area, with suction taken from a point within 12 inches of floor level
	2	2	Within 3 feet of any fill or dispensing point, extending in all directions
Specific areas adjacent to classified locations	Unclassified	Unclassified	Areas adjacent to classified locations where flammable vapors are **not** likely to be released, such as stock rooms, switchboard rooms, and other similar locations, where mechanically ventilated at a rate of four or more air changes per hour or designed with positive air pressure or where effectively cut off by walls or partitions
Repair garage, minor (where Class I liquids or gaseous fuels are **not** transferred or dispensed*)	2	2	Entire space within any pit, belowgrade work area, or subfloor work area that is not ventilated
	2	2	Up to 18 inches above floor level, extending 3 feet horizontally in all directions from opening to any pit, belowgrade work area, or subfloor work area that is **not ventilated**
	Unclassified	Unclassified	Entire space within any pit, belowgrade work area, or subfloor work area that is provided with ventilation of at least $(1\ ft^3/min./ft^2)$ of floor area, with suction taken from a point within 12 inches of floor level
Specific areas adjacent to classified locations	Unclassified	Unclassified	Areas adjacent to classified locations where flammable vapors are **not** likely to be released, such as stockrooms, switchboard rooms, and other similar locations, where mechanically ventilated at a rate of four or more air changes per hour or designed with positive air pressure, or where effectively cut off by walls or partitions

*Includes draining of Class I liquids from vehicles.

•**Author's note**: Understanding Table 511.3(C) with arrows:

↖ Major and Minor Repair Garages ↖ Heavier - Than- Air Fuel (Class I fuel such as propane).

◀ Class I, where flammable gases, flammable liquid-produced vapors, or combustible liquid-produced vapors are or may be present.

↻ Division (Group D), flammable gas, flammable liquid-produced vapor mixed with air that may burn or explode.

↻ Zone (Group IIA), atmospheres containing acetone, ammonia, ethyl alcohol, gasoline, methane, propane, or flammable gas, flammable liquid-produced vapor mixed with air that may burn or explode. *Group IIA is equivalent to Class I, Group D as described in 500.6(A)(4).*

◀ Repair garage, **major** (where Class I liquids or gaseous fuels are transferred or dispensed*)

◀III Class I, Division 1, also Zone 1 (Group IIA) entire space within any pit, belowgrade work area, or subfloor work area that is **not ventilated**.

◀ Class I, Division 2, also Zone 2 (Group IIA) entire space within any pit, belowgrade work area, or subfloor work area that is provided with ventilation of at least (**1 ft³/min./ft²**) of floor area, with suction taken from a point within 12 inches of floor level. *The definition of Zone 2 is functionally identical to NEC Division 2 location, where hazardous concentrations occur only under accidental or unusual operating conditions.*

◀ Unclassified definition: locations determined to be neither Class I, Division 1; Class I, Division 2; Class I, Zone 0; Class I, Zone 1; Class I, Zone 2; Class II, Division 1, Class II, Division 2; Class III, Division 1, Class III, Division 2; Zone 20; Zone 21; Zone 22; nor any combination thereof.

Table 511.3(C) Extent of Classified Locations for Major and Minor Repair Garages with Heavier - Than- Air Fuel

Location	Class I Division (Group D)	Class I Zone (Group IIA)	Extent of Classified Location
Repair garage, **major** ◀ (where Class I liquids or gaseous fuels are transferred or dispensed*)	1 ◀III	1 ◀III	Entire space within any pit, belowgrade work area, or subfloor work area that is **not ventilated**.
	2 ◀	2 ◀	Entire space within any pit, belowgrade work area, or subfloor work area that is provided with ventilation of at least (**1 ft³/min./ft²**) of floor area, with suction taken from a point within 12 inches of floor level
	2	2	Up to 18 inches above floor level of the room, except as noted below, for entire floor area
	Unclassified	Unclassified	Up to 18 inches above floor level of the room where room is provided with ventilation of at least (**1 ft³/min./ft²**) of floor area, with suction taken from a point within 12 inches of floor level

511.3(D). Repair Garages, Major. Where vehicles using lighter-than-air gaseous fuels (such as hydrogen and natural gas) are repaired or stored, hazardous area classification guidance is found in Table 511.3(D).

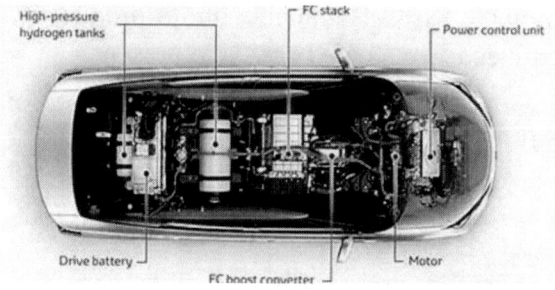

How is Natural Gas Formed?
•Characteristics: Lighter than air, mostly made up of methane, usually found near underground petroleum.
•Natural gas is colorless, odorless, and tasteless.

Table 511.3(D) Extent of Classified Locations for Major Repair Garages with Lighter - Than - Air Fuel

Location	Class I		Extent of Classified Location
	Division[2]	Zone[3]	
Repair garage, **major** (where lighter - than - air gaseous fueled[1] vehicles are repaired or stored)	2	2	Wthin 18 inches of ceiling, except as noted below
	Unclassified	Unclassified	Within 18 inches of ceiling where ventilation of at least ($1 \text{ ft}^3/\text{min./ft}^2$) of floor area, with suction taken from a point within 18 inches of the highest point in ceiling
Specific areas **adjacent** to classified locations	Unclassified	Unclassified	Areas adjacent to classified locations where flammable vapors are **not** likely to be released, such as stock rooms, switchboard rooms, and other similar locations, where mechanically ventilated at a rate of four or more air changes per hour or designed with positive air pressure or where effectively cut off by walls or partitions

[1]Includes fuels such as hydrogen and natural gas, but **not** LPG
[2]For hydrogen (lighter than air) Group B, or natural gas Group D
[3]For hydrogen (lighter than air) Group IIC or IIB + H2, or natural gas IIA

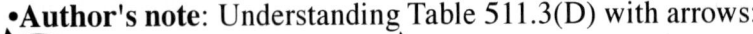

•**Author's note**: Understanding Table 511.3(D) with arrows:

Major Repair Garages ◀ ▰ Lighter - Than- Air Fuel (fuel such as hydrogen and natural gas).

◀▬ Class I, where flammable gases, flammable liquid-produced vapors, or combustible liquid-produced vapors are or may be present.

⟲ **Division**[2] for hydrogen (lighter than air) Group B, or natural gas Group D ⟲ **Zone**[3] for hydrogen (lighter than air) Group IIC or IIB + H2, or natural gas IIA.

Group IIC: Atmospheres containing acetylene, hydrogen, or flammable gas, flammable liquid produced vapor, or combustible liquid produced vapor mixed with air that may burn or explode.

Note: This grouping is equivalent to Class I, Groups A and B.

Group IIB. Atmospheres containing acetaldehyde, ethylene, or flammable gas, flammable liquid produced vapor, or combustible liquid produced vapor mixed with air that may burn or explode.

Note: This grouping is equivalent to Class I, Group C.

Group IIA: Atmospheres containing acetone, ammonia, ethyl alcohol, gasoline, methane, propane, or flammable gas, flammable liquid produced vapor, or combustible liquid produced vapor mixed with air that may burn or explode.

Note: This grouping is equivalent to Class I, Group D.

◀▰ Repair garage, **major** (where lighter - than - air gaseous fueled[1] vehicles are repaired or stored) includes fuels such as hydrogen and natural gas, but **not** LPG.

Table 511.3(D) Extent of Classified Locations for Major Repair Garages with Lighter - Than - Air Fuel

Location	Class I		Extent of Classified Location
	Division[2] ⟲	Zone[3] ⟲	
Repair garage, **major** ◀▰ (where lighter - than - air gaseous fueled[1] vehicles are repaired or stored)	2	2	Wthin 18 inches of ceiling, except as noted below
	Unclassified	Unclassified	Within 18 inches of ceiling where ventilation of at least (**1 ft³/min./ft²**) of floor area, with suction taken from a point within 18 inches of the highest point in ceiling
Specific areas **adjacent** to classified locations	Unclassified	Unclassified	Areas adjacent to classified locations where flammable vapors are **not** likely to be released, such as stock rooms, switchboard rooms, and other similar locations, where mechanically ventilated at a rate of four or more air changes per hour or designed with positive air pressure or where effectively cut off by walls or partitions

[1]Includes fuels such as hydrogen and natural gas, but **not** LPG
[2]For hydrogen (lighter than air) Group B, or natural gas Group D
[3]For hydrogen (lighter than air) Group IIC or IIB + H2, or natural gas IIA

Examples of the Tables

Table 511.3(C). Floor Areas

The entire floor area up to a level of 18" above the floor **shall be considered unclassified where there is mechanical ventilation providing** a minimum of four air changes per hour or one cubic foot per minute of exchanged air for each square foot of floor area. Ventilation shall provide for air exchange across the entire floor area, and exhaust air taken within 12" of floor.

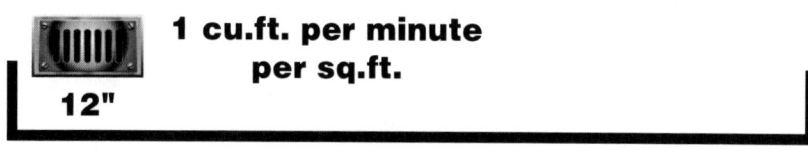

Up to a level of 18" above the floor. For each floor, the entire area up to a level of 18" above the floor shall be a Class I, Division 2 location.

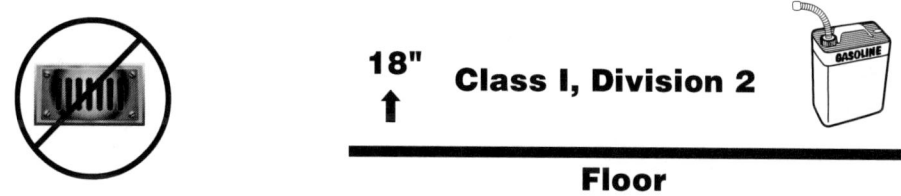

Ceiling Areas

In major repair garages, where lighter-than-air gaseous fuels (such as natural gas or hydrogen) vehicles are repaired or stored, the area within 18" of the ceiling **shall be considered unclassified where ventilation** of at least one cubic foot per minute per square foot of ceiling area taken from a point not more than 18" of the highest point in the ceiling is provided.

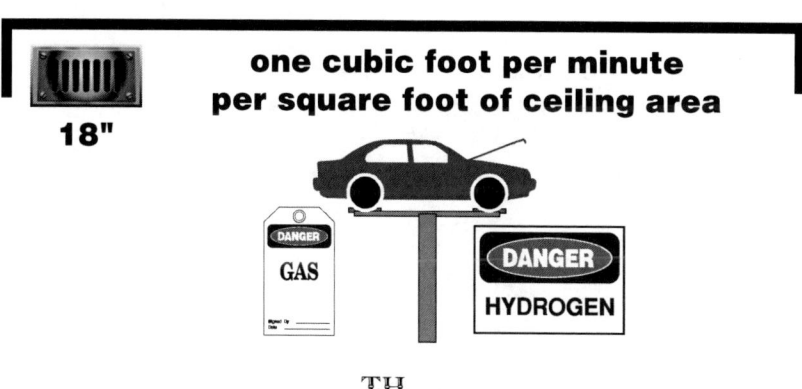

In major repair garages where lighter-than-air gaseous fuel (such as natural gas or hydrogen) vehicles are repaired or stored, ceiling spaces that are **not ventilated** per **Table 511.3(D)** shall be classified as Class I, Division 2.

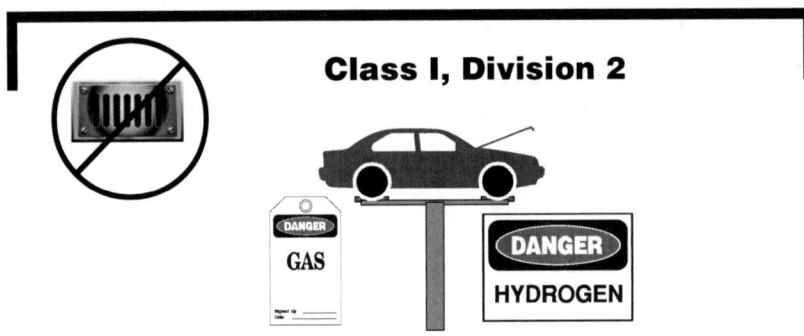

Any pit or depression **not ventilated** shall be a Class I, Division 1 location.

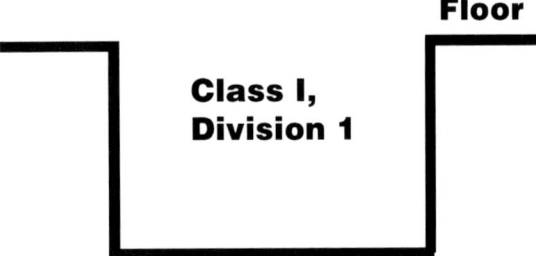

In minor repair garages, any pit, belowgrade work area, or subfloor work area where Class I liquids are **not** transferred that is provided with exhaust ventilation at a rate of not less than one cubic foot per minute for each square foot of floor area at all times that the building is occupied or when vehicles are parked in or over this area and where exhaust is taken from a point within 12" of the floor of the pit, belowgrade work area, or subfloor work area is unclassified.

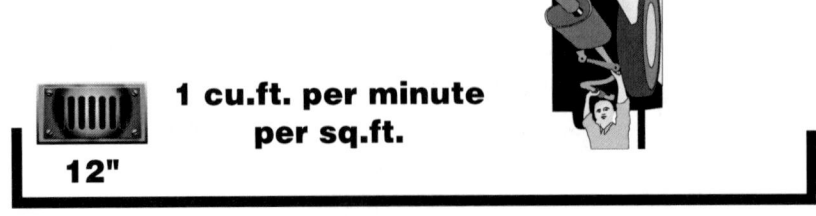

The Code allows areas adjacent to classified locations in which flammable vapors are not likely to be released, such as stock rooms, switchboard rooms, etc. to be unclassified if they are mechanically ventilated at a rate of four or more changes of air per hour or designed with positive air pressure, or where effectively cut off by walls or partitions.

**4 or more changes of air per hour
or
effectively cut off by walls or partitions**

511.4 Wiring and Equipment in Class I Locations.

511.4(A). Class I wiring shall conform to the wiring rules of Article 501.

511.4(B). Class I equipment shall conform to the rules of Article 501.

511.4(B)(1). Where fuel-dispensing units (other than liquid petroleum gas, which is prohibited) are located within buildings, the requirements of Article 514 shall govern.

Article 514

Where mechanical ventilation is provided in the dispensing area, the control shall be interlocked so that the dispenser cannot operate without ventilation, as prescribed in 500.5(B)(2).

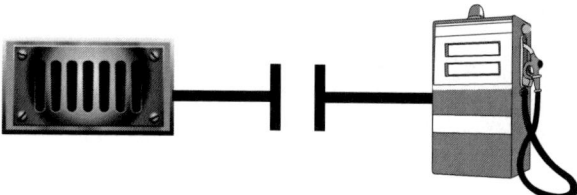

511.4(B)(2). Portable lighting equipment shall be equipped with handle, lampholder, hook, and substantial guard attached to the lampholder or handle. All exterior surfaces that might come in contact with battery terminals, wiring terminals, or other objects shall be of nonconducting material or shall be effectively protected with insulation.

Lampholders shall be of an unswitched type and shall **not** provide means for plug-in of attachment plugs. The outer shell shall be of molded composition or other suitable material.

Unless the lamp and its cord are supported or arranged in such a manner that they cannot be used in the locations classified in 511.3, they shall be of a type identified for Class I, Division 1 locations.

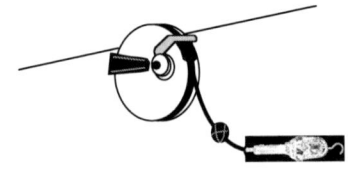

A cord for a handlamp with a retractable cord reel must be short enough to prevent the light from reaching closer than 18" of the floor, otherwise the light would have to be *identified* for use in a Class I, Division 1 location.

511.7 Wiring and Equipment Installed Above Class I locations.

511.7(A)(1). All fixed wiring above Class I locations shall be in:

- metal raceways
- ENT
- liquidtight flexible metal conduit
- Type MI cable
- Type AC cable
- PLTC cable
- Type ITC cable

- rigid PVC
- flexible metal conduit
- liquidtight flexible nonmetallic conduit
- Type MC cable
- manufactured wiring systems
- Type TC cable

- Cellular metal floor raceways or cellular concrete floor raceways shall be permitted to be used only for supplying ceiling outlets or extensions to the area below the floor, but such raceways shall have no connections leading into or through any Class I location above the floor.

511.7(A)(2). For pendants, flexible cord suitable for the type of service and listed for hard usage shall be used.

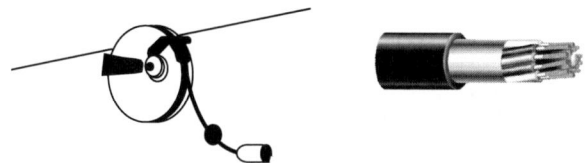

511.7(B)(1). Fixed electrical equipment above a Class I location shall be located above the level of any defined Class I location or shall be *identified* for the location.

(a) Equipment that is less than 12' above the floor level and that might produce arcs, sparks, or particles of hot metal (such as switches, motors, generators, charging panels, cutout switches, or other equipment) having make-and-break or sliding contacts, must be of the totally enclosed type or be constructed so that sparks or hot metal particles cannot escape. •Receptacles, lamps, and lamp holders are not covered by this rule.

(b) Lamps and lampholders for fixed lighting located over lanes through which vehicles are commonly driven, or that may otherwise be exposed to physical damage must be located not less than 12' above the floor level, unless of the totally enclosed type or so constructed that sparks or hot metal particles cannot escape.

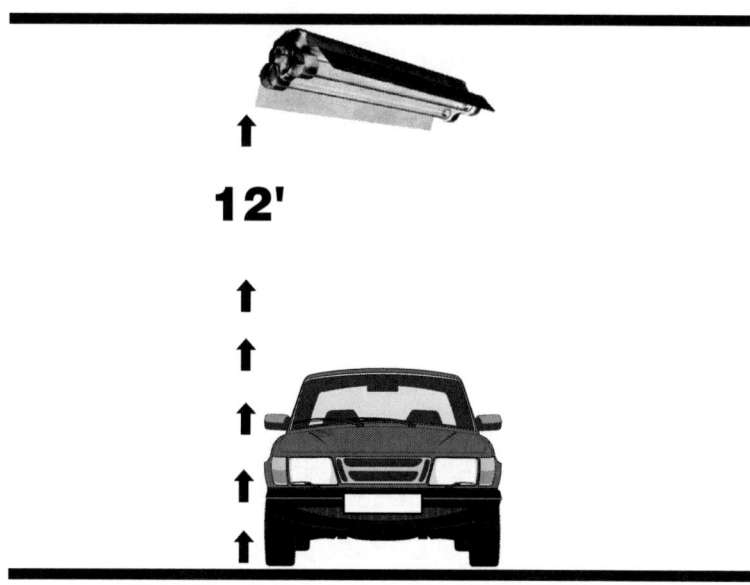

12'

511.9. Seals conforming to the requirements of 501.15 and 501.15(B)(2) shall be provided and shall apply to horizontal as well as vertical boundaries of Class I locations.

511.10(A). Battery chargers and their control equipment, and batteries being charged, shall not be located within locations classified in 511.3.

511.10(B)(1). Electric vehicle charging equipment shall be installed in accordance with Article 625, except as noted in 511.10(B)(2) and (B)(3). Flexible cords shall be of a type identified for extra-hard usage.

511.10(B)(2). No connector for electric vehicle charging equipment shall be located within a Class I location.

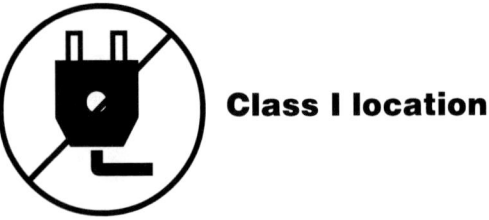

Class I location

511.10(B)(3). Where a cord is suspended overhead for electric vehicle charging equipment, it must be arranged so the lowest point of sag is at least 6" above the floor.

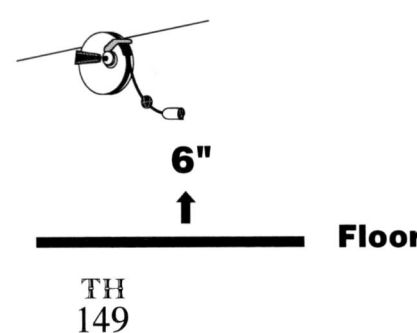

6"

Floor

511.12. All 125 volt single-phase 15 and 20 amp receptacles installed in areas where electrical diagnostic equipment, electrical hand tools, or portable lighting devices are planned for use must provide GFCI protection for personnel as required in 210.8(B).

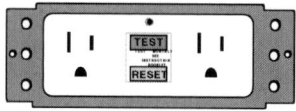  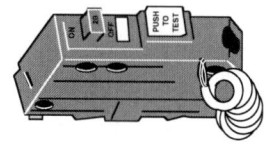

511.16(A). All metal raceways, metal armor or metallic sheath on cables, and all non-current-carrying metal parts of fixed or portable electrical equipment, regardless of voltage, shall be grounded per Article 250.

511.16(B). Grounding in Class I locations shall follow 501.30.

511.16(B)(1). Where a circuit supplies portables or pendants and includes a grounded conductor, receptacles, plugs, connectors, etc. shall be of the grounding type, and the grounded conductor of the flexible cord shall be connected to the screw shell of any lampholder or to the grounded terminal of any utilization equipment supplied.

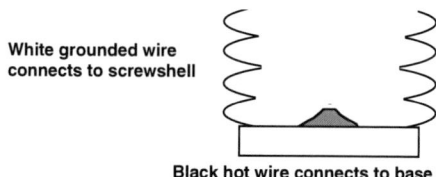

White grounded wire connects to screwshell

Black hot wire connects to base

511.16(B)(2). Approved means shall be provided for maintaining continuity of the **equipment grounding conductor** between the fixed wiring system and the non-current-carrying metal portions of pendant fixtures, portable lamps, and portable utilization equipment.

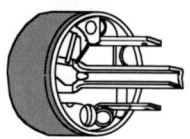

 •**Author's note**: To summarize Article 511, the principal concern is a leak of gasoline from a vehicle. Repair garages usually have large quantities of combustible oils, but they are usually below their flash point at room temperature. Article 511 rules apply to garages using electrical equipment, open flames, or welding as part of the repair operation. Parking garages or automobile dealer showrooms are not likely to be considered hazardous, even though these showrooms will have some form of electrical equipment. The risk of explosion is minimal, since work on the fuel tank is not being performed. Some parking garages do require hazardous classification, particularly if fuel is being dispensed within the parking garage. Hydraulic lifts have replaced some servicing pits. However, pits are becoming common in lubritoriums that provide express oils changes and lubrication.

ARTICLE 513
Aircraft Hangars

513.1. This Article applies to buildings inside of which aircraft are stored, serviced, or repaired. Aircraft containing Class I flammable liquids or Class II combustible liquids whose temperatures are above their flash points. This does not include locations used exclusively for aircraft that have *never* contained such liquids or gases, such as a plant which manufacture aircraft, or where they are stored or housed only after the fuel has been drained and properly purged.

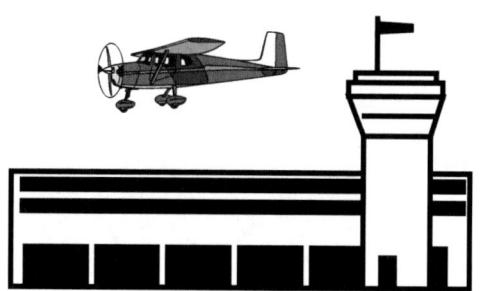 

Article 100 Part III Definitions.

Article 100 Part III. Aircraft Painting Hangar. An aircraft hangar constructed for the express purpose of spray/dipping/applications and provided with dedicated ventilation supply and exhaust.

Article 100 Part III. Mobile Equipment. Equipment with electric components suitable to be moved only with mechanical aids or is provided with wheels for movement by person(s) or powered devices.

Article 100 Part III. Portable Equipment. Equipment with electric components suitable to be moved by a single person without mechanical aids.

513.3. Classification of Locations.

Where the term "Class I" is used with respect to Zone classification within this article of the Code, it shall apply to Zone 0, Zone 1, and Zone 2 designations.

513.3(A). Any pit or depression below the level of the hangar floor shall be a Class I, Division 1 or Zone 1 location that shall extend up to said floor level.

513.3(B). The entire area of the hangar, including any adjacent and communicating areas not suitably cut off from the hangar or ventilated, shall be classified as a Class I, Division 2 or Zone 2 location up to a level 18" above the floor.

513.3(C). The area within 5' horizontally from the aircraft power plant(s) or aircraft fuel tank(s) shall be classified as Class I, Division 2 or Zone 2 location that shall extend upward from the floor to a level 5' above the upper surface of wings and of engine enclosures.

513.3(D). Adjacent areas in which flammable liquids or vapors are not likely to be released, such as stock rooms, electrical control rooms, etc., shall not be classified as hazardous where adequately ventilated and where effectively cut off from the hangar itself by walls or partitions.

•*Note: See sketch on the next page outlining these dimensions.*

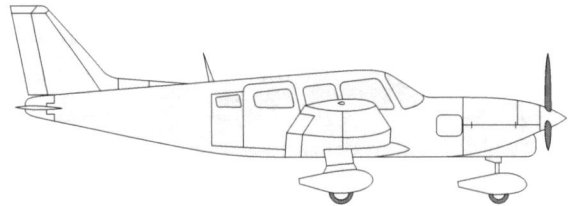

VERTICAL LIMITS

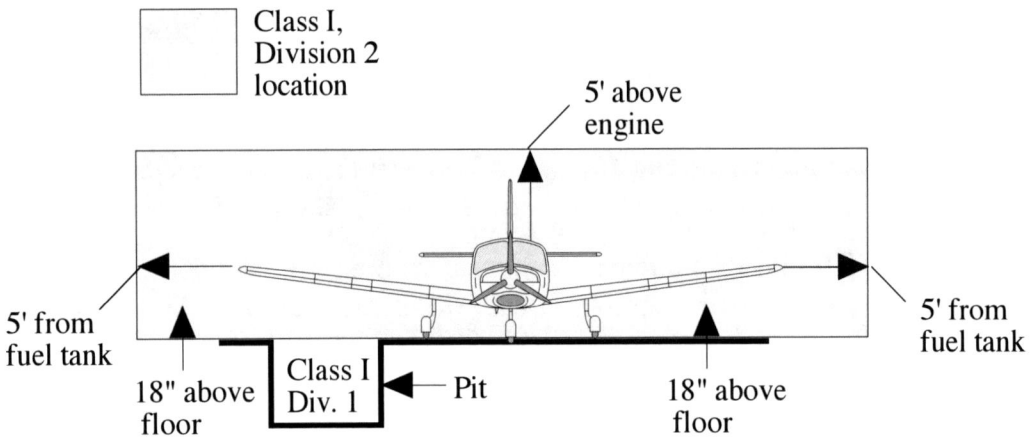

Class I, Division 2 location

5' above engine

5' from fuel tank

18" above floor

Class I Div. 1

Pit

18" above floor

5' from fuel tank

HORIZONTAL LIMITS

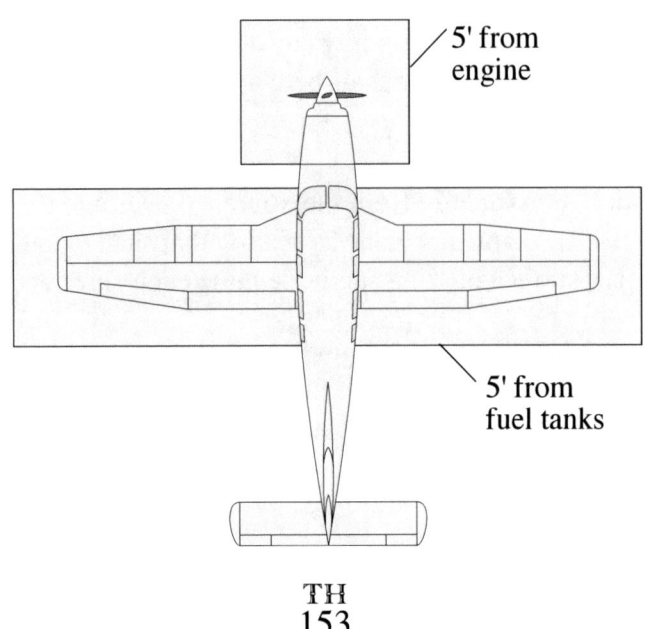

5' from engine

5' from fuel tanks

513.3 Classification of Locations. Where the term "Class I" is used with respect to Zone classification within this article of the Code, it shall apply to Zone 0, Zone 1, and Zone 2 designations.

513.4 Wiring and Equipment in Class I Locations.

513.4(A). All wiring and equipment that is or may be installed or operated within any of the Class I locations shall comply with Article 501 for the division or Article 505 for the zone in which they are used.

Attachment plugs and receptacles in Class I locations shall be identified for Class I locations or shall be designed such that they cannot be energized while the connections are being made or broken. This is to prevent an arc or spark from the receptacle or plug while being connected or disconnected. This can cause an explosion in a Class I location with flammable fuel present.

Receptacle and plugs must be of a Class I type or have a switch to de-energize the circuit before unplugging or plugging in.

513.4(B). Electric wiring, outlets, and equipment (including lamps) on or attached to stanchions, rostrums, or docks that are located in a Class I location shall comply with Article 501 or 505 for the division in which they are used.

Definition of rostrum: a raised platform.

513.7 Wiring and Equipment NOT Installed in Class I Locations.

513.7(A). Fixed wiring in an aircraft hangar above or outside of the hazardous (classified) location shall be installed in metal raceways or shall be Type MI, TC, or MC cable.

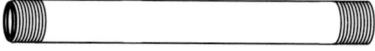 

Exception: Adjacent areas in which flammable liquids or vapors are not likely to be released, such as stock rooms, electrical control rooms, etc., where adequately ventilated and where effectively cut off from the hangar itself by walls or partitions shall be permitted to be any suitable wiring method from Chapter 3.

513.7(B). Flexible cords for pendants must be identified for hard usage and **must contain an equipment grounding conductor**.

513.7(C). Equipment that can emit sparks or hot metal particles, mounted less than 10' above the classified (hazardous) location must be totally enclosed or must have a method of preventing the escape of sparks and hot metal particles that could fall into the hazardous location.

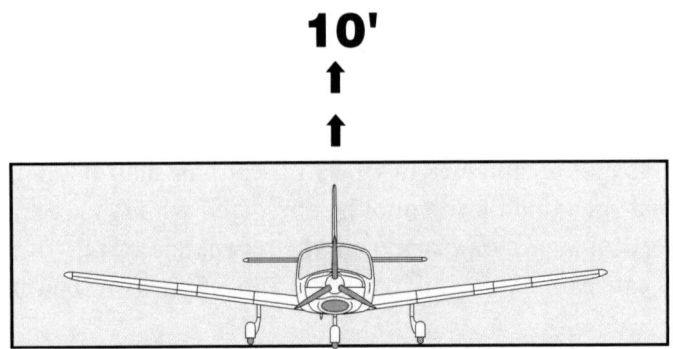

Exception: Adjacent areas in which flammable liquids or vapors are not likely to be released, such as stock rooms, electrical control rooms, etc., where adequately ventilated and where effectively cut off from the hangar itself by walls or partitions shall be permitted to be of the general-purpose type.

513.7(D). Lampholders of metal-shell, fiber-lined types shall **not** be used for fixed incandescent lighting.

513.7(E). Where stanchions, rostrums, or docks that are **not** located in a Class I location wiring and equipment shall comply with 513.7, except that such wiring and equipment not more than 18" above the floor in any position shall comply with 513.4(B). Receptacle and attachment plugs shall be of the locking type that will not readily disconnect.

513.7(F). Mobile stanchions with electric equipment complying with 513.7(E) shall carry at least one permanently affixed warning sign with the following words or equivalent:

> **WARNING**
> **KEEP 5 FEET CLEAR OF AIRCRAFT**
> **ENGINES AND FUEL TANK AREAS**

or

> **WARNING**
> **KEEP 1.5 METERS CLEAR OF AIR-**
> **CRAFT ENGINES AND FUEL TANK**
> **AREAS**

513.8. Underground Wiring.

513.8(A). All wiring installed in or under the hangar floor must comply with Class I, Division 1 rules. Where such wiring is located in vaults, pits, or ducts, adequate drainage shall be provided.

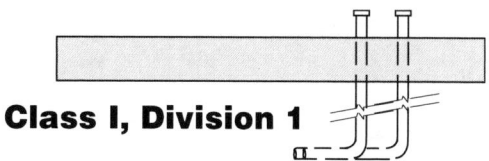

Class I, Division 1

513.8(B). Uninterrupted raceways that are embedded in a hangar floor or buried beneath the hangar floor are considered within the Class I location above the floor, regardless of the point at which the raceway descends below or rises above the floor.

513.9. Seals shall be provided in accordance with 501.15 or 505.16. Sealing requirements specified shall apply to horizontal as well as to vertical boundaries of Class I locations.

513.10 Special Equipment.

513.10(A)(1). When the aircraft is stored in a hangar, and whenever possible, while the aircraft is undergoing maintenance the aircraft electrical systems shall be de-energized.

513.10(A)(2). Aircraft batteries shall **not** be charged where installed in an aircraft located inside or partially inside a hangar.

513.10(B). Aircraft battery chargers shall **not** be located or operated within any Class I location defined in 513.3 and shall preferably be located in a separate building or in adjacent areas in which flammable liquids or vapors are not likely to be released, such as stock rooms, electrical control rooms, etc., where adequately ventilated and where effectively cut off from the hangar itself by walls or partitions. Mobile chargers shall carry at least one permanently affixed warning sign with the following words or equivalent:

> **WARNING**
> **KEEP 5 FEET CLEAR OF AIRCRAFT**
> **ENGINES AND FUEL TANK AREAS**

Tables, racks, trays, and wiring shall not be located within a Class I location and shall comply with Article 480.

513.10(C)(1). External power sources for energizing aircraft shall be designed and mounted so that all electrical equipment and fixed wiring will be at least 18" above floor level and shall not be operated in a Class I location area within 5' horizontally from the aircraft power plant(s) or aircraft fuel tank(s) shall be classified as Class I, Division 2 or Zone 2 location that shall extend upward from the floor to a level 5' above the upper surface of wings and of engine enclosures.

513.10(C)(2). Mobile energizers shall carry at least one permanently affixed warning sign with the following words or equivalent:

> **WARNING**
> **KEEP 5 FEET CLEAR OF AIRCRAFT**
> **ENGINES AND FUEL TANK AREAS**

513.10(C)(3). Flexible cords for aircraft energizers and ground support equipment shall be identified for the type of service and extra-hard usage and shall include an **equipment grounding conductor.**

513.10(D) Mobile Servicing Equipment with Electrical Components.

513.10(D)(1). This section requires that vacuum cleaners, air compressors, air movers, and other mobile equipment having electric wiring and equipment not suitable for Class I, Division 2 locations or Zone 2 locations must be mounted so that all fixed wiring and equipment will be at least 18" above the floor. This equipment must not be operated in a Class I location area within 5' horizontally from the aircraft power plant(s) or aircraft fuel tank(s) shall be classified as Class I, Division 2 or Zone 2 location that shall extend upward from the floor to a level 5' above the upper surface of wings and of engine enclosures and shall carry at least one permanently affixed warning sign with the following words or equivalent:

> **WARNING**
> **KEEP 5 FEET CLEAR OF AIRCRAFT**
> **ENGINES AND FUEL TANK AREAS**

513.10(D)(2). Flexible cords for mobile equipment must be suitable for the type of service and identified for extra-hard usage and must contain an **equipment grounding conductor**.

Attachment plugs and receptacles must be identified for the location in which they are installed and provide a point for connection of the **equipment grounding conductor**.

513.10(D)(3). Equipment that is not identified as suitable for Class I, Division 2 locations must not be operated in locations where maintenance operations are likely to release flammable liquids or vapors in the process.

513.10(E). Due to so much portable equipment being used in hangars, this section requires portable lighting and utilization equipment:
•Be identified for the location when it is lighting equipment.
•Use flexible cords rated for extra-hard use.
•Each cord must contain an equipment grounding conductor.
•Be suitable for use in Class I, Division 2 or Zone 2 locations when it's utilization equipment.

513.12. All 125 volt single-phase 15 and 20 amp receptacles installed in areas where electrical diagnostic equipment, electrical hand tools, or portable lighting devices are planned for use must provide GFCI protection for personnel as required in 210.8(B).

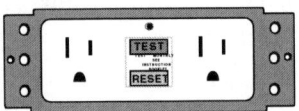  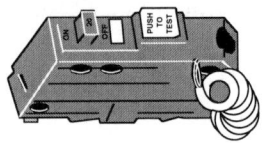

513.16(A). All metal raceways, metal armor or metallic sheath on cables, and all non-current-carrying metal parts of fixed or portable electrical equipment, regardless of voltage, shall be grounded per Article 250.

513.16(B)(1). Where a circuit supplies portables or pendants and includes a grounded conductor, receptacles, plugs, connectors, etc. shall be of the grounding type, and the grounded conductor of the flexible cord shall be connected to the screw shell of any lampholder or to the grounded terminal of any utilization equipment supplied.

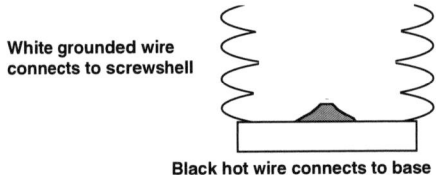

White grounded wire connects to screwshell

Black hot wire connects to base

511.13(B)(2). Approved means shall be provided for maintaining continuity of the **equipment grounding conductor** between the fixed wiring system and the non-current-carrying metal portions of pendant fixtures, portable lamps, and portable utilization equipment.

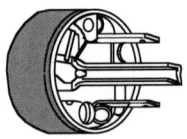

 •**Author's note**: To summarize Article 513, the likelihood of a fuel leak is high, because a small amount of fuel is routinely drained from sumps as part of a preflight inspection. Unfortunately, many of these preflight inspections are conducted in a hangar.

Aviation gasoline (AVGAS) is limited primarily to smaller aircraft. It is similar in many respects to automotive gasoline. Of all the aviation fuels, AVGAS is the most flammable. Jet A is the least flammable of the common aviation fuels. Static electricity is a significant concern while fueling aircraft.

ARTICLE 514
Motor Fuel Dispensing Facilities

514.1. This article applies to motor fuel dispensing facilities, marine/motor fuel dispensing facilities, motor fuel dispensing facilities located inside buildings, and fleet vehicle motor fuel dispensing facilities.

Article 100 Part III - The definition of a motor fuel dispensing facility is that portion of a property where motor fuels are stored and dispensed from fixed equipment into fuel tanks of motor vehicles or marine craft or into approved containers, including all equipment used in connection therewith.

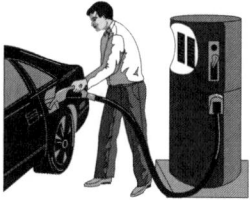  

Informational Note: Other areas within the service station used sales rooms, offices, service and repair bays, etc. must comply with the rules of Articles 510 and 511.

514.3. Classification of Locations.

Where the term "Class I" is used with respect to Zone classification within this article of the Code, it shall apply to Zone 0, Zone 1, and Zone 2 designations.

514.3(A). Where the authority having jurisdiction can satisfactorily determine that flammable liquids such as gasoline with a flash point below 100°F will **not** be handled, such a location will not be required to be classified (hazardous).

Some diesel and kerosene stations can be treated as nonhazardous locations determined by their flash points.

514.3(B)(1). Class I locations. Table 514.3(B)(1) shall be applied where Class I liquids are stored, handled, or dispensed and shall be used to *delineate* and classify motor fuel dispensing facilities and commercial garages as defined in Article 511. For aboveground tanks, follow Table 515.3. A Class I location shall not extend beyond an unpierced wall, roof, or other solid partition.

Definition of delineate: to indicate or represent by drawn or painted lines, to mark the outline.

**Aboveground tanks
Article 515**

514.3(B)(2). Table 514.3(B)(2) shall be used to *delineate* and classify areas where compressed natural gas (CNG), liquefied natural gas (LNG), compressed or liquefied hydrogen, (LPG) gas, or combinations of these, are dispensed as motor vehicle fuels along with Class I or Class II liquids that are also dispensed as motor vehicle fuels.

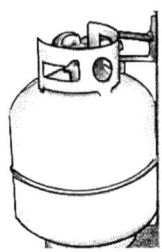

Where CNG or LNG dispensers are installed beneath a canopy or enclosure, either the canopy or the enclosure shall be designed to prevent accumulation or entrapment of ignitible vapors, or all electrical equipment shall be suitable for Class I, Division 2 hazardous (classified) locations. Dispensing devices for LPG shall be located not less than 5' from any dispensing device for Class I liquids.

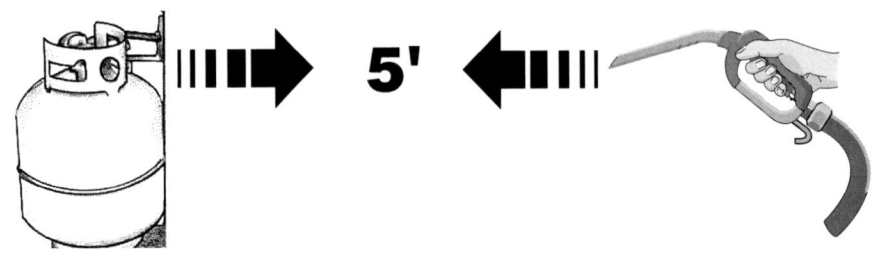

Table 514.3(B)(1).

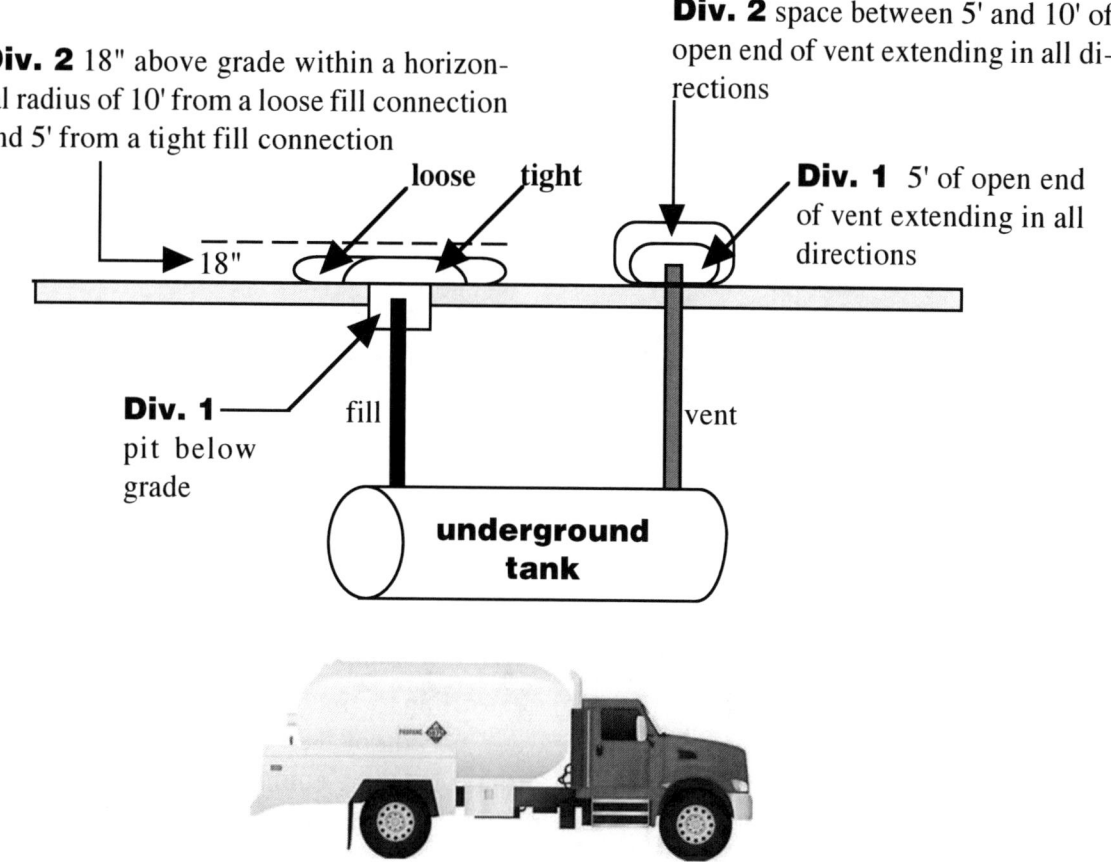

Div. 2 18" above grade within a horizontal radius of 10' from a loose fill connection and 5' from a tight fill connection

Div. 2 space between 5' and 10' of open end of vent extending in all directions

Div. 1 5' of open end of vent extending in all directions

loose   tight

Div. 1
pit below grade

fill

vent

underground tank

Note: The connection from the fuel truck to the fill pipe on the tank can be a tight connection or a loose connection. With a loose connection, the Division 2 is extended to a 10' radius.

Table 514.3(B)(1) sets up a 20' diameter, 18" high **Division 2** area around each fill-pipe for the underground gasoline tanks at a gas station.

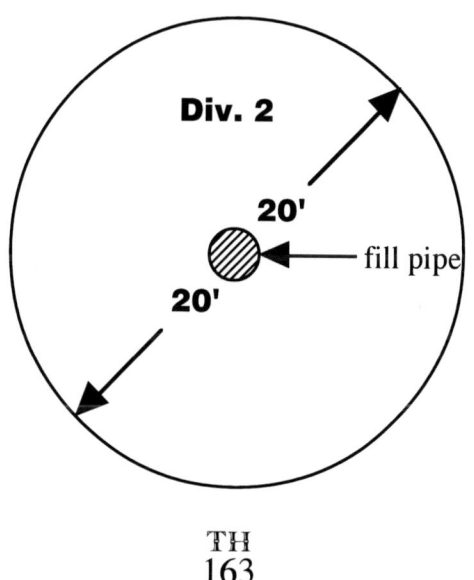

Div. 2

20'

20'

fill pipe

Table 514.3(B)(1).

Dispensing Device

Div. 1 Entire space within any pit or box below grade level, any part of which is within the Division 1 or Division 2, Zone 1 or Zone 2. *Any wiring or equipment that is installed beneath any part of a Div.1 or Div.2 location to the point where the wiring method is brought up out of the ground. This means the Div.1 area may extend far **beyond** the 20' radius perimeter around the dispensing pumps. The Div.1 area extends to the point where the conduit comes up to the panelboard, light, or sign.*

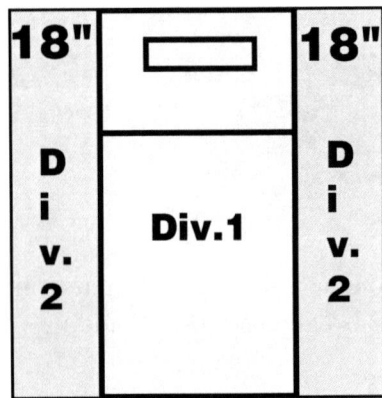

Div. 2 within 18" horizontally in all directions extending to grade from the dispenser enclosure or that portion of the dispenser enclosure containing liquid-handling components.

Table 514.3(B)(1) sets up a 20' diameter, 18" high **Division 2** area around **outdoor** dispenser.

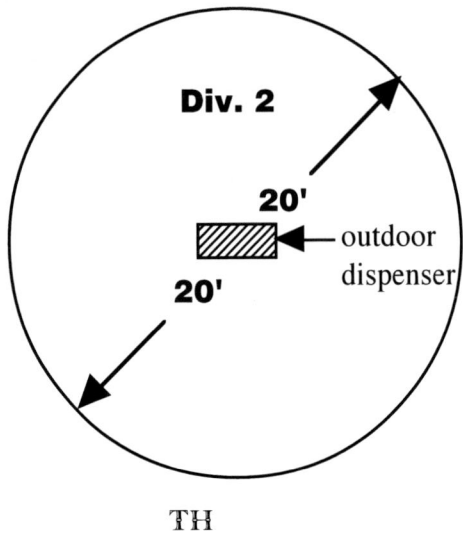

Table 514.3(B)(1).

Indoor Dispensing Device

Table 514.3(B)(1) sets up a 20' diameter, 18" high **Division 2** area around **indoor** dispenser with **mechanical ventilation**.

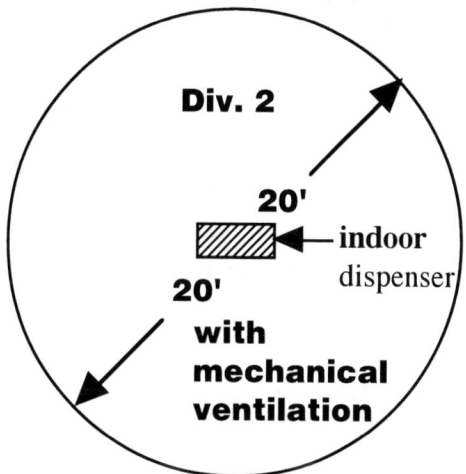

Table 514.3(B)(1) sets up a 25' diameter, 18" high **Division 2** area around **indoor** dispenser with **gravity ventilation**.

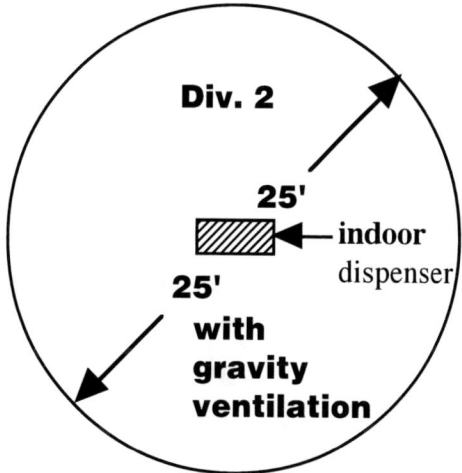

Table 514.3(B)(1).

Overhead Dispensing Device

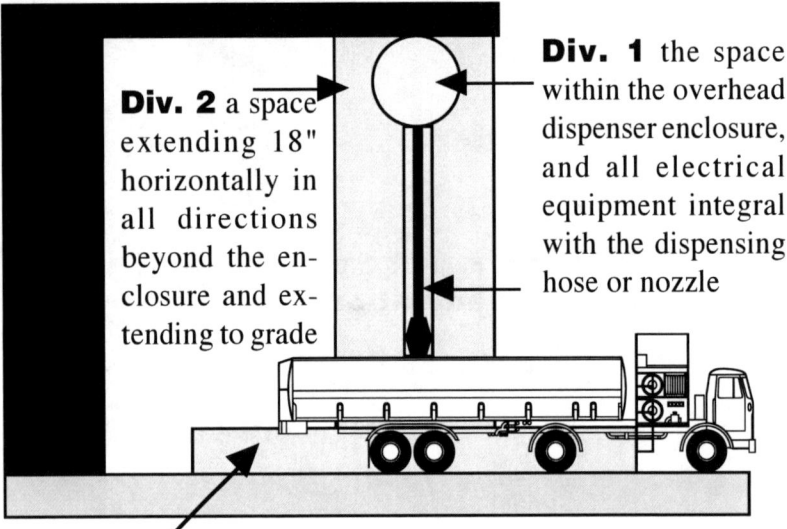

Div. 2 a space extending 18" horizontally in all directions beyond the enclosure and extending to grade

Div. 1 the space within the overhead dispenser enclosure, and all electrical equipment integral with the dispensing hose or nozzle

Div. 2 up to 18" above grade level within 20' horizontally measured from a point vertically below the edge of any dispenser enclosure

Remote Pump Outdoors

Table 514.3(B)(1) any pit or box below grade level if any part is within a horizontal distance of 10' from any edge of pump is a **Division 1** location.

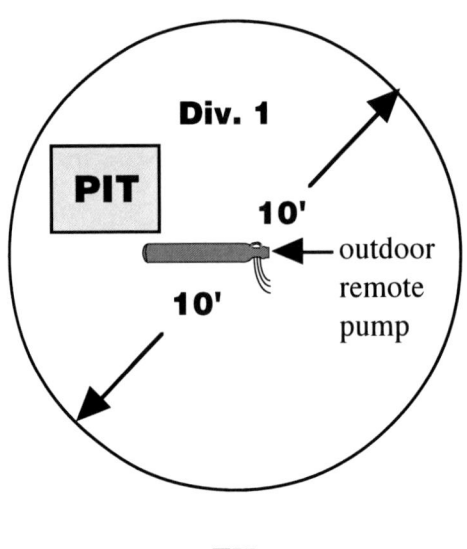

Table 514.3(B)(1).

Remote Pump Outdoors

Table 514.3(B)(1) within 3' of any edge of pump, extending in all directions. Also up to 18" above grade level within 10' horizontally from any edge of the pump is a **Division 2** location.

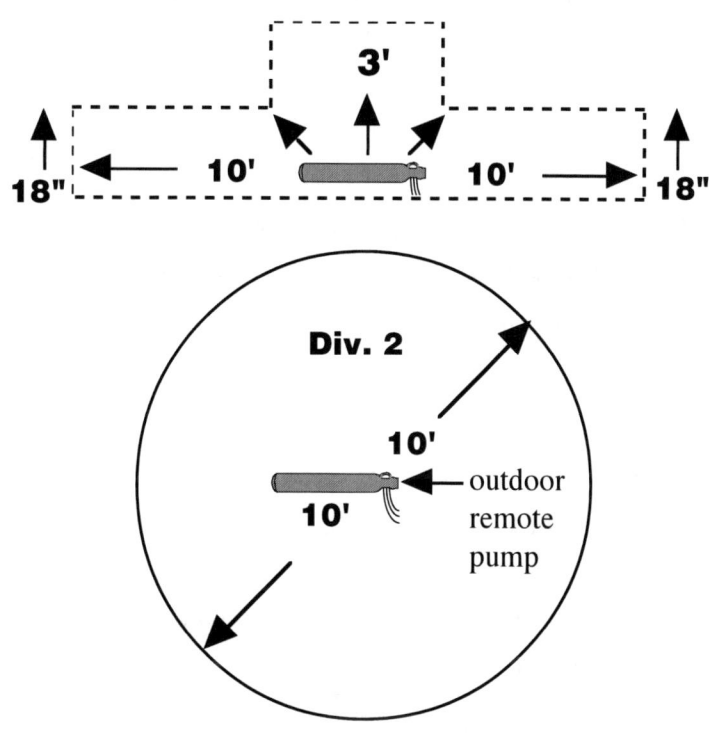

Remote Pump Indoors

Table 514.3(B1) entire space within any pit is a **Division 1** location.

Div. 1

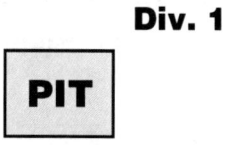

Table 514.3(B)(1) within 5' of any edge of pump, extending in all directions. Also up to 3' above grade level within 25' horizontally from any edge of the pump is a **Division 2** location.

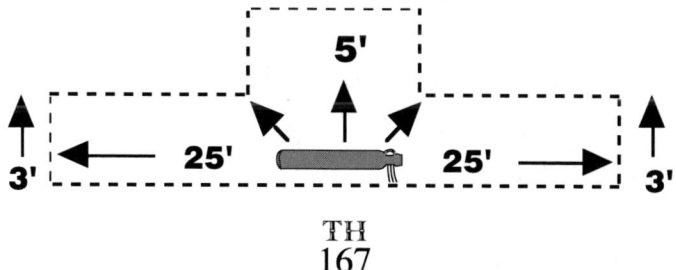

Table 514.3(B)(1).

Sales, Storage, and Rest Rooms

Table 514.3(B)(1) these rooms are **unclassified** (nonhazardous), however, if there is any opening to these rooms within the extent of a Division 1 or Division 2 location, the entire room shall be classified as that Division.

Vapor Processing Systems Pits

Table 514.3(B)(1) any pit or box below grade level, any part of which is within a Division 1 or Division 2 classified location or that houses any equipment used to transport or process vapors is a **Division 1** location.

Vapor Processing Equipment Located Within Protective Enclosures

Table 514.3(B)(1) within any protective enclosure housing vapor processing equipment is a **Division 2** location.

Vapor Processing Equipment NOT Within Protective Enclosures

Table 514.3(B)(1) the space within 18" in all directions of equipment containing flammable vapor or liquid extending to grade level and up to 18" above grade level within 10' horizontally of vapor processing equipment is a **Division 2** location.

Equipment Enclosures

Table 514.3(B)(1) any space within the enclosure where vapor or liquid is present under normal operating conditions is a **Division 1** location.

Vacuum-Assist Blowers

Table 514.3(B)(1) the space within 18" in all directions extending to grade level and up to 18" above grade level within 10' horizontally.

Table 514.3(B)(2). Electrical Equipment Classified Areas for Dispensing Devices

Compressed Natural Gas

Table 514.3(B)(2) the entire space within the dispenser enclosure is a Class I, **Division 1** location. 5' in all directions from the dispenser location is a **Division 2** location.

Liquefied Natural Gas

Table 514.3(B)(2) the entire space within the dispenser enclosure is a Class I, **Division 1** location. 10' in all directions from the dispenser location is a **Division 2** location.

Liquefied Petroleum Gas

Table 514.3(B)(2) the entire space within the dispenser enclosure; 18" from the exterior surface of the dispenser enclosure to an elevation of 4' above the base of the dispenser; the entire pit or open space beneath the dispenser and within 20' horizontally from any edge of the dispenser when the pit or trench is **not** mechanically ventilated is a Class I, **Division 1** location. Up to 18" aboveground and within 20' horizontally from any edge of the dispenser enclosure, including pits or trenches within this area when provided with mechanical ventilation is a **Division 2** location.

514.4. All electrical equipment and wiring installed in Class I locations shall comply with Article 501.

Exception: Rigid PVC is **not** required to be encased in 2" of concrete if buried 24" deep.

514.7. Wiring and equipment installed above Class I locations shall comply with 511.7.

514.8. Underground wiring shall be installed in threaded rigid metal conduit or threaded IMC. Any portion of electrical wiring or equipment below a Division 1 or Division 2 location shall be sealed within 10' of the point of emergence above grade. Except for listed explosionproof reducers at the conduit seal, there shall be no union, coupling, box, or fitting between the conduit seal and the point of emergence above grade.

Exception 1: Type MI cable is permitted.

Exception 2: Type PVC conduit and Type RTRC conduit is permitted where buried not less than 24". Rigid steel or IMC shall be used for the last 2' of the underground run to emergence **or** to the point of connection to the above ground raceway, and an equipment grounding conductor shall be installed.

•**Author's note**: Exception 2 requires the 2' length of metal conduit to be used on the end of the PVC even when the conduit does not turn up, but passes horizontally into the nonhazardous area of a basement. The metal conduit is needed to provide for the installation of a sealing fitting since the conduit is emerging from a Class I, Division 1 location below ground and a seal is required at the crossing of the boundary between the hazardous location and the nonhazardous location.

514.9 Sealing

514.9(A). A listed seal shall be provided in each conduit run entering or leaving a dispenser or any cavities or enclosures in direct communication therewith. The sealing fitting or listed explosionproof reducer at the end of the seal shall be the first fitting after the conduit emerges from the earth or concrete.

LEAVING ⊽ ⊼ ENTERING

514.9(B). Additional seals at the boundary shall be provided in accordance with 501.15.

501.15(A)(4). This section requires a seal in each and every conduit that leaves the Class I, Division 1 location, whether it passes into a Division 2 location or into a nonhazardous location. This required seal may be installed on either side of the boundary and within 10' of the boundary.

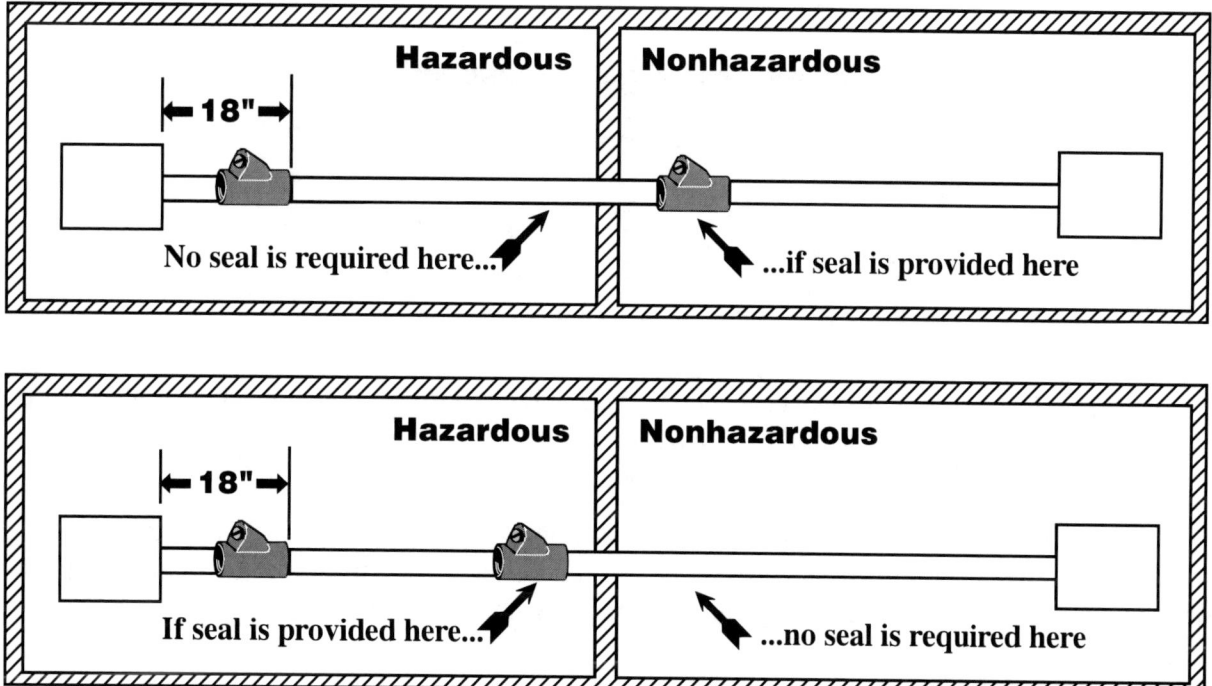

Hazardous **Nonhazardous**

←18"→

No seal is required here... ...if seal is provided here

Hazardous **Nonhazardous**

←18"→

If seal is provided here... ...no seal is required here

501.15(B)(2). Class I, Division 2 boundary, the seal is permitted on either the Division 2 or nonhazardous side of the boundary. It must be installed in a manner that will minimize the gas or vapor that can enter the conduit system within the Division 2 location and be communicated beyond the seal.

Rigid metal conduit or threaded IMC conduit must be used between the sealing fitting and the point at which the conduit leaves the Division 2 location.

A threaded connection must be used at the sealing fitting, and no fittings, unions, etc. except an explosionproof reducer at the sealing fitting can be installed between the sealing fitting and the point at which the conduit leaves the Division 2 location.

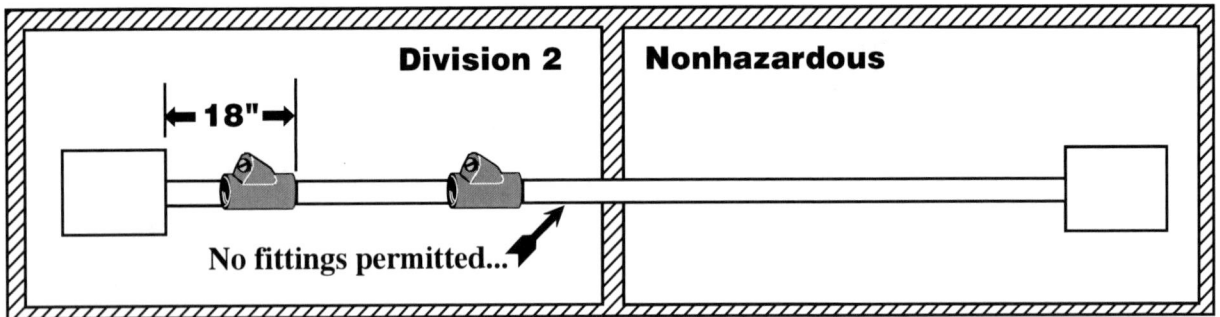

501.15(B)(2) **Exception 1**. A continuous run of metal conduit passing completely through a Class I, Division 2 location without any fittings within the Division 2 location, and not less than 12" beyond each of the boundaries, is not required to be sealed if both ends are in nonhazardous locations.

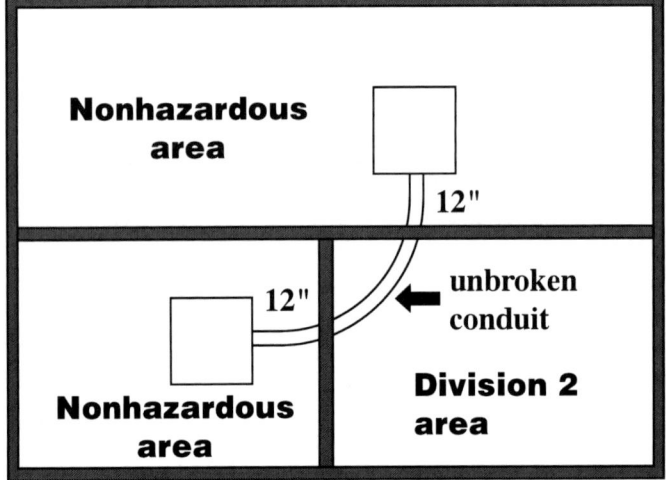

501.15(B)(2) Exception 2. No seal is needed in the conduit run from a Division 2 to a nonhazardous area where a transition is made in the nonhazardous location from a conduit to cable tray, cablebus, ventilated busway, Type MI cable or open wiring.

The principle here is that a Division 2 location is one that seldom contains the hazardous atmosphere. This, in combination with an outdoor termination to a wiring method that is incapable of serving as a means of conducting the hazardous agent, means that chance of ignition is very slight.

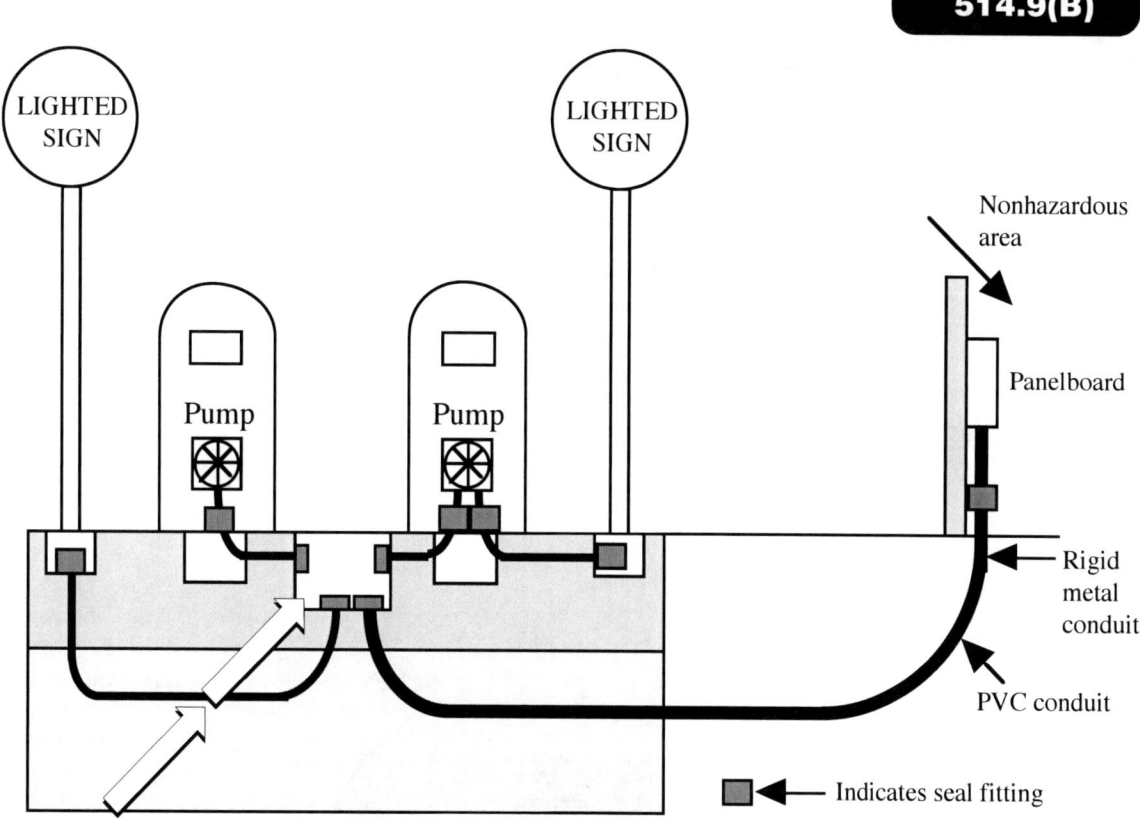

•The explosionproof box is approved as raintight and has integral sealing wells. All the conduits connecting to the box are sealed without need for separate individual sealing fittings.

•The lighted signs must satisfy section 511.7(B)(1)(b) which states: Lamps and lamp holders for fixed lighting located over lanes through which vehicles are commonly driven, or that may otherwise be exposed to physical damage must be located not less than 12' above the floor level, unless of the totally enclosed type or so constructed that sparks or hot metal particles cannot escape.

•Normally, panelboards are located in a nonhazardous location so that a seal is shown where the conduit emerges from underground.

•Rigid steel or IMC shall be used for the last 2' of the underground run to emergence **or** to the point of connection to the above ground.

514.11(A). Emergency Electrical Disconnects. Fuel dispensing systems shall be provided with one or more clearly identified emergency shutoff devices or electrical disconnects. Such devices shall be installed in approved locations but not less than 20 feet or more than 100 feet from the fuel dispensing devices that they serve. Emergency shutoff devices or electrical disconnects shall disconnect power to all dispensing devices; to all remote pumps serving the dispensing devices; to all associated power, control, and signal circuits; and to all other electrical equipment in the hazardous (classified) locations surrounding the fuel dispensing devices.

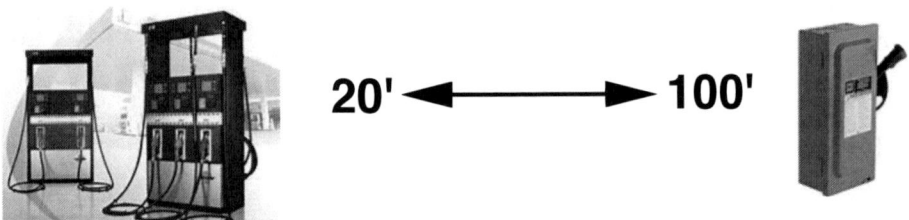

514.11(B). At attended motor fuel dispensing facilities, the devices or disconnects shall be readily accessible to the attendant.

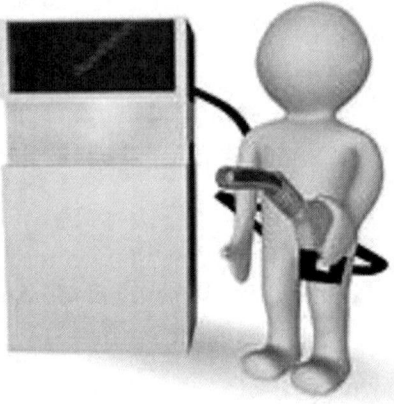

514.11(C). At unattended motor fuel dispensing facilities, the devices or disconnects shall be readily accessible to patrons and at least one additional device or disconnect shall be readily accessible to each group of dispensing devices on an individual island.

514.16. All metal raceways, metal armor or metallic sheath on cables, and all non-current-carrying metal parts of fixed and portable electrical equipment, regardless of voltage, shall be grounded per Article 250. Grounding in Class I locations shall comply with 501.30.

•**Author's note**: To summarize Article 514, you could say the most frequently encountered hazardous locations are automotive service stations. Gasoline is the most widely used flammable liquid. It has a flash point of approximately -40°F, it is readily ignitible in ordinary air. In automotive gasoline dispensing stations, the principal concern is that gasoline will be spilled during dispensing or will leak from the tank of the vehicle. The electrical equipment requirements are intended to ensure the electrical system is not the ignition source.

The service station with gasoline dispensing is a **Class I Group D** hazardous location.

GROUP D: Atmospheres such as acetone, alcohol, ammonia, benzine, benzol, butane, gasoline, hexane, lacquer solvent vapors, naphtha, natural gas, propane, or gases or vapors equivalent in hazard.

Since it is a **Class I location,** the rules of **Article 501** will apply. To refresh your memory, it would be good to read Article 501 again. When wiring a service station, the electrician will be concerned if it's a Division 1 or a Division 2 location as the rules in Article 501 must be followed.

DIVISION 1

A Class I, Division 1 hazardous location is defined as follows:
• Those locations in which ignitible concentrations of flammable gases or vapors **can exist under normal operating condition**.
• Those locations in which ignitible concentrations of such gases or vapors may **exist frequently** because of repair or maintenance operations or because of leakage.
• Those locations in which breakdown or faulty operation of equipment or processes **might release** ignitible concentrations of flammable gases or vapors and might cause simultaneous failure of electric equipment in such a way as to directly cause the electrical equipment to become a source of ignition.

DIVISION 2

A Class I, Division 2 hazardous location is defined as follows:
• In which volatile flammable liquid produced vapors or flammable gases are handled, processed, or used, but in which the liquids, vapors, or gases **will normally be confined within closed containers** or closed systems from which they can escape only in case of accidental rupture or breakdown of such containers or systems or in case of abnormal operation of equipment.
• In which ignitible concentrations of **gases or vapors are normally prevented** by positive mechanical ventilation and which might become hazardous through failure or abnormal operation of ventilating equipment.
• That is adjacent to a Class I, Division 1 location, and to which ignitible concentrations of gases or vapors might **occasionally** be communicated unless such communication is prevented by adequate positive-pressure ventilation from a source of clean air and effective safeguards against ventilation failure are provided.

•*Circle your choice of answer and* **write the Code section where it was found***.*

1. A point located 24" above grade level and 20 feet from the edge of an indoor remote gas pump is considered ____.

(a) Class I, Group D, Division 2   (b) Class I, Group D, Division 1
(c) Class I, Group C, Division 2   (d) Class I, Group C, Division 1

2. Fixed wiring, which is to provide external power to aircraft hangers, shall be installed at least ____ above floor level.

(a) 12"   (b) 18"   (c) 24"   (d) 30"

3. In commercial garages using electrical hand tools, portable lights, etc., ground fault protection shall be provided for ____.

(a) receptacles in pits below floor level only
(b) receptacles located in adjacent bathrooms only
(c) receptacles within 18" above the floor only
(d) all receptacles in the service area

4. A propane-dispensing unit is located outdoors, 50 feet from an office in which the branch circuit supplying the unit originates. Conduit seals shall be required ____.

(a) where the conduit emerges from the ground at the office only
(b) where the conduit emerges from the ground at the dispensing unit only
(c) where the conduit emerges from the ground at both the dispensing unit and at the office
(d) No seals are required for propane gas

5. Aircraft hangar attachment plugs and receptacles in Class I locations shall be designed so they cannot be energized while ____.

(a) the aircraft is within 20'   (b) the connections are being made or broken
(c) the voltage is above 30   (c) all of these

6. In a major repair garage, the pit shall be classified ____ unless provisions are made for ventilation.

(a) Class I, Division 2 (b) Class II, Division 2 (c) Class II, Division 1 (d) Class I, Division 1

7. Fuel dispensing systems shall be provided with one or more clearly identified emergency shutoff devices or electrical disconnects. Such devices shall be installed in approved locations but not less than ____feet or more than ____ feet from the fuel dispensing devices that they serve.

(a) 10, 50   (b) 20, 100   (c) 25, 50   (d) 35, 65

8. Portable lighting equipment in commercial garages shall be equipped with ____ and substantial guard attached to the lampholder or handle. All exterior surfaces that might come in contact with battery terminals, wiring terminals, or other objects shall be of nonconducting material or shall be effectively protected with insulation.

(a) handle   (b) receptacle   (c) AFCI protection   (d) identified for Class III locations

9. Aircraft batteries shall not be _____ where installed in an aircraft located inside or partially inside a hangar.

(a) charged   (b) removed   (c) connected   (d) de-energized

10. Underground wiring for a motor fuel dispener shall be installed in ____.

(a) threaded rigid metal conduit
(b) threaded steel intermediate metal conduit
(c) rigid non-metallic conduit buried not less than 24"
(d) Any of the above

11. At attended motor fuel dispensing facilities, the devices or disconnects shall be ___ to the attendant.

(a) readily accessible   (b) accessible   (c) with in 4'   (d) with in 5'

12. All fixed wiring above Class I locations in a repair garage shall be in ____.

I. flexible nonmetallic conduit   II. rigid nonmetallic conduit   III. TC cable

(a) I only   (b) II only   (c) I and II only   (d) I, II and III

•*Circle your choice of answer and* **write the Code section where it was found**.

1. Parking garages used for parking or storage and where no repair work is done, open flame, welding, or the use of volatile flammable liquids are ____.

(a) Class I   (b) Class II   (c) Class III   (d) unclassified

2. At unattended motor fuel dispensing facilities, the devices or disconnects shall be readily accessible to patrons and at least one additional device or disconnect shall be readily accessible to each group of dispensing devices on a/an ____.

(a) individual island   (b) pump circuit   (c) underground tank   (d) device

3. Table 514.3(B)(1) shall be applied where Class I liquids are stored, handled, or dispensed and shall be used to ____ and classify motor fuel dispensing facilities and commercial garages as defined in Article 511.

(a) identify   (b) mark   (c) delineate   (b) unclassify

4. In commercial garages, all 125v single-phase, 15 and 20 amp receptacles where ____ are to be used, shall provide GFCI protection for personnel.

I.   portable lighting equipment
II. electrical hand tools
III. electrical automotive diagnostic equipment

(a) I only   (b) II only   (c) III only   (d) I, II and III

5. Which of the following about an aircraft hangar is **true**?

I.   Any area below the floor level shall be considered a Class I, Division 1 location up to the floor level.
II. The area within 5' horizontally of aircraft power plants or fuel tanks shall be considered a Class I, Division 2 location extending from the floor to a level 5' above the upper surface of wings and engine enclosures.

(a) I only   (b) II only   (c) both I and II   (d) neither I nor II

6. Storerooms and similar areas adjacent to aircraft hangars but effectively isolated shall be designated ____.

(a) Class I, Division 2 (b) Class II, Division 1 (c) Class II, Division 2 (d) shall not be classified

7. An approved seal shall be provided in each conduit run entering or leaving a dispenser or any cavities or enclosures in direct communication therewith. The sealing fitting shall be _____ .

(a) concrete-tight
(b) 3/4" minimum thickness
(c) the last fitting after the conduit emerges from the earth or concrete
(d) the first fitting after the conduit emerges from the earth or concrete

8. In minor repair garages, generally the floor area to a height of 18" above floor level is designated as ____ where ventilation is not provided.

(a) Class I, Division 1 (b) Class I, Division 2 (c) Class II, Division 2 (d) Class II, Division 1

9. What is the minimum burial depth for RTRC conduit in a dispensing station Class I, Division 1 location?

(a) 18"   (b) 24"   (c) 30"   (d) cannot be used in Class I, Division 1 location

10. Lighting fixtures installed over vehicle lanes inside a commercial garage shall be installed a minimum of ____ feet.

(a) 8   (b) 10   (c) 12   (d) 15

11. Flexible cords for aircraft energizers and ground support equipment shall ____.

I.   be approved for extra-hard usage
II. include a grounded conductor
III. be suitable for the type of service

(a) I only   (b) I and III only   (c) I and II only   (d) I, II and III

12. Articles ____ through ____ cover occupancies or parts of occupancies that are or may be hazardous because of atmospheric concentrations of flammable liquids, gases, or vapors, or because of deposits or accumulations of materials that may be readily ignitible.

(a) 517 through 520   (b) 511 through 517   (c) 514 through 517   (d) 514 through 600

ARTICLE 515
Bulk Storage Plants

515.1. This article covers electrical equipment and wiring in the bulk storage plant area where flammable liquids are received by tank vessel, pipelines, tank car, or tank vehicle and are stored for the purpose of distributing such liquids by tank vessel, pipeline, tank car, tank vehicle, portable tank, or container.

515.3. Classification of Locations.

Where the term "Class I" is used with respect to Zone classification within this article of the Code, it shall apply to Zone 0, Zone 1, and Zone 2 designations.

515.3. Class I Locations. Table 515.3 shall be applied where Class I flammable liquids are stored, handled, or dispensed and shall be used to classify bulk storage plants. The classified location shall not extend beyond a floor, wall, roof, or other solid partition that has no communicating openings.

Informational Note 1: The extent of the area classifications shown in Table 515.3 are based on the understanding that the installation meets the applicable rules of NFPA 30-2018, Chapter 5, in all respects. Should this not be the case, the authority having jurisdiction has the authority to classify the extent of the classified space.

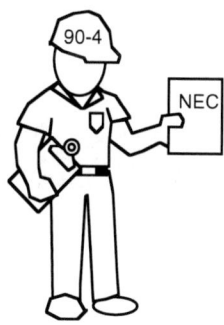

Informational Note 2: See 514.3(C) through (E) for gasoline dispensing stations in marinas and boatyards.

Table 515.3. Indoor equipment installed where flammable vapor-air mixtures can exist under normal operation (*see Informational Note*)

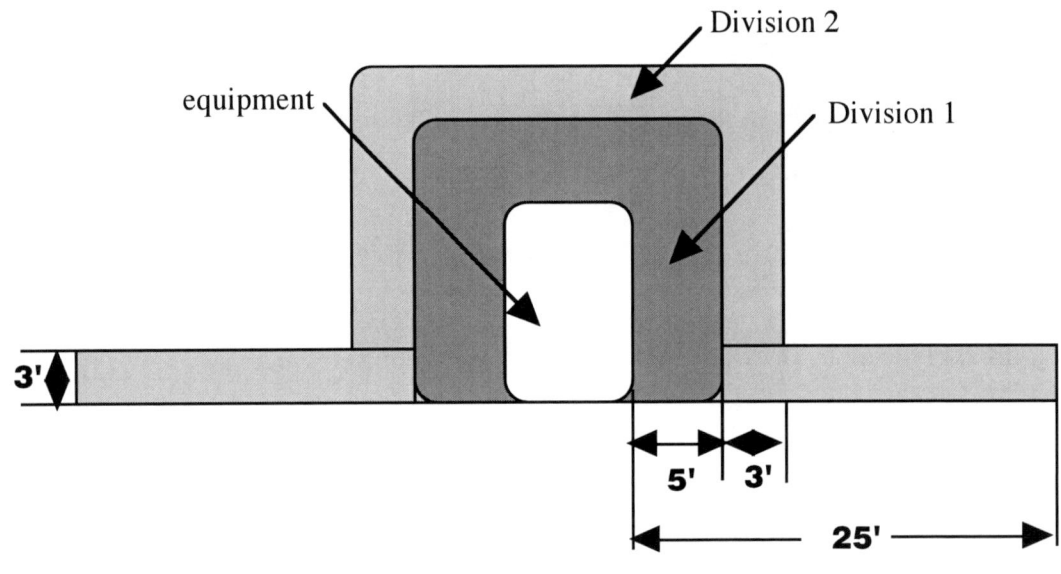

Outdoor equipment installed where flammable vapor-air mixtures can exist under normal operation

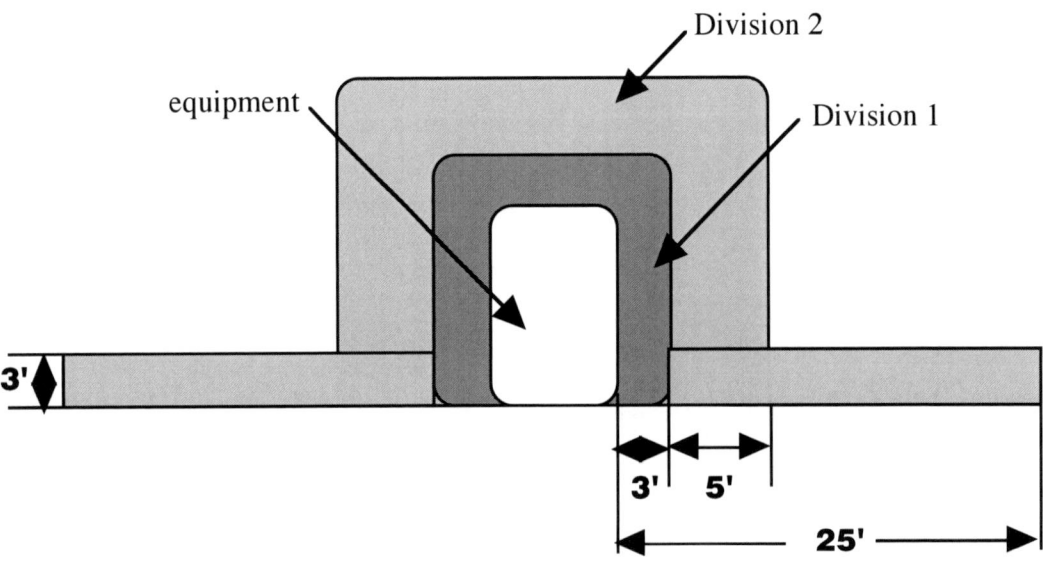

Table 515.3. Tank storage installations inside buildings.

Class I, Division 1: All equipment located below grade level.

Class I, Division 2: All equipment located at or above grade level.

Tank - aboveground, fixed roof

Class I, Division 1: Inside fixed roof tank. Area inside dike where dike height is greater than the distance from the tank to the dike for more than 50% of the tank circumference.

Tank - aboveground, floating roof

With fixed outer roof	Class I, Division 1 - Area between the floating roof and the fixed roof sections and within the shell
With no fixed outer roof	Class I, Division 1 - Area above the floating roof and within the shell
Tank vault - interior	Class I, Division 1 - Entire interior volume, if Class I liquids are stored within
Underground tank fill opening	Class I, Division 1 - Any pit, box, or space below grade level, if any part is within a Division 1 or 2, or Zone 1 or 2 classified location Class I, Division 2 - Up to 18" above grade level within a horizontal radius of 10' from a loose fill connection, and within a horizontal radius of 5' from a tight fill connection
Vent - discharging upward	Class I, Division 1 - Area inside of vent piping or within 3' of open end of vent, extending in all directions Class I, Division 2 - Area between 3' and 5' of open end of vent, extending in all directions

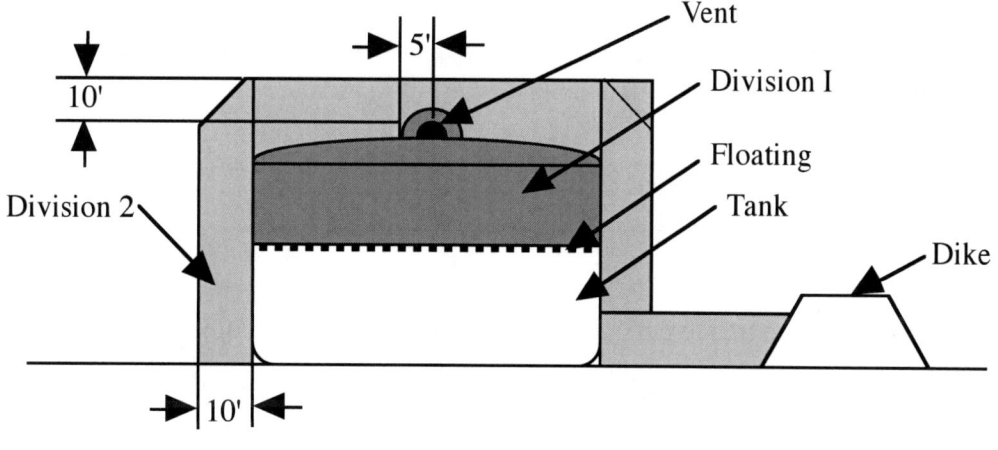

Drum and container filling - outdoors or indoors.

Class I, Division 1: Area inside the drum or container. Within 3' of vent and fill openings, extending in all directions.

Class I, Division 2: Area between 3' and 5' from vent or fill openings, extending in all directions; also, up to 18" above floor or grade level within a horizontal radius of 10' from vent or fill opening.

Pumps, bleeders, withdrawal fittings.
INDOORS

Class I, Division 2: Within 5' of any edge of such devices, extending in all directions; also, up to 3' above floor or grade level within 25' horizontally from any edge of such devices.

OUTDOORS

Class I, Division 2: Within 3' of any edge of such devices, extending in all directions; also, up to 18" above floor or grade level within 10' horizontally from any edge of such devices.

Pits and sumps WITHOUT MECHANICAL VENTILATION.

Class I, Division 1: Entire area within a pit or sump if any part is within a Division 1 or 2, or Zone 1 or 2, classified location.

WITH ADEQUATE MECHANICAL VENTILATION

Class I, Division 2: Entire area within a pit or sump if any part is within a Division 1 or 2, or Zone 1 or 2, classified location.

Containing valves, fittings, or piping, and not within a Division 1 or 2, or Zone 1 or 2, classified location.

Class I, Division 2: Entire pit or sump.

Table 515.3.

Drainage ditches, separators, impounding basins
OUTDOORS.

Class I, Division 2: Area up to 18" above ditch, separator, or basin; also, area up to 18" above grade within 15' horizontally from any edge.

INDOORS.

Class I, Division 2: Same classified area as pits.

Tank vehicle and tank car loading through open dome.

Class I, Division 1: Area inside tank. Within 3' edge of dome extending in all directions.

Class I, Division 2: Area between 3' and 15' from edge of dome, extending in all directions.

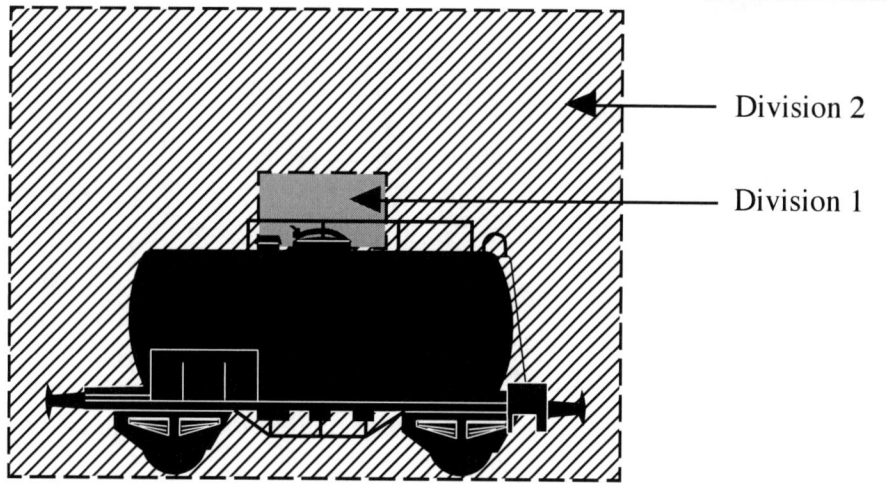

Loading through bottom connections with atmospheric venting.

Class I, Division 1: Area inside tank. Within 3' of point of venting to atmosphere, extending in all directions.

Class I, Division 2: Area between 3' and 15' from point of venting to atmosphere, extending in all directions; also, up to 18" above grade within a horizontal radius of 10' from point of loading connection.

Loading through closed dome with atmospheric venting.

Class I, Division 1: Within 3' of open end of vent, extending in all directions.

Class I, Division 2: Area between 3' and 15' from open end of vent, extending in all directions; also, within 3' of edge of dome, extending in all directions.

Loading through closed dome with vapor control.

Class I, Division 2: Within 3' of point of connection of both fill and vapor lines extending in all directions.

Table 515.3. Bottom loading with vapor control or any bottom unloading.

Class I, Division 2: Within 3' of point of connections, extending in all directions; also up to 18" above grade within a horizontal radius of 10' from point of connections.

Storage and repair garage for tank vehicles.

Class I, Division 1: All pits or spaces below floor level.

Class I, Division 2: Area up to 18" above floor or grade level for entire storage or repair garage.

Garages for other than tank vehicles.

Ordinary. If there is any opening to these rooms within the extent of an outdoor classified location, the entire room shall be classified the same as the area classification at the point of the opening.

Office and rest rooms.

Ordinary. If there is any opening to these rooms within the extent of an indoor classified location, the room shall be classified the same as if the wall, curb, or partition did not exist.

Outdoor drum storage.

Ordinary.
Inside rooms or storage lockers used for the storage of Class I liquids.

Class I, Division 2: Entire room.

Indoor warehousing where there is no flammable liquid transfer.
Ordinary. If there is any opening to these rooms within the extent of an indoor classified location, the room shall be classified the same as if the wall, curb, or partition did not exist.

Office and rest rooms.
Unclassified, if there is any opening to these rooms within the extent of an indoor classified location, the room shall be classified the same as if the wall, curb, or partition did not exist.

Piers and wharves.

Class I, Division 2: 25' horizontally in all directions on the pier side from that portion of the hull containing cargo tanks.
From the water level to 25' above the cargo tanks at their highest position.

Additional locations required by the presence of sources of flammable liquids on the berth, or by the Coast Guard or other regulations.

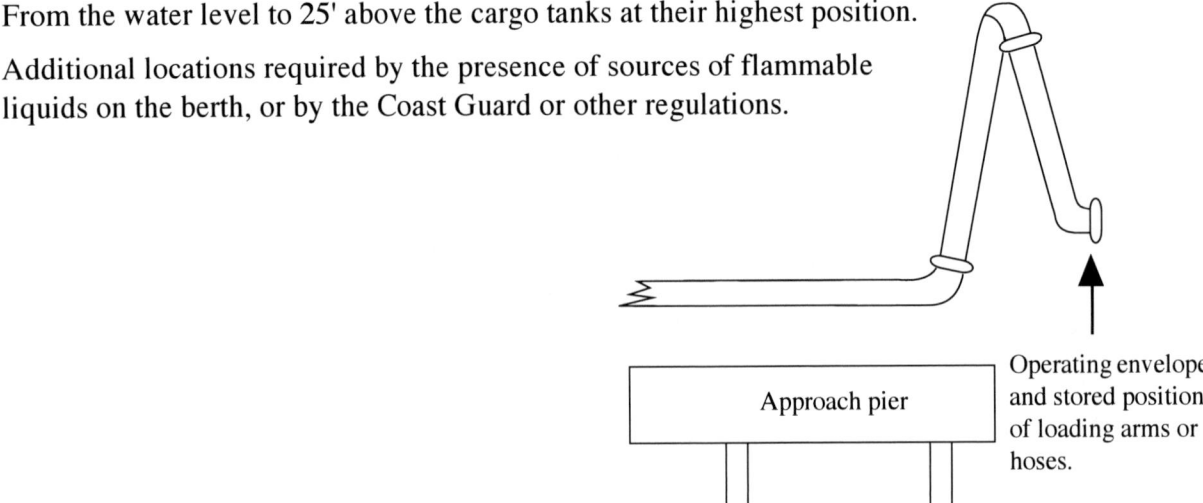

Operating envelope and stored position of loading arms or hoses.

Approach pier

Informational Note: See section 7.3 of NFPA 30-2018, *Flammable and Combustible Liquids Code*, for additional information.

515.4. All electrical wiring and equipment within the Class I locations defined in 515.3 shall comply with Article 501 or Article 505.

Exception: As permitted in 515.8.

515.7(A). All fixed wiring above Class I locations shall be in metal raceways or Schedule 80 PVC, Type RTRC marked with suffix -XW, or be Type MI, TC, PLTC, PLTC-ER, ITC, ITC-ER or MC cable.

515.7(B). Fixed equipment that may produce arcs, sparks, or particles of hot metal, such as lamps and lampholders for fixed lighting, cutouts, switches, receptacles, motors, etc. having make-and-break or sliding contacts, shall be of the totally enclosed type or be constructed so as to prevent the escape of such.

515.7(C). Portable lamps and their flexible cords shall follow the provisions of Article 501 or 505 for the class of location above which they are connected or used.

515.8(A). Underground wiring shall be installed in threaded rigid metal conduit or threaded IMC or, where buried under not less than 2' of cover, shall be permitted in rigid PVC or a listed cable. Where PVC or Type RTRC, or a listed cable is used, not less than the last 2' of the conduit run to the conduit point of emergence from the underground location or to the point of connection above ground must be in rigid steel or IMC. Where cable is used, it shall be enclosed in threaded rigid or IMC from the point of the lowest buried cable level to the point of connection above ground.

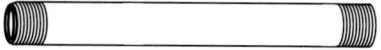

515.8(B). In Class I, Divisions 1 and 2, it is important to use conductor and cable insulations that will not be attacked by the process fluids. Where condensed vapors or liquids may collect on, or come in contact with, the insulation must be of a type identified for the conditions used. The insulation may be required to be protected by a lead sheath or other approved means.

515.8(C). Where Type PVC conduit, Type RTRC conduit, or cable with a nonmetallic sheath is used, an equipment grounding conductor is required.

515.9. Sealing requirements shall apply to horizontal as well as to vertical boundaries of Class I locations. Buried raceways and cables under Class I locations shall be considered to be within a Class I, Division 1 or Zone 1 location.

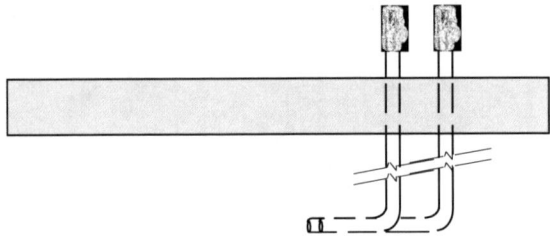

515.10. Where gasoline or other volatile flammable liquids or liquefied flammable gases are dispensed at bulk stations, Article 514 shall apply.

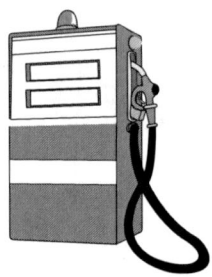

515.16. All metal raceways, metal armor or metallic sheath on cables, and all non-current-carrying metal parts of fixed or portable electrical equipment, regardless of voltage, shall be grounded and bonded per Article 250. Grounding and bonding in Class I, Division 1 and 2 locations shall comply with 501.30 and 505.25 for Class I, Zone 0, 1, and 2 locations.

•**Author's note**: To summarize Article 515, bulk storage plants are facilities where gasoline or other volatile flammable liquids are stored in large capacity tanks sometimes referred to as a "tank farm."

The loading and unloading of fuel is done at a high flow rate which can result in the generation of static electricity. Static charges can be kept at safe levels with proper bonding.

Vapor is often lost into the atmosphere during loading and unloading operations. Vapor recovery units are provided to recapture the lost vapor.

Marine terminals handle large amounts of fuel at high flow rates. Corrosion is a problem at marine fuel dispensing stations. Salt water can attack the electrical equipment and wiring. Corrosion has caused **discontinuity in the equipment grounding path of metal conduit systems.** It can also lead to stray voltages in equipment, which may be hazardous to personnel. Equipment in such locations must be corrosion resistant in order to ensure that the hazardous protection will be effective.

Gas spills on a boat are very hazardous, because the vapors will tend to accumulate at the bottom of the boat.

ARTICLE 516
Spray Application, Dipping, and Coating Processes Using Flammable or Combustible Materials

FLASHPOINT

Part I. General

516.1. Article 516 covers the regular or frequent application of flammable liquids, combustible liquids, and combustible powders by spray operations and the application of flammable liquids, or combustible liquids at temperatures above their flashpoint by spraying, dipping, coating, printing or other means.

516.3. Classification of Locations.

Where the term "Class I" is used with respect to Zone classification within this article of the Code, it shall apply to Zone 0, Zone 1, and Zone 2 designations.

Definition of Spray Area. Any fully enclosed, partly enclosed, or unenclosed area in which dangerous quantities of flammable or combustible vapors, mists, residues, dusts, or deposits are present due to the operation of spray process, including:
(1) any area in the direct path of a spray application process;
(2) the interior of a spray booth, spray room, or limited finishing workstation, as herein defined;
(3) the interior of any exhaust plenum, eliminator section, or scrubber section;
(4) the interior of any exhaust duct or exhaust stack leading from a spray application process;
(5) the interior of any air recirculation path up to and including recirculation particulate filters;
(6) any solvent concentrator (pollution abatement) unit or solvent recovery (distillation) unit; and
(7) the inside of a membrane enclosure.

The following are **not** part of the spray area:
(1) fresh air make-up units;
(2) air supply ducts and air supply plenums;
(3) recirculation air supply ducts downstream of recirculation particulate filters; and
(4) exhaust ducts from solvent concentrator (pollution abatement) units.

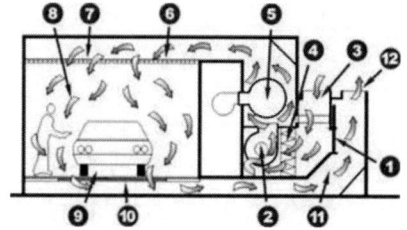 

Unenclosed spray areas are locations outside of buildings or are localized operations within a larger room or space. Such are normally provided with some local vapor extraction/ventilation system. In automated operations, the area limits are the maximum area in the direct path of spray operations. In manual operations, the area limits are the maximum area of spray when aimed at 90° to the application surface.

Limited Finishing Workstation. An apparatus that is capable of confining the vapors, mists, residues, dusts, or deposits that are generated by a spray application process but does not meet the requirements of a spray booth or spray room, as herein defined.

Membrane Enclosure. A temporary enclosure used for the spraying of workpieces that cannot be moved into a spray booth where open spraying is not practical due to proximity to other operations, finish quality, or conerns such as the collection of overspray.

Temporary membrane enclosures are used in the marine industry to paint yachts that are too large to fit in a spray booth. The standard not only makes painting safer but eases the concerns of fire marshals and regulators who oversee this work.

Spray Booth. A power-ventilated enclosure for a spray application operation or process that confines and limits the escape of the material being sprayed, including vapors, mists, dusts, and residues that are produced by the spraying operation and conducts or directs these materials to an exhaust system.

A spray booth is an enclosure or insert within a larger room used for spray/coating/dipping applications. A spray booth can be fully enclosed or have open front or face and can include separate conveyor entrance and exit. The spray booth is provided with a dedicated ventilation exhaust with supply air from the larger room or from dedicated air supply.

Outdoor Spray Area. A spray area that is outside the confines of a building or that has a canopy or roof that does not limit the dissipation of the heat of a fire or dispersion of flammable vapors and does not restrict fire-fighting access and control. For the purpose of this standard, an outdoor spray area can be treated as an unenclosed spray area.

Spray Room. A power-ventilated fully enclosed room used exclusively for open spraying of flammable or combustible materials.

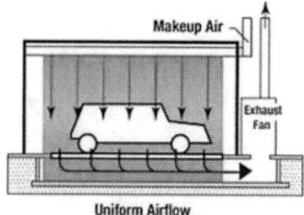

Unenclosed Spray Area. Any spray area that is not confined by a limited finishing workstation, spray booth, or spray room, as herein defined.

Part II. Open Containers

516.4. Area Classification. For open containers, supply containers, waste containers, spray gun cleaners, and solvent distillation units that contain Class I liquids that are located in ventilated areas, area classification shall be in accordance with the following:

(1) The area within 3 feet in all directions from any such container or equipment and extending to the floor or grade level shall be classified Class I, Division 1 or Class I, Zone 1, whichever is applicable.

(2) The area extending 2 feet beyond the Division 1 or Zone 1 location shall be classified as Class I, Division 2 or Class I, Zone 2, whichever is applicable.

(3) The area extending 5 feet horizontally beyond the area described in 516.4(2) up to a height of 18" above the floor or grade level shall be classified as Class I, Division 2 or Class I, Zone 2, whichever is applicable.

(4) The area inside any tank or container shall be classified as Class I, Division 1 or Class I, Zone 0, whichever is applicable.

(5) Sumps, pits, or below grade channels within 10 feet horizontally of a vapor source shall be classified as Class I, Division 1 or Zone 1. If the sump, pit, or channel exceeds beyond 10 feet from the vapor source, it shall be provided with a vapor stop or it shall be classified as Class I, Divsion 1 or Zone 1 for its entire length.

For the purposes of electrical area classification, the Division and the Zone system shall **not** be intermixed for any given source of release.

Electrical wiring and utilization equipment installed in these areas shall be suitable for the location, as shown in Figure 516.4 on the next page.

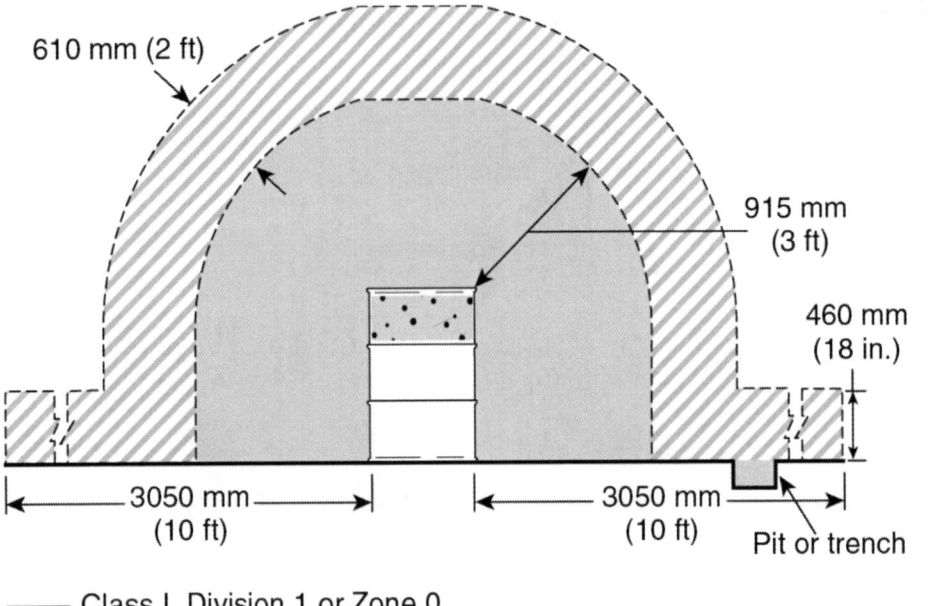

	Class I, Division 1 or Zone 0 (e.g., vapor space in container)
	Class I, Division 1 or Zone 1
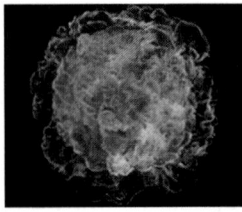	Class I, Division 2 or Zone 2

Part III. Spray Application Processes

516.5. For spray application processes, the area classification is based on quantities of flammable vapors, combustible mists, residues, dusts, or deposits that are present or might be present in quantities sufficient to produce ignitible or explosive mixtures with air.

516.5(B). The interior of any open or closed container or vessel of a flammable liquid shall be considered Class I, Division 1, or Class I, Zone 0, as applicable.

516.5(D)(1). Unenclosed Spray Processes

Electrical wiring and utilization equipment located outside but within 20 feet horizontally and 10 feet vertically of an enclosed spray area and not separated from the spray area by partitions extending to the boundries of the area designated as Division 2, Zone 2 or Zone 22 (shown below) shall be suitable for Class I, Division 2; Class I, Zone 2; Class 2, Division 2; or Zone 22 locations, whichever is applicable.

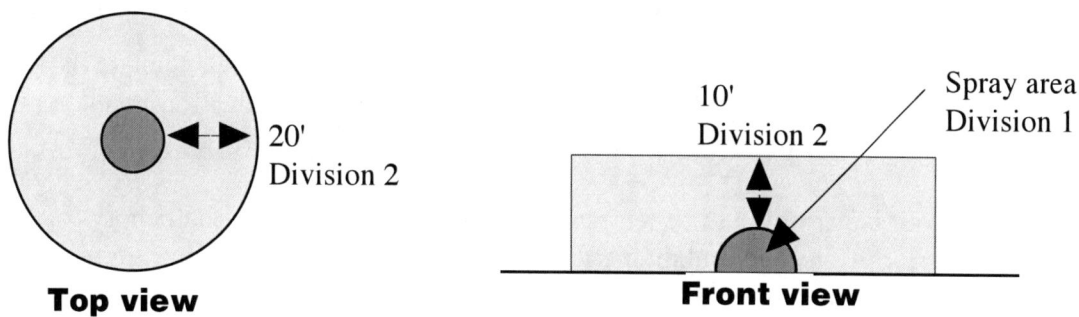

Top view

Front view

516.5(D)(2). Closed-Top, Open-Face, and Open-Front Spray Booths and Spray Rooms

If spray application operations are conducted within a closed-top. open-face, or open-front booth or room, as shown below, any electrical wiring or utilization equipment located outside of the booth or room but within 3 feet of any opening shall be suitable for Class I, Division 2; Class I, Zone 2; Class II, Division 2; or Zone 22 locations shall extend from the edges of the open face or open front of the booth or room.

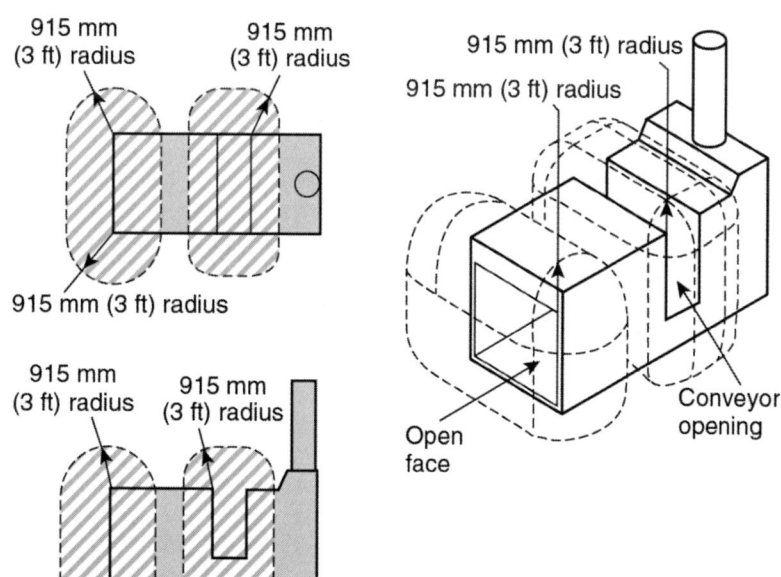

515.5(D)(3). Open-Top Spray Booths

For spraying operations conducted within an open top spray booth, the space 3 feet vertically above the booth and within 3 feet of other booth openings shall be considered Class I, Division 2; Class I, Zone 2; Class II, Division 2; or Zone 22 whichever is applicable.

516.5(D)(4). Enclosed Spray Booths and Spray Rooms

For spray application operations confined to an enclosed spray booth or room, electrical area classification shall be as follows:

(1) The area within 3 feet of any opening shall be classified as Class I, Division 2; Class I, Zone 2; Class II, Division 2; or Zone 22 locations, whichever is applicable, as shown in sketch below.

(2) Where automated spray application equipment is used, the area outside the access doors shall be unclassified provided the **door interlock** prevents the spray application when the door is open.

•*Interlocked* shall mean that the spray application equipment cannot be operated unless the exhaust ventilation system is operating and functioning properly and spray application is automatically stopped if the exhaust ventilation system fails.

(3) Where exhaust air is permitted to be recirculated, both of the following shall apply:

a. The interior of any recirculation path from the secondary particulate filters up to and including the air supply plenum shall be classified as Class I, Division 2; Class I, Zone 2; Class II, Division 2; or Zone 22 locations, whichever is applicable.

b. The interior of fresh air supply ducts shall be **unclassified**.

(4) Where exhaust air is not recirculated, the interior of fresh air supply ducts and fresh air supply plenums shall be **unclassified**.

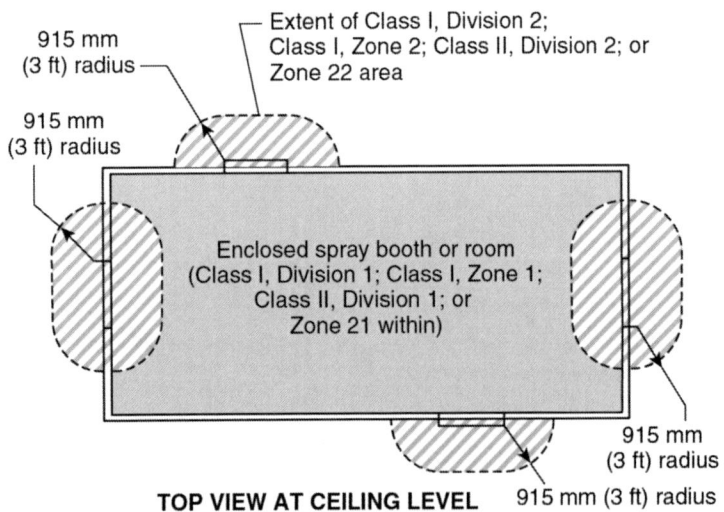

TOP VIEW AT CEILING LEVEL

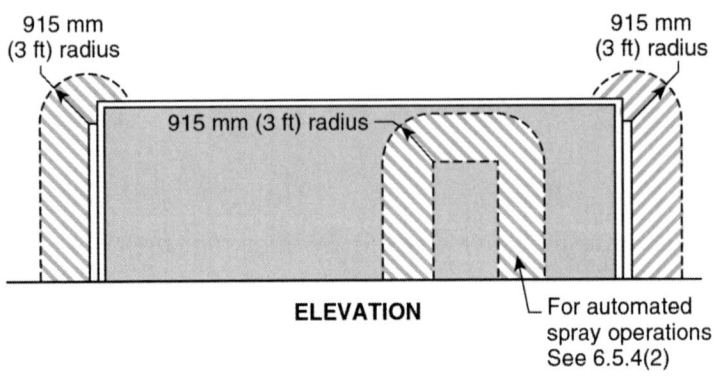

ELEVATION

516.5(D)(5). Limited Finishing Workstations

(a) For limited finishing workstations, the area inside the 3 feet space horizontally and vertically beyond the volume enclosed by the outside surface of the curtains or partitions shall be classified as Class I, Division 2; Class I, Zone 2; Class II, Division 2; or Zone 22 as shown below .

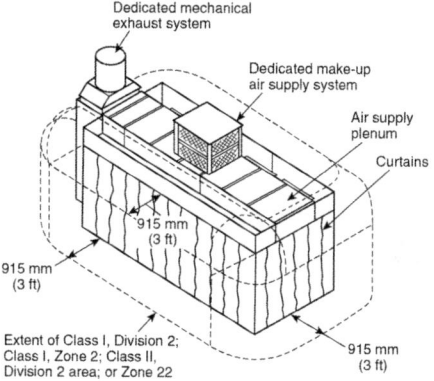

(b) A limited finishing workstation shall be designed and constructed to have all of the following:

(1) A dedicated make-up air supply
(2) Curtains or partitions that are noncombustible or limited combustible
(3) A dedicated mechanical exhaust and filtration system
(4) An approved automatic extinguishing system

(c) The amount of material sprayed in a limited finishing workstation shall not exceed one gallon in any 8 hour period.

8 HOURS

(d) Curtains or partitions shall be fully closed during any spray operations.

516.5(D)(5)(e). The equipment within the limited finishing workstation shall be *interlocked* such that the spray application equipment cannot be operated unless the exhaust ventilation system is operating and functioning properly and spray application is automatically stopped if the exhaust ventilation system fails.

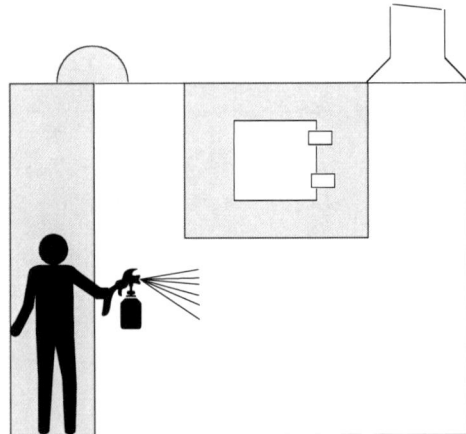

516.5(D)(5)(f). Any limited finishing workstation used for spray application operations shall not be used for any operation that is capable of producing sparks or particles of hot metal or for operations that involve open flames or electrical utilization equipment capable of producing sparks or particles of hot metal.

516.5(D)(5)(g). Where industrial air heaters are used to elevate the air temperature for drying, curing, or fusing operations, a high limit switch shall be provided to automatically shut off the drying apparatus if the air temperature in the limited finishing workstation exceeds the maximum discharge-air temperature allowed by the standard that the heater is listed to or 200°F, whichever is less.

516.5(D)(5)(h). A means shall be provided to show that the limited finishing workstation is in the drying or curing mode of operation and that the limited finishing workstation is to be unoccupied.

516.5(D)(5)(i). Any containers of flammable or combustible liquids shall be removed from the limited finishing workstation before the drying apparatus is energized.

516.5(D)(5)(j). Portable spot-drying, curing, or fusion apparatus shall be permitted to be used in a limited finishing workstation, provided that it is not located within the hazardous (classified) location when spray application operations are being conducted.

516.5(D)(5)(k). Recirculation of exhaust air shall be permitted when the provisions of 516.(D)(4) and (3) are both met.

(3) Where exhaust air is permitted to be recirculated, both of the following shall apply:

    a. The interior of any recirculation path from the secondary particulate filters up to and including the air supply plenum shall be classified as Class I, Division 2; Class I, Zone 2; Class II, Division 2; or Zone 22 locations, whichever is applicable.

    b. The interior of fresh air supply ducts shall be **unclassified**.

516. 6 Wiring and Equipment in Class I Locations

(A) Wiring and Equipment - Vapors. All electrical wiring and equipment within the Class I location (containing vapor only - not residues) defined in 516.5 shall comply with the applicable provisions of Article 501 or Article 505, as applicable.

516.6(B). Wiring in rigid metal conduit, IMC, MI cable, metal boxes containing no splices, taps, or terminal connections, no electrical equipment may be installed in spray areas containing vapors and residues unless specifically listed for the location.

516.6(C). Luminaires shall be permitted to be installed as follows:
(1) Luminaires, like that shown below, that are attached to the walls or ceiling of a spray area but that are outside any classified area and are separated from the spray area by glass panels shall be suitable for use in unclassified locations. Such fixtures shall be serviced from outside the spray area.

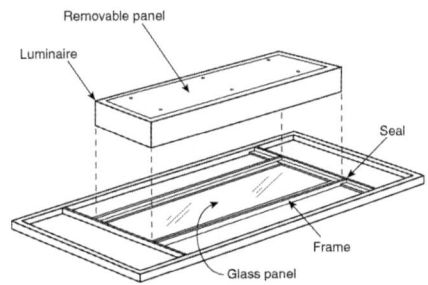

(2) Luminaires, like that shown above, that are attached to the walls or ceiling of a spray area; that are separated from the spray area by glass panels and that are located within a Class I, Division 2; a Class I, Zone 2; or Zone 22 location shall be suitable for such location. Such fixtures shall be serviced from outside the spray area.

(3) Luminaires, like that shown below, that are an integral part of the walls or ceiling of a spray area shall be permitted to be separated from the spray area by glass panels that are an integral part of the fixture. Such fixtures shall be listed for use in Class I, Division 2; a Class I, Zone 2; or Zone 22 locations, whichever is applicable, and also shall be listed for accumulations of deposits of combustible residues. Such fixtures shall be serviced from outside the spray area.

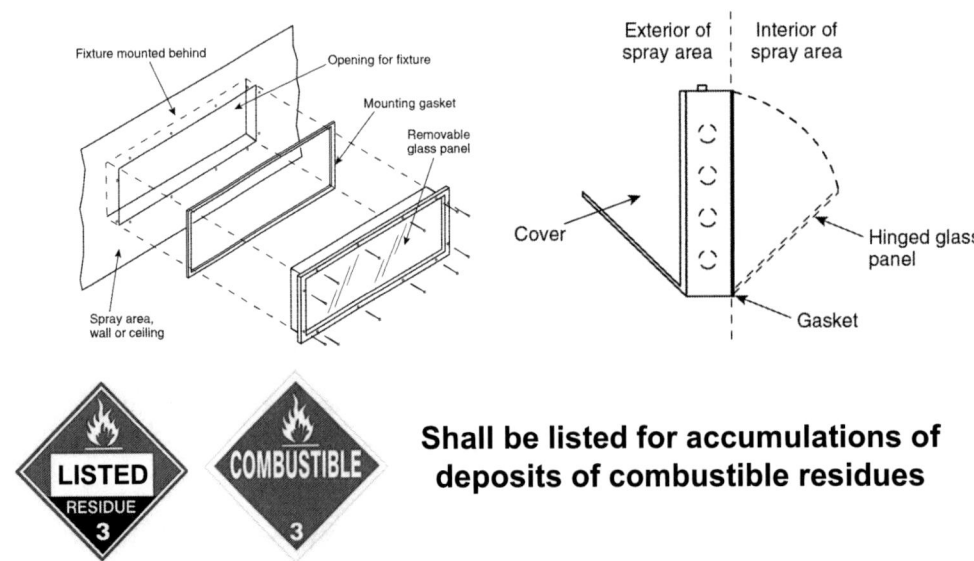

Shall be listed for accumulations of deposits of combustible residues

516.6(C)(4). Glass panels used to separate luminaires from the spray area or that are an integral part of the luminaire shall meet the following requirements.

(a) Panels for light fixtures or for observation shall be of heat-treated glass, laminated glass, wired glass, or hammered-wired glass and shall be sealed to confine vapors, mists, residues, dusts, and deposits to the spray area.

Exception: Listed spray booth assemblies that have vision panels constructed from other materials shall be permitted.

(b) Panels for light fixtures shall be separated from the fixture to prevent surface temperature of the panel exceeding 200°F.

(c) The panel frame and method of attachment shall be designed to not fail under fire exposure before the vision panel fails.

516.6(D). In general, portable electric lamps or other electrical utilization equipment shall not be used in the spray area. There are two exceptions:

Exception 1: Where portable electric lamps are required for operations in spaces not readily illuminated by fixed lighting within the spraying area, they shall be of the type identified for Class I, Division 1 or Zone 1 locations where readily ignitible residues may be present.

516.6(D) Exception 2. Where portable electric drying apparatus is used in spray booths and the following requirements are met.

(1) The apparatus and its electrical connections are not located within the spray enclosure during spray operations.

(2) Electrical equipment within 18" of the floor is identified for Class I, Division 2 or Class I, Zone 2 locations.

(3) All metallic parts of the drying apparatus are electrically bonded and grounded.

(4) Interlocks are provided to prevent the operation of spray equipment while drying apparatus is within the spray enclosure, to allow for a 3-minute purge of the enclosure before energizing the drying apparatus and to shut off drying apparatus on failure of the ventilation system.

 **3 Minute Purge**

 **Author's note**: The intent is to keep hot apparatus that could ignite volatile vapor or residue in the spraying booth out of the area while the mixture is present. This is a very flammable area.

516.6(E). Electrostatic spraying or deterring equipment shall be installed and used only as provided in section 516.10.

516.7. Wiring and Equipment Not Within Class I and II Locations

516.7(A). All fixed wiring above Class I and II locations shall be in metal raceways, Type PVC or Type RTRC conduit, or electrical nonmetallic tubing, or MI, TC, or MC cable. Cellular metal floor raceways shall be permitted only for supplying ceiling outlets or as extensions to the area below the floor of a Class I or II location, but such raceways shall have no connections leading into or passing through the Class I or II location above the floor unless suitable seals are provided.

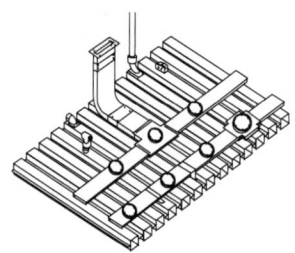

516.7(B). Equipment that may produce arc, sparks, or particles of hot metal, where installed above a Class I or II location shall be of the totally enclosed type or be constructed to prevent the escape of such.

516.10(A). Fixed Electrostatic Equipment. When the charging or atomizing device is attached to a mechanical support or manipulator (including robotic, but not hand-held devices) they must comply with the following:

(1) Power and control equipment such as transformers, high voltage supplies, control apparatus, and all other portions of the equipment, must be installed outside of the Class I location, or be identified for the location.

Exception: High-voltage grids, electrodes, electrostatic atomizing heads, and their connections shall be permitted within the Class I location.

516.10(A)(2). Electrodes and electrostatic atomizing heads must be adequately supported in permanent locations and effectively insulated from ground. Electrodes and electrostatic atomizing heads that are permanently attached to their bases, supports, reciprocators, or robots are considered to comply with this requirement.

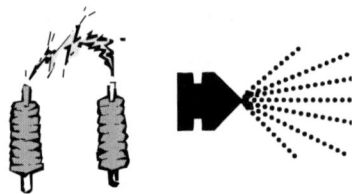

516.10(A)(3). High-voltage leads must be properly insulated and protected from mechanical damage or exposure to destructive chemicals. Any exposed element operating at high voltage must be effectively and permanently supported on suitable insulators and effectively guarded against accidental contact or grounding.

516.10(A)(4). Goods being coated must be supported on conveyors or hangers. The conveyor or hanger must be arranged (1) to ensure that the parts being coated are electrically connected to ground with a resistance of 1 megohm or less and (2) to prevent parts from swinging.

1 megohm or less

516.10(A)(5). Electrostatic apparatus must be equipped with automatic means that will rapidly de-energize the high-voltage elements under any of the following conditions:
(1) Stoppage of ventilating fans or failure of ventilating equipment from any cause.

(2) Stoppage of the conveyor carrying goods through the high-voltage field unless stoppage is required by the spray process.
(3) Occurrence of excessive current leakage at any point in the high voltage system.
(4) Primary voltage input to the power supply de-energized.

516.10(A)(6). All electrically conductive objects in the spray area, except those objects required by the process to be at high voltage, must be adequately grounded. This requirement applies to paint containers, wash cans, guards, hose connectors, brackets, and any other electrically conductive objects or devices in the area.

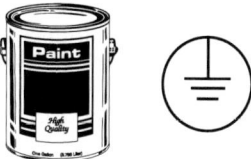

516.10(A)(7). Safeguards such as adequate booths, fencing, railings, interlocks, etc. must be placed about the equipment, or incorporated within it, so that they assure that a safe separation of the process is maintained.

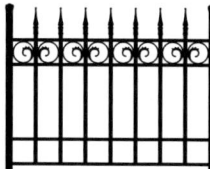

516.10(A)(8). Signs must be conspicuously posted to designate the process zone as dangerous with regard to fire and accident, identify the grounding requirement for all electrically conductive objects in the spray area, and restrict access to qualified personnel only.

516.10(A)(9). All insulators must be kept clean and dry.

516.10(A)(10). Spray equipment that cannot be classified as nonincendive must comply with:

(a) Conveyors or hangers must be arranged so that they will maintain a safe distance of at least twice the sparking distance between the goods being painted, and electrodes, electrostatic atomizing heads, or charged conductors. Warnings defining this safe distance must be posted.
(b) The equipment must provide an automatic means of rapidly de-energizing the high-voltage elements in the event the distance between the goods being painted and the electrodes or electrostatic atomizing heads falls below the specified minimum safe distance.

516.10(B). Electrostatic hand-spraying equipment and devices used in connection with paint-spraying operations must be of the listed types and comply with the following:

(1) High-voltage circuits must neither produce a spark of sufficient intensity to ignite the most readily ignitible of those vapor-air mixtures likely to be encountered, nor result in appreciable shock hazard upon coming in contact with a grounded object under all normal operating conditions.

The electrostatically charged exposed elements of the hand gun must be capable of being energized only by an actuator that also controls the coating material supply.

(2) Power equipment such as transformers, power packs, control apparatus, and all other electric portions of the equipment, must be located outside of the Class I location, or be identified for the location.

Exception: The hand gun itself and its connections to the power supply, can be located within the Class I location.

(3) The handle of the spraying gun must be electrically connected to ground by a metallic connection, and it must be constructed so that in normal operating position, the operator is in intimate electrical contact with the grounded handle to prevent the buildup of a static charge on the operator's body.

Signs indicating the necessity for grounding other persons entering the spray area must be conspicuously posted.

516.10(B)(4). All electrically conductive objects in the spraying area must be adequately grounded. This applies to paint containers, wash cans, etc. in the area.

The equipment must carry a prominent, permanently installed warning regarding the necessity for this grounding feature.

516.10(B)(5). Objects being painted must be maintained in metallic contact with the conveyor or other grounded support. The area of contact must be sharp points or knife edges where possible. Points of support of the object must be concealed from random spray where feasible. Where the objects being sprayed are supported from a conveyor, the point of attachment to the conveyor must be located in a position where it will not collect spray material during normal operation.

Hooks must be regularly cleaned to ensure adequate grounding of 1 megohm or less.

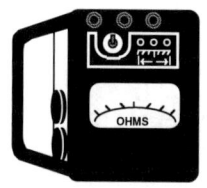 **1 megohm or less**

516.10(C). Powder Coating. Powder Coating processes in which combustible dry powders are applied include hazards associated with combustible dusts. The degree to which it is hazardous depends upon the chemical composition of the material, particle size, shape, and distribution.

516.10(C)(1). Electric equipment and sources must comply with Article 502. Portable electric lamps and other utilization equipment must not be used within a Class II location during operation of the finishing processes. When such lamps or equipment are used during cleaning or repairing operations, they must be of a type identified for Class II, Division 1 locations, and all exposed metal parts must be effectively grounded.

Exception: Portable electric luminaires are permitted in the spraying area when they are required for operations in spaces not readily illuminated by fixed lighting. They must be of a type identified for Class II, Division 1 locations where readily ignitible residues might be present.

516.10(C)(2). The provisions of 516.10(A) and 516.10(C)(1) shall apply to fixed electrostatic spraying equipment.

516.10(C)(3). The provisions of 516.10(B) and 516.10(C)(1) shall apply to fixed electrostatic hand-spraying equipment.

516.10(C)(4). Electrostatic fluidized beds and associated equipment shall be of identified types. Any discharge produced by the high-voltage circuits when the charging electrodes of the bed are approached or contacted by a grounded object must not be of sufficient intensity to ignite any powder-air mixture likely to be encountered, nor result in any appreciable shock hazard.

(a) Transformers, power packs, control apparatus, and all other electric portions of the equipment must be located outside the powder-coating area, or must otherwise comply with the rules for Class II locations.

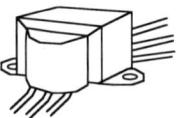

Exception: Charging electrodes and their connections to the power supply are permitted within the powder-coating area.

(b) All electrically conductive objects within the powder-coating area must be adequately grounded. The powder-coating equipment must carry a prominent, permanently installed warning regarding the necessity for grounding these objects.

516.10(C)(4).

(c) Objects being coated must be maintained in electrical contact (less than 1 megohm) with the conveyor or other support in order to ensure proper grounding. Hangers must be regularly cleaned to ensure effective electrical contact. Areas of electrical contact must be sharp points or knife edges where possible.

(d) The electric equipment and compressed-air supplies must be **interlocked** with a ventilation system so that the equipment cannot be operated unless the ventilating fans are in operation.

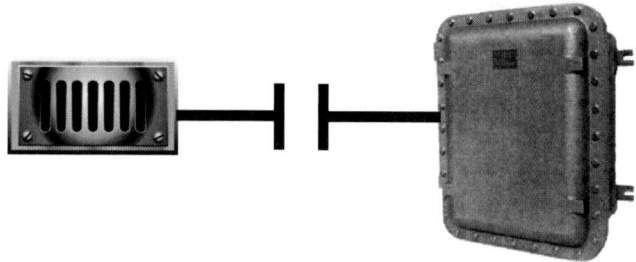

516.16. All metal raceways, the metal armors or metallic sheath on cables, and all non-current carrying metal parts of fixed or portable electrical equipment, regardless of voltage, shall be grounded and bonded as provided in Article 250. Grounding and bonding shall comply with 501.30, 502.30, or 505.25, as applicable.

Part IV. Spray Application Operations in Membrane Enclosures

516.18 Area Classification for Temporary Membrane Enclosures. Electrical area classification shall be as follows:

(1) The area within the membrane enclosure shall be considered a Class I, Division 1 area as shown in sketch.

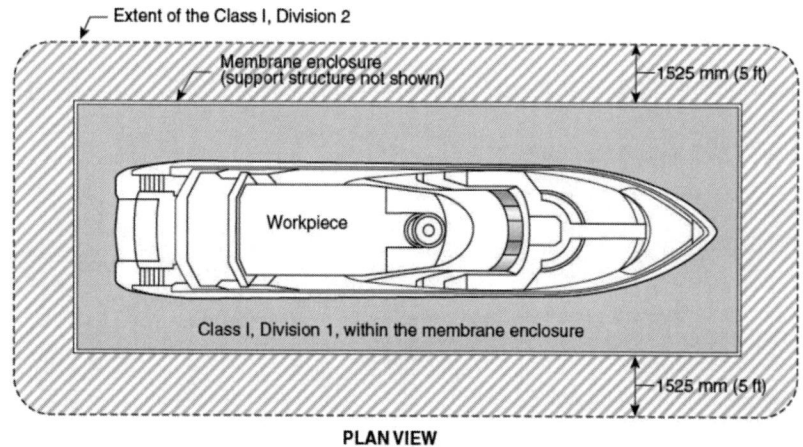

— Extent of the Class I, Division 2

Membrane enclosure
(support structure not shown)

1525 mm (5 ft)

Workpiece

Class I, Division 1, within the membrane enclosure

1525 mm (5 ft)

PLAN VIEW

(2) A 5 foot zone outside of the membrane enclosure shall be considered a Class I, Division 2 area as shown in sketch.

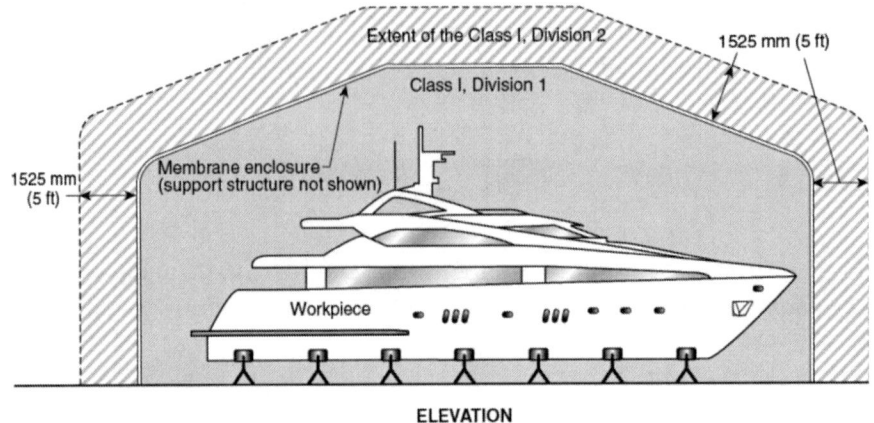

ELEVATION

516.23. Electrical wiring and utilization equipment used within the classified areas inside and outside of a membrane enclosure during spray painting shall be suitable for the location and shall comply with all of the following:

(1) All power to the workpiece shall be removed during spray painting.

(2) Workpiece shall be grounded.

(3) Spray paint equipment shall be grounded.

(4) Scaffolding shall be bonded to the workpiece and grounded by an approved method.

Part V. Printing, Dipping, and Coating Processes

516.29. Classification is based on quantities of flammable vapors, combustible mists, residues, dusts, or deposits that are present or might be present in quantities sufficient to produce ignitible or explosive mixtures with air. Electrical wiring and electrical utilization equipment located adjacent to open processes shall comply with the requirements as follows:

(1) Electrical wiring and electrical utilization equipment located in any sump, pit or below grade channel that is within 25 feet horizontally of a vapor source, as defined in this standard, shall be suitable for Class I, Division 1 or Class I, Zone 1 locations. If the sump, pit, or channel extends beyond 25 feet of the vapor source, it shall be provided with a vapor stop, or it shall be classified as Class I, Division 1 or Class I, Zone 1 for its entire length.

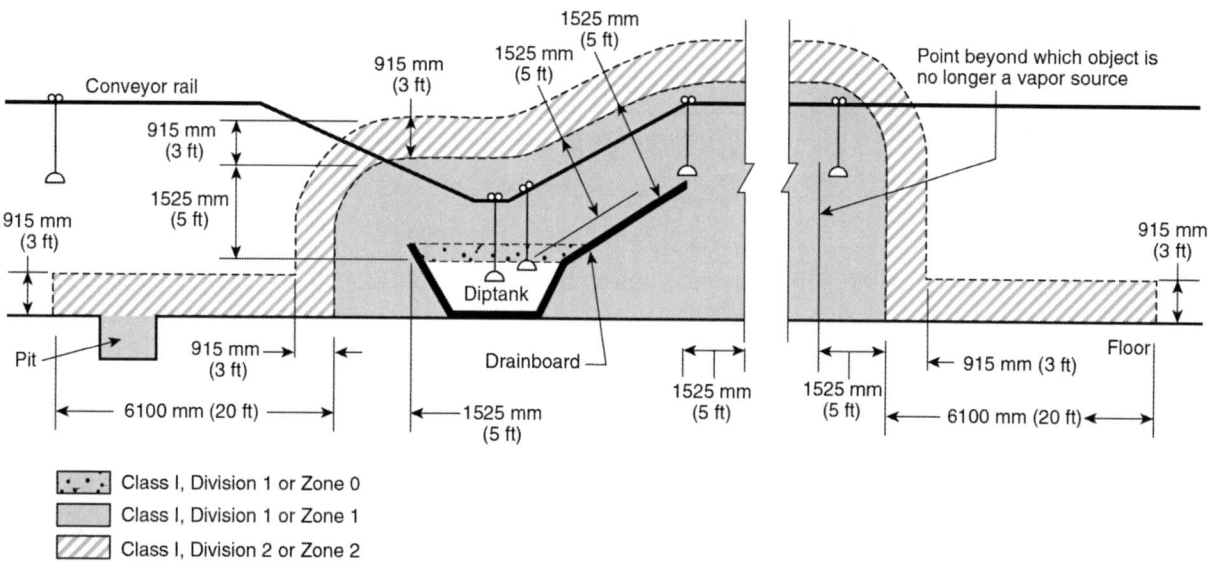

(2) Electrical wiring and electrical utilization equipment located within 5 feet of a vapor source shall be suitable for Class I, Division 1 or Class I, Zone 1 locations. The space inside a dip tank , ink fountain, ink reservoir, or ink tank shall be classified as Class I, Division 1 or Class I, Zone 0, whichever is applicable.

(3) Electrical wiring and electrical utilization equipment located within 3 feet of the Class I, Division 1 or Class I, Zone 1 location shall be suitable for Class I, Division 2 or Class I, Zone 2 locations, whichever is applicable.

(4) The space 3 feet above the floor and extending 20 feet horizontally in all directions from the Class I, Division 1 or Class I, Zone 1 location shall be classified as Class I, Division 2 or Class I, Zone 2, and electrical wiring and electrical utilization equipment located within this space shall be suitable for Class I, Division 2 or Class I, Zone 2, whichever is applicable.

(5) This space shall be permitted to be nonclassified for the purpose of electrical installations if the surface area of the vapor source does not exceed 5 feet squared, the contents of the dip tank, ink fountain, ink reservoir, or ink tank do not exceed 5 gallons, and the vapor concentration during operating and shutdown periods does not exceed 25% of the lower flammable limit.

 **25%**

516.35. Areas adjacent to enclosed dipping and coating processes shall be classified as follows:

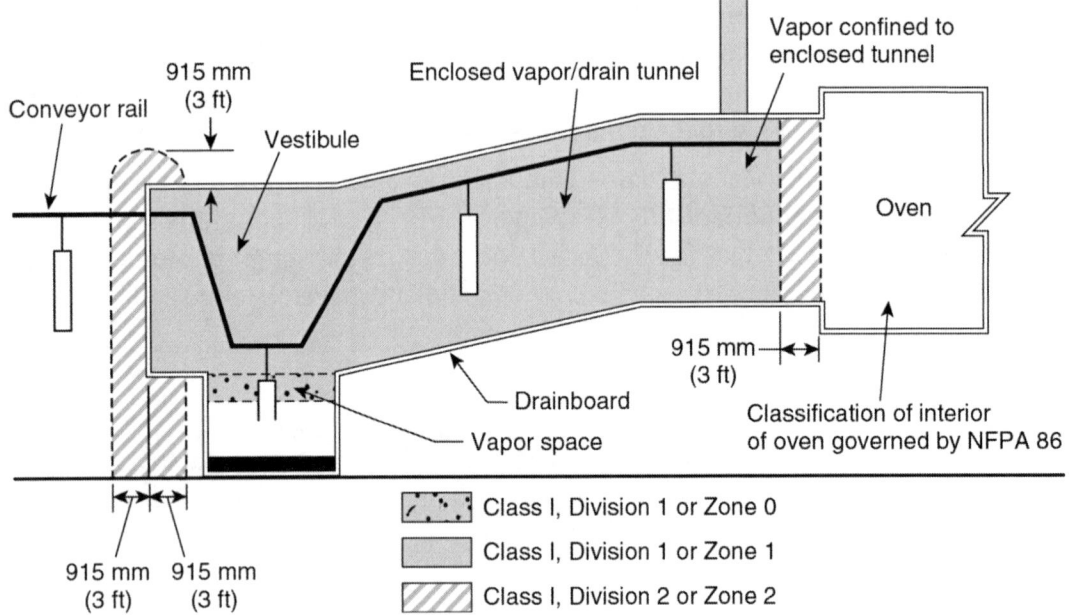

(1) The interior of any enclosed dipping and coating processor coating process or apparatus shall be a Class I, Division 1 or Class I, Zone 1 location, and electrical wiring and electrical utilization equipment located within this space shall be suitable for Class I, Division 1 or Class I, Zone 1 locations, whichever is applicable. The area inside the dip tank shall be classified as Class I, Division 1 or Class I, Zone 0, whichever is applicable.

(2) The space within 3 feet in all directions from any opening in the enclosure and extending to the floor or grade level shall be classified Class I, Division 2 or Class I, Zone 2, and electrical wiring and electrical utilization equipment located in this space shall be suitable for Class I, Division 2 or Class I, Zone 2, whichever is applicable.

(3) All other spaces adjacent to an enclosed dipping or coating process or apparatus shall be classified as nonhazardous for purposes of electrical installations.

516.36. Open containers, supply containers, waste containers, and solvent distillation units that contain Class I liquids shall be located in areas ventilated in accordance with 516.4

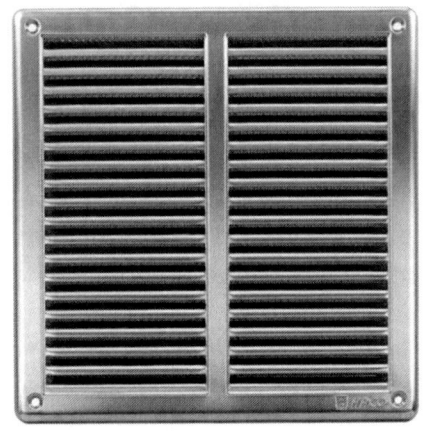

516.37. For printing, coating, and dipping equipment where the process area is enclosed by glass panels that are sealed to confine vapors and mists to the inside of the enclosure, luminaires that are attached to the walls or ceilings of a process enclosure and that are located outside of any classified area shall be permitted to be of general purpose construction. Such luminaires shall be serviced from outside the enclosure.

516.40. All persons and all electrically conductive objects, including any metal parts of the process equipment or apparatus, containers of material, exhaust ducts, and piping systems that convey flammable or combustible liquids, shall be electrically grounded.

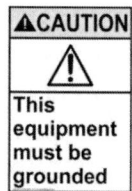

Provisions shall be made to dissipate static electric charges from all nonconductive substrates in printing processes.

Author's note: The safety of life and property from fire or explosion in the spray application of flammable paints and finishes and combustible powders depends on the extent, arrangement, maintenance, and operation of the process.

An analysis of actual experience in the industry demonstrates that the largest fire losses and greatest fire frequency have occurred where good practice standards were not observed.

Spray application is a common practice in industrial facilities, ranging from auto body shops to large assembly lines. The most common atomizing device for fluid coatings is the air-spray gun. The gun uses high-pressure jets of air to break up the fluid into a high pressure mist. Another fluid-coating gun, the airless atomizer, sprays by hydraulic means without compressed air. Fluid pressures can range from 300 psi to 3000 psi.

An electrostatic spray gun uses an atomizing head with a high-voltage electrical input that charges the paint droplets. Voltages applied to the gun range from 35,000 to over 100,000 volts.

Powder coating is a process in which dry organic powder is suspended in air and charged electrostatically from a high-voltage direct current power supply. The powder is directed toward the workpiece and is held in place by the electrostatic charge.

Most spray operations are performed in a spray booth. A booth not only limits the extent of overspray, but it can also limit the extent of a hazardous location.

Overspray deposits are a spray application problem, regardless of the type of spray application confinement system used. If allowed to build up, these deposits may present operational problems and a fire hazard.

Static electricity can be a significant problem in electrostatic as well as nonelectrostatic air and airless spraying systems. Means must be provided to prevent static charges from reaching dangerous potentials. The problem can be especially severe with electrostatic systems, since the coating material is intentionally charged.

Robots or manipulators are very common in large assembly operations. They are used to operate paint spray guns. The majority of the paint spray robots have intrinsically safe electrical circuits. However, the spray gun is not intrinsically safe.

The dipping and coating process includes a number of processes that use flammable or combustible materials, such as oil quenching, painting, impregnating, priming, and cleaning. Many of the coating or dipping materials are used above their flash points.

The proper maintenance and operation of processes and process areas where flammable and combustible materials are handled and applied are critical with respect to the protection of life and property from fire or explosion.

ARTICLE 517
Health Care Facilities

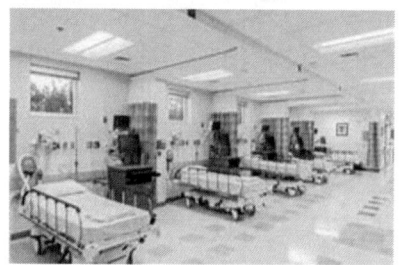

Part I. General

517.1. This article applies to electrical construction and installation criteria in health care facilities that provide service to human beings. Requirements for essential and emergency electrical systems in hospitals have also been covered in this article.

Any specific type of health care location, such as a doctor's or dental office whether the location is an occupancy by itself or is part of a larger facility such as a hospital, or it may be located in a school building, a mall, or a similar location.

Veterinary facilities are not included in this article.

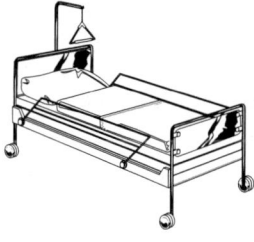

517.2. There are over 40 definitions included in this section.

The definition of ambulatory health care facilities, such as outpatient surgery centers, free-standing emergency medical centers, and hemodialysis units correlate with the definition of the same term in NFPA 99, *Standard for Health Care Facilities*.

The definition of anesthetizing location recognizes that in an emergency it may be necessary to administer an anesthetic almost anywhere in a health care facility.

Definitions of hospital, nursing home, limited care facility, and ambulatory health care facility correlate with the definitions in NFPA *101, Life Safety Code*.

The definition of patient care area applies to hospitals as well as patient care areas in outpatient facilities.

II. Wiring and Protection

517.10(A). Part II shall apply to patient care areas of all health care facilities.

517.10(B). Part II shall **not** apply to the following:
(1) Business offices, corridors, waiting rooms, and the like in clinics, medical and dental offices, and outpatient facilities.

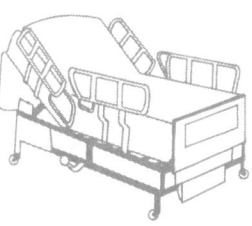

(2) Areas of nursing homes and limited care facilities wired in accordance with Chapters 1 through 4 where these areas are used exclusively as patient sleeping rooms.

(3) Areas used exclusively for any of the following purposes:
a. Intramuscular injections (immunizations)   b. Psychiatry and psychotherapy
c. Alternative medicine   d. Optometry

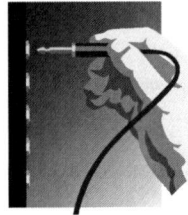

517.11. Construction Criteria.

This article is to specify the installation criteria and wiring methods that minimize electrical hazards by the maintenance of adequately low potential differences only between exposed conductive surfaces that are likely to become energized and could be contacted by a patient.

Informational Note: In a health care facility, it is difficult to prevent the occurrence of a conductive or capacitive path from the patient's body to some grounded object, because that path may be established accidentally or through instrumentation directly connected to the patient. For example, the insertion of a catheter may render a patient much more vulnerable to the effects of an electric current. It is essential that those responsible for the design, installation, and maintenance be familar with this note.

517.12. Except as modified with this article, wiring methods shall follow the rules of Chapters 1 through 4.

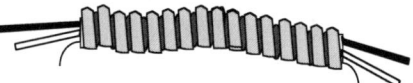

517.13(A). All branch circuits serving patient care spaces shall be provided with a ground path in the metal raceway or metal cable armor or sheath that qualifies as an **equipment grounding conductor** per 250.118.

517.13(B). The grounding terminals of all receptacles, metal boxes and enclosures containing receptacles and all non-current carrying conductive surfaces of fixed electric equipment likely to become energized that are subject to personal contact, operating at over 100 volts, shall be grounded by an insulated copper conductor that is clearly identified along its entire length by **green insulation**.

Copper - Insulated Equip. Grounding conductor

Exception #1: For other than isolated ground receptacles, an insulated equipment bonding jumper that directly connects to the **equipment grounding conductor** is permitted to connect the box and receptacle(s) to the **equipment grounding conductor.**

Exception #2: Luminaires more than 7' 6" above the floor and switches located outside of the patient care vicinity shall not be required to be grounded by an **insulated equipment grounding conductor**.

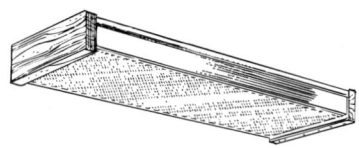

Author's note: The grounding requirements of section 517.13 for patient care areas are not limited to just patient rooms. Other areas, such as examining rooms, therapy areas, certain corridors, etc. are also included. Also, 517.13 is not limited to just hospitals. The grounding requirements are also required for patient care spaces in other health care facilities, such as nursing homes, clinics, medical and dental offices.

This is a redundant grounding approach as the metal raceway must qualify as an **equipment grounding conductor**, and the raceway must contain an insulated copper equipment grounding conductor.

517.14. The **equipment grounding** terminal buses of the normal and essential branch-circuit panelboards serving the same individual patient vicinity shall be bonded together with an insulated continuous copper conductor not smaller than #10. Where two or more panelboards serving the same individual patient vicinity are served from separate transfer switches on the emergency system, the **equipment grounding** terminal buses of those panelboards shall be bonded together with an insulated continuous copper conductor not smaller than #10. Although required to be "continuous," the wording of this section recognizes terminating this conductor at ground buses and terminals as satisfying the requirement for a "continuous" conductor.

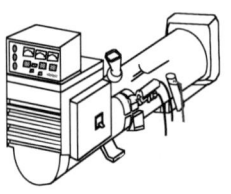 **#10 or larger**

517.16. An isolated ground receptacle, if used, shall not defeat the purposes of the safety features of the grounding systems detailed in 517.13.

517.16(B)(1). The grounding terminals of isolated ground receptacles installed in branch circuits for patient care spaces shall be connected to an **insulated equipment grounding conductor** in accordance with 250.146(D) in addition to the **equipment grounding conductor** path required in 517.13(A).

517.16(B)(2). The **insulated grounding conductor** required in 517.13(B)(1) shall be clearly identified along its entire length by green insulation.

Informational Note #1: This type of installation is typically used where a reduction of electrical noise is necessary, and parallel grounding paths are to be avoided.

Informational Note #2: Care should be taken in specifying a system containing isolated ground receptacles, because the grounding impedance is controlled only by the grounding wires and does not benefit from any conduit or building structure in parallel with the grounding path.

517.17 Ground Fault Protection.

517.17(A). The requirements of this section shall apply to hospitals and other buildings (including multiple occupancy buildings) with critical care (Category 1) spaces or utilizing electrical life support equipment and buildings that provide the required essential utilities or services for the operation of critical care (Category 1) spaces or electrical life support equipment.

517.17(B). At least one additional level of ground-fault protection is required for health care facilities where ground-fault protection is used on service equipment. Where the installation of ground-fault protection is made on the normal service disconnecting means, each feeder must be provided with similar protective means. This requirement is to prevent a catastrophic outage. By applying appropriate selectivity at each level, the ground fault can be limited to a single feeder, and thereby, service may be maintained throughout the balance of the health care facility.

The additional levels of ground-fault protection shall **not** be installed on the load side of an essential electrical system transfer switch.

517.17(C). This section requires that selection of the tripping time of the main GFP be such that each feeder GFP will operate to open a ground fault on the feeder, without opening the service GFP.

The separation of ground fault protection time current characteristics shall conform to the manufacturer's recommendations and shall consider all required tolerances and disconnect operating time to achieve 100% selectivity.

517.17(D). To make sure of the proper hookup of the ground-fault protection system, a performance test is required to ensure compliance with 517.17(C) and provides 100% selectivity. A written record of this test shall be provided for the inspector per 230.95(C).

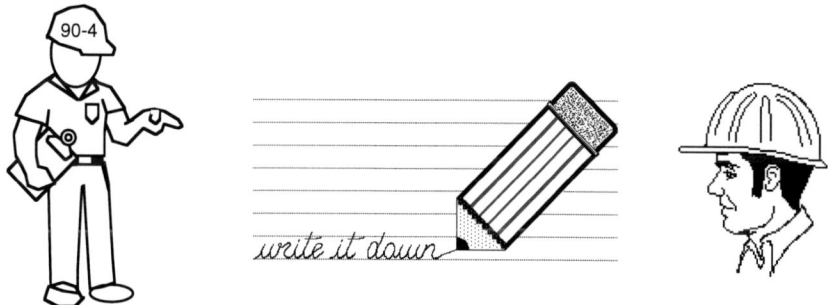

517.18. General Care (Category 2) Spaces.

517.18(A). Two branch circuits, one from the emergency system and one from the normal system shall be supplied to each patient bed location. All branch circuits from the normal system shall originate in the same panelboard. The branch circuit serving patient bed locations shall **not** be part of a multiwire branch circuit.

Exception 1: Branch circuits serving only special-purpose outlets or receptacles, such as portable X-ray outlets, shall **not** be required to be served from the same distribution panel.

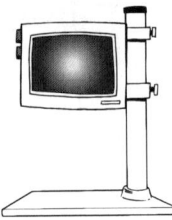

Exception 2: Requirements of 517.18(A) shall **not** apply to patient bed locations in nursing homes, outpatient facilities, clinics, medical offices, limited care facilities, etc.

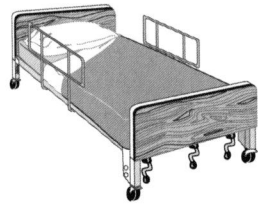

Exception 3: Allows both of the two required branch circuits to be supplied by the emergency system, provided they are supplied by two separate transfer switches. Two emergency branch circuits have a higher reliability than one normal and one emergency branch circuit.

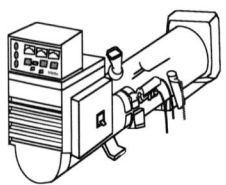

517.18(B). Receptacles at patient bed locations in "General Care Areas" must be "listed hospital grade" and so identified. The minimum of eight required receptacles at each such bed location may be either single, duplex, or quadruplex types, or any combination of the three. All receptacles shall be listed "hospital grade" and shall be so identified. Each receptacle shall be grounded by means of an insulated copper conductor sized per 250.122.

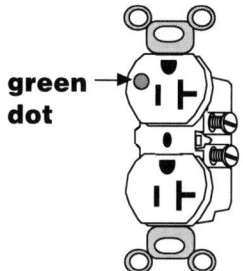

green
dot →

Listed "Hospital Grade" receptacle green dot

Exception 1: This section does **not** apply to psychiatric, substance abuse, and rehabilitation hospitals meeting 517.10(B)(2).

Exception 2: Psychiatric security rooms shall **not** be required to have receptacle outlets installed in the room.

Informational Note: It is **not** intended that there be a total, immediate replacement of existing non-hospital grade receptacles. It is intended, that non-hospital grade receptacles be replaced with hospital grade receptacles upon modification of use, renovation, or as existing receptacles need replacement.

Author's note: Some design specifications require hospital receptacles to be installed with the equipment grounding pin on the "top." This is not a Code requirement, but I personally feel it's a good idea to have the grounding pin on top.

    The Code book does NOT state which way, you can install the receptacle either way. Code standards do not require the grounding pin to be in any special orientation.

    Some prefer to install the receptacle with the grounding pin "down." They say the receptacle looks as if it's smiling!

    Some feel if the grounding pin is "down" an angle cord cap oriented *incorrectly* will put stress on the cord while in use. With the grounding pin "down," if a cord cap were to work loose in the receptacle, the grounding pin would be the last element to separate from the receptacle.

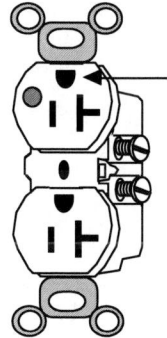

    With the grounding pin installed in the "up" position, some feel there is a measure of protection to the "hot circuit." If conductive material were to fall on the receptacle, it would first come into contact with the grounding pin, if it was installed in the "up" position.

    In some cases, specifications on the drawing will state how the receptacles are to be installed. **Hospital** specifications often require for Sensitive Patient areas, the receptacles be installed with the **grounding pin facing in the "UP" position**.

517.18(C). Category 2 General Care Pediatric Locations. Receptacles located within the rooms, bathrooms, playrooms, activity rooms, and patient care areas of designated pediatric locations shall be listed and identified tamper resistant or shall employ a listed tamper resistant cover.

Author's note: A tamper-resistant receptacle is one that would make it extremely difficult to insert a pin, paper clip, or similar small metal object into a slot on the receptacle. This section recognizes the use of listed tamper resistant covers instead of "tamper-resistant" receptacles. Receptacles are available with rotating slot covers or internal contact mechanisms which make it necessary to use a cord plug cap to gain access to energized parts.

517.19. Category 1 Critical Care Spaces.

517.19(A). Two branch circuits, one or more from the emergency system and one or more from the normal system shall be supplied to each patient bed location in critical care spaces. All branch circuits from the normal system shall originate in the same panelboard. At least one branch circuit from the emergency system shall supply an outlet(s) only at that bed location. Emergency system receptacles shall be identified and shall indicate the panelboard and circuit number supplying them. The branch circuit serving patient bed locations shall **not** be part of a multiwire branch circuit.

 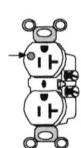 **Supplied from panel H93, circuit #3**

The electrical receptacles or the cover plates for the electrical receptacles supplied from the life safety and critical branches shall have a distinctive color or marking so as to be readily indentifiable.

Exception 1: Branch circuits serving only special-purpose receptacles or equipment in category 1 critical care spaces shall be permitted to be served by other panelboards.

Exception 2: Critical care (Category 1) spaces served from two separate transfer switches on the emergency system shall **not** be required to have circuits from the normal system.

517.19(B)(1). Each patient bed shall be provided with a minimum 14 receptacles, at least one of which shall be connected to either of the following:
(1) The normal branch circuit required in 517.19(A).
(2) A critical branch circuit supplied by a different transfer switch than the other receptacles at the same patient bed location.

CRITICAL CARE SPACES

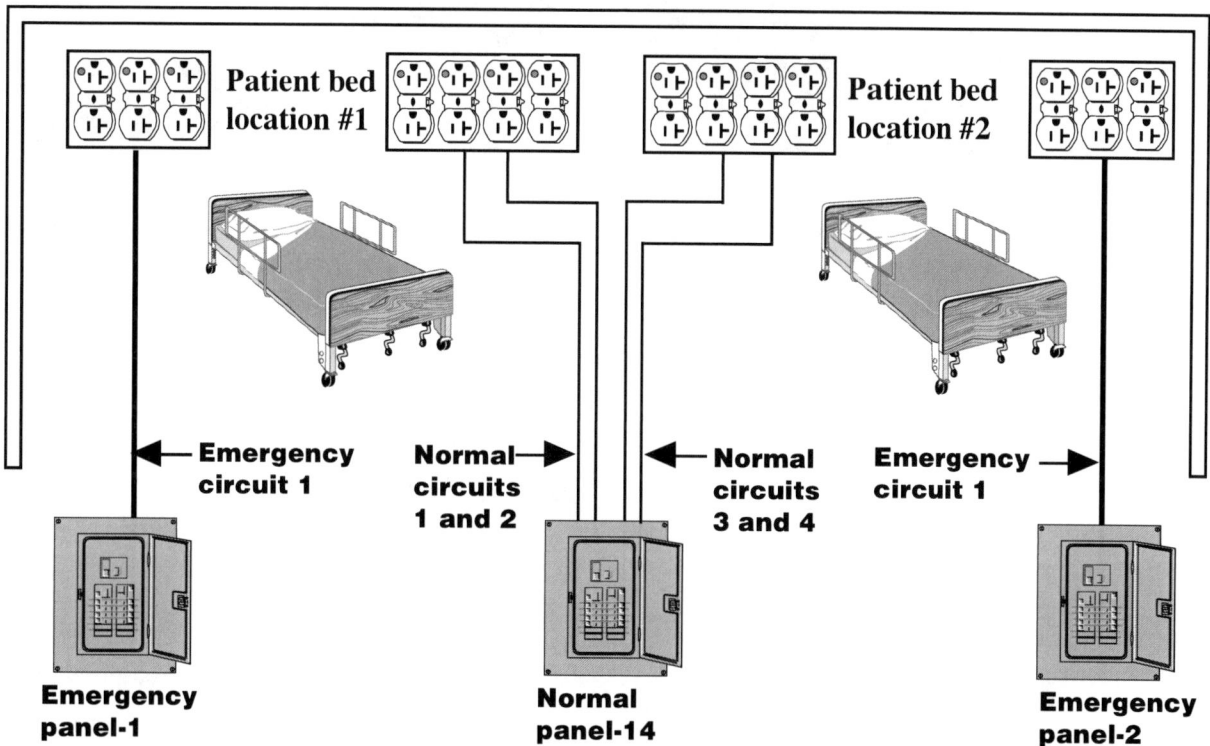

517.19(B)(2). The receptacles required shall be of the single, duplex, or quadruplex type or any combination thereof. All receptacles, whether six or more, shall be listed "hospital grade" and shall be so identified. Each receptacle shall be grounded to the reference point by means of an insulated **copper equipment grounding conductor**. The best point to call a reference grounding point is the grounding bus in the distribution panel, which is the transition point between the branch-circuit grounding wires and the feeder grounding wires.

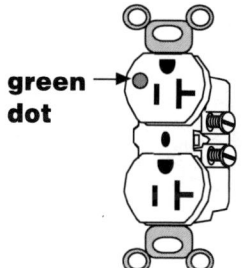

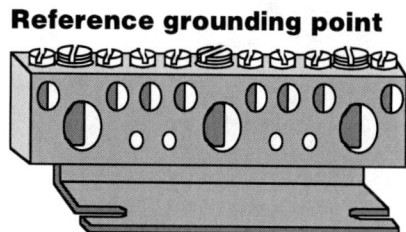

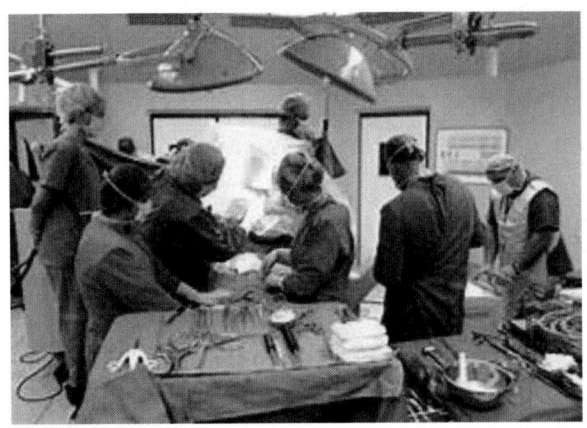 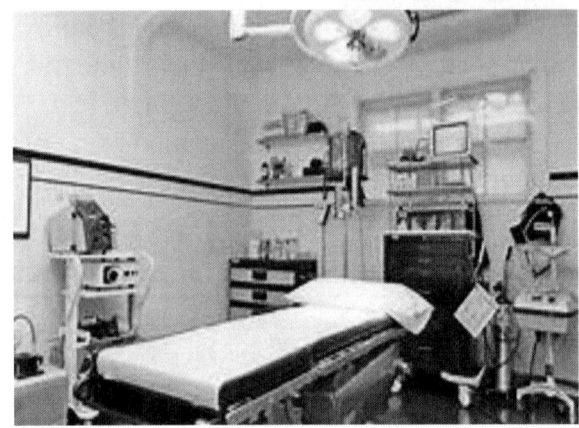

517.19(C)(1). Each operating room shall be provided with a minimum of 36 receptacles divided between at least two branch circuits. At least 12 receptacles, but no more than 24, shall be connected to either of the following:

(1) The normal system branch circuit required in 517.19(A)

(2) A critical branch circuit supplied by a different transfer switch than the other receptacles at the same location

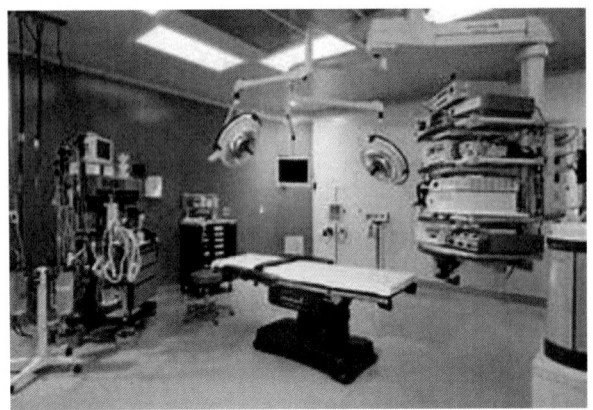 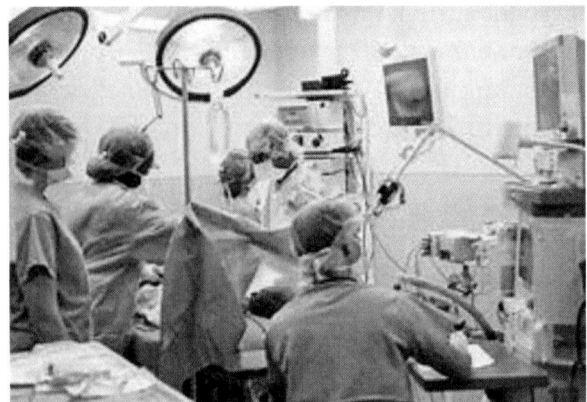

517.19(D). A patient equipment grounding point is **not** mandatory. When a patient equipment grounding point is used in a patient vicinity, it must be grounded to the ground terminal of all grounding-type receptacles in the patient vicinity by means of a minimum #10 copper conductor looped to all of the receptacles or by individual #10 conductors run from the patient grounding point to each receptacle.

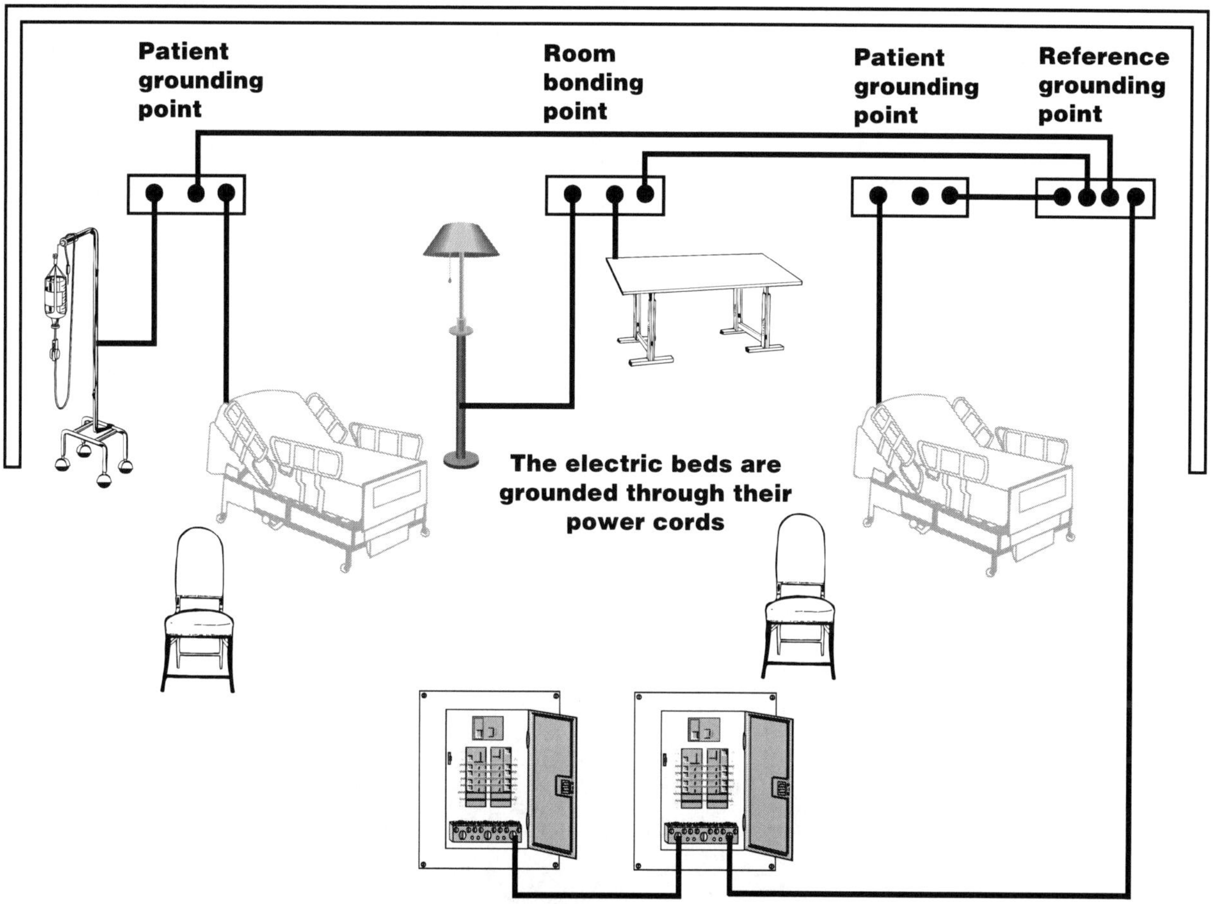

Patient grounding point

Room bonding point

Patient grounding point

Reference grounding point

The electric beds are grounded through their power cords

Bonding to the equipment grounding bus is required. Conductor must be at least #10 copper

Informational Note: Where there is no patient equipment grounding point, it is important that the distance between the reference grounding point and the patient vicinity be as short as possible to minimize any potential differences.

Author's note: Some have disagreed with grounding every piece of exposed metal in the patient's room. Doing this may actually increase the shock hazard. Because a shock occurs when a person touches two surfaces with a voltage difference between the surfaces, the fewer surfaces that are intentionally grounded, the better. A metal door frame or a metal window frame that is not likely to become energized is not required to be grounded. It was not good safety engineering to propose that metal furniture in a patient's room be intentionally grounded.

517.19(E). A bonding-type connection is required for a **feeder** in metal conduit or MI, MC cable. Grounding of enclosures and equipment, such as panelboards and switchboards, shall be ensured by one of the following means at each termination point or junction point of the conduit or metal cable:

(1) A grounding bushing and a continuous copper bonding jumper, sized per 250.122, with the bonding jumper connected to the junction enclosure or the ground bus of the panel.

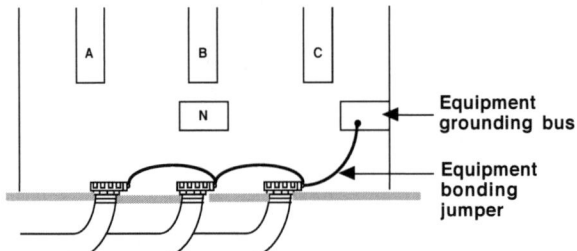

(2) Connection of feeder raceways or MI or MC cable to **threaded hubs** or bosses on terminating enclosures.

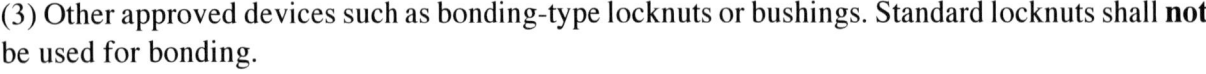

(3) Other approved devices such as bonding-type locknuts or bushings. Standard locknuts shall **not** be used for bonding.

 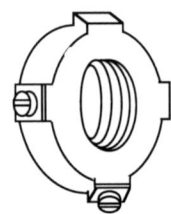 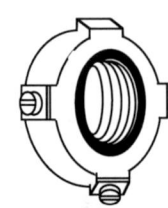 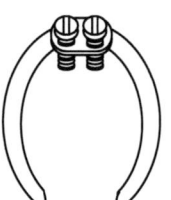 

BONDING BUSHING   **NONINSULATED THROAT BUSHING**   **INSULATED THROAT BUSHING**

517.19(F). Isolated power systems shall be permitted to be used for category 1 critical care spaces, if used, the isolated power system equipment shall be listed as isolated power equipment. The isolated power system shall be designed and installed per 517.160.

Exception: The audible and visual indicators of the line isolation monitor shall be permitted to be located at the nursing station for the area being served.

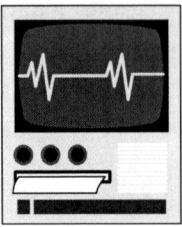

517.19(G). Where an isolated ungrounded power source is used and limits the first-fault current to a low magnitude, the **equipment grounding conductor** associated with the secondary circuit shall be permitted to be run outside the enclosure of the power conductors in the same circuit.

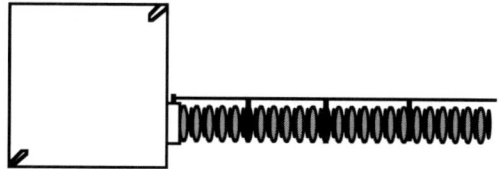

Informational Note: Although it is permitted to run the grounding conductor outside of the conduit, it is safer to run it with the power conductors to provide better protection in case of a second ground fault.

517.19(H). Receptacles intended for special pieces of equipment, like mobile X-ray equipment, must have their equipment grounding conductor extented to a reference point within the branch-circuit panelboard that supplies the patient area. Where such a circuit is served from an isolated ungrounded system, the **equipment grounding conductor** shall **not** be required to be run with the power conductors; however, the equipment grounding terminal of the special-purpose receptacle shall be connected to the reference grounding point.

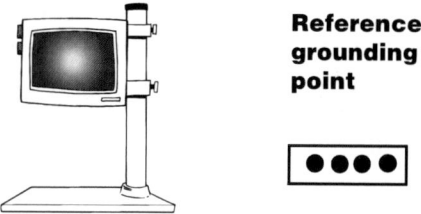

Reference grounding point

517.20. Wet Procedure Locations.

517.20(A). Wet procedure location patient care areas shall be provided with special protection against electric shock by one of the following means:
(1) Power distribution system that inherently limits the possible ground fault current due to a first fault to a low value, without interrupting the power supply
(2) Power distribution system in which the power supply is interrupted if the ground fault current does, in fact, exceed the trip value of a Class A GFCI.

Exception: Branch circuits supplying only listed, fixed therapeutic and diagnostic equipment shall be permitted to be supplied from a normal grounded service, single or three phase system, provided that:
(a) Wiring for grounded isolated circuit does not occupy the same raceway, and
(b) All conductive surfaces of the equipment are connected to an **insulated copper equipment grounding conductor**.

517.20(B). Where an isolated power system is utilized, the isolated power equipment shall be listed as isolated power equipment, and the isolated power system shall be designed and installed per 517.160.

Informational Note: For requirements for installation of therapeutic pools and tubs, see Part VI of Article 680.

 **Author's note:** The definition of **isolated power system** is: A system comprising an isolation transformer or its equivalent, a line isolation monitor, and its ungrounded circuit conductors.

517.21. The intent of this section is to exempt receptacles installed in the critical care (Category 1) spaces where the toilet and basin are installed within the patient room from being GFCI protected. Since patients are bedridden, the critical care spaces are not the same as other patient areas.

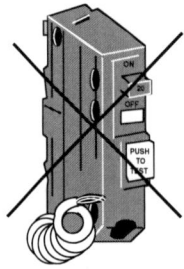 

III. Essential Electrical System

517.25. Essential electrical systems are covered for hospitals, clinics, medical and dental offices, outpatient facilities, nursing homes, residential custodial care facilities, and other health care facilities for patient care. The essential electrical system for these facilities shall comprise a system capable of supplying a limited amount of lighting and power service, which is considered essential for life safety and orderly cessation of procedures during the time normal electrical service is interrupted for any reason.

Definition: **Essential Electrical System.** A system comprised of alternate sources of power and all connected distribution systems and ancillary (auxiliary) equipment, designed to ensure continuity of electrical power to designated areas and functions of a health care facility during disruption of normal power sources, and also designed to minimize disruption within the internal wiring system.

•Author's note: Hospitals have been evolving for the past few decades in both size and complexity, and in many cases have grown from a single structure to multiple buildings. A primary challenge is to provide a high-quality source of electrical power that is backed up with highly reliable emergency and standby power systems to ensure uninterrupted flow of electricity to the entire facility, during crisis and natural disasters.

Unlike most standard commercial buildings, delivering emergency and standby power to health care facilities is a major undertaking due to its complexity and size. It involves many different systems consisting of alternate sources of power, switching equipment, controls, and distribution equipment.

For the most part, hospitals fall under the risk Category 1, where equipment and systems are expected to work and be available at all times, and their failure is likely to cause major injury or death to patients, staff, or visitors. The Category 2 spaces are areas of the hospital where failure of equipment or a system is likely to cause minor injury to patients, staff, or visitors, but no risk to life.

A single generator may not be able to sufficiently handle the total capacity of life safety and critical loads in larger facilities. For larger hospitals, it is highly recommended to use multiple generators controlled by paralleling switchgear.

Hospitals are considered as a place of healing and caregiving, unlike other buildings, hospitals are expected to maintain and continue their operation without any interruptions or long delays.

The hospital electrical system is very complex and must comply with several codes and standards that have undergone extensive changes in recent years and will likely continue due to changes in technology.

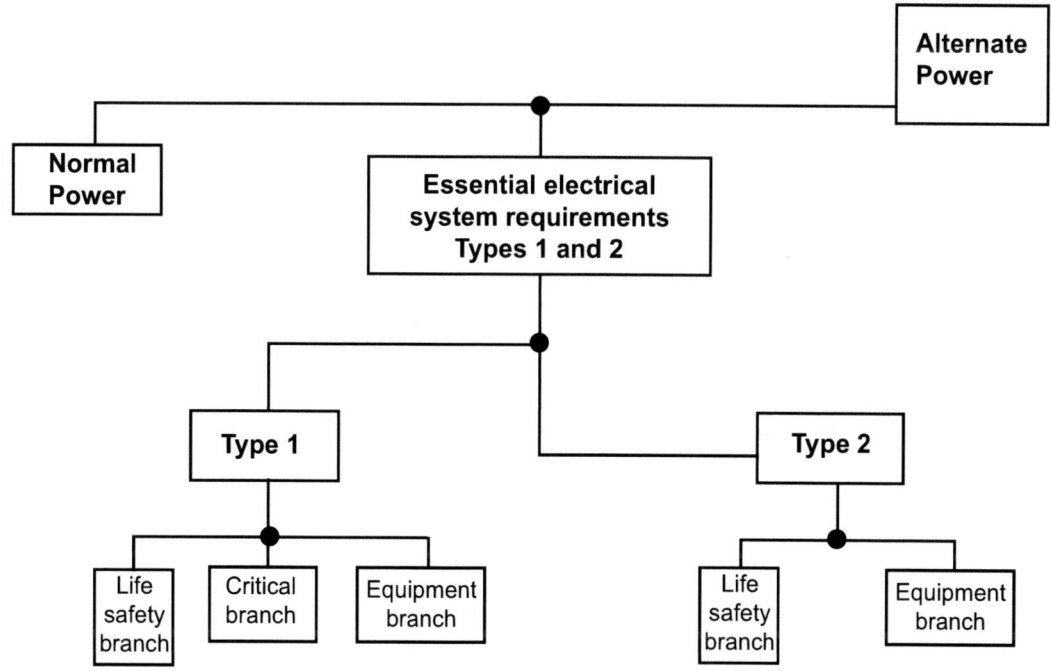

517.26. The life safety branch of the essential electrical system shall meet the requirements of Article 700, except as amended by Article 517.

(1) Section 700.4 shall not apply.

(2) Section 700.10(D) shall not apply.

(3) Section 700.17 shall be replaced with the following: Branch circuits that supply emergency lighting shall be installed to provide service from a source complying with 700.12 when normal supply for lighting is interrupted or where single circuits supply luminaires containing secondary batteries.

(4) Section 700.32 shall not apply.

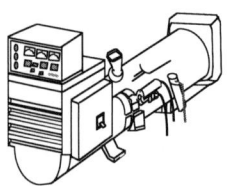

517.29(A). The requirements of Part III, 517.29 through 517.35, shall apply to Type 1 essential electrical systems. Type 1 systems shall be required for Category 1 (critical care) spaces. Type 1 systems shall be permitted to serve Category 2 (general care), Category 3 (basic care), and Category 4 (support) spaces.

517.29(B). Critical care (Category 1) spaces shall be served only by a Type 1 essential electrical system. Category 1 spaces shall not be served by a Type 2 EES.

517.30 Sources of Power.

(A) Essential electrical systems shall have a minimum of the following two independent sources of power: a normal source generally supplying the entire electrical system and one or more alternate source(s) for use when power is interrupted.

(B) Types of Power Sources.

(1) Generating Units. Where the normal source consists of generating units on the premises, the alternate source shall be either another generating set or an external utility service.

(2) Fuel cell systems shall be permitted to serve as the alternate source for all or part of an essential electrical system provided the following conditions apply:

(1) Installation of fuel cells shall comply with the requirements in Parts I through VII of Article 692 for 1000 volts or less and Part VIII for over 1000 volts.

(2) N + 1 units shall be provided where N units have sufficient capacity to supply the demand loads of the portion of the system served.

(3) Systems shall be able to assume loads within 10 seconds of loss of normal power source.

(4) Systems shall have a continuing source of fuel supply, together with sufficient on-site fuel storage for the essential system type.

(5) A connection shall be provided for a portable diesel generator to supply life safety and critical portions of the distribution system.

517.31 Requirements for the Essential Electrical Systems for Hospitals

517.31(A). Separate Branches. Type 1 Essential electrical systems for hospitals shall be comprised of three separate systems capable of supplying a limited amount of lighting and power service, that is considered essential for life safety and effective hospital operation during the time the normal electrical service is interrupted for any reason. These three branches are *life safety, critical, and equipment.*

The division between the branches shall occur at transfer switches where more than one transfer switch is required.

Definition: **Life Safety Branch**. A system of feeders and branch circuits supplying power for lighting, receptacles, and equipment essential for life safety that is automatically connected to alternate power sources by one or more transfer switches during interruption of the normal power source.

Definition: **Critical Branch**. A system of feeders and branch circuits supplying power for task illumination, fixed equipment, select receptacles, and select power circuits serving areas and functions related to patient care that are automatically connected to alternate power sources by one or more transfer switches during interruption of the normal power source.

Definition: **Equipment system**. A system of feeders and branch circuits arranged for delayed, automatic, or manual connection to the alternate power source and that serves primarily 3-phase power equipment.

517.31(B). The number of transfer switches to be used shall be based on reliability and design. Each branch of the essential electrical system shall have one or more transfer switches.

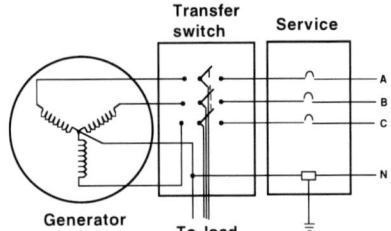

One transfer switch and downstream distribution system shall be permitted to serve one or more branches in a facility with a maximum demand on the essential electrical system of 150 kVA

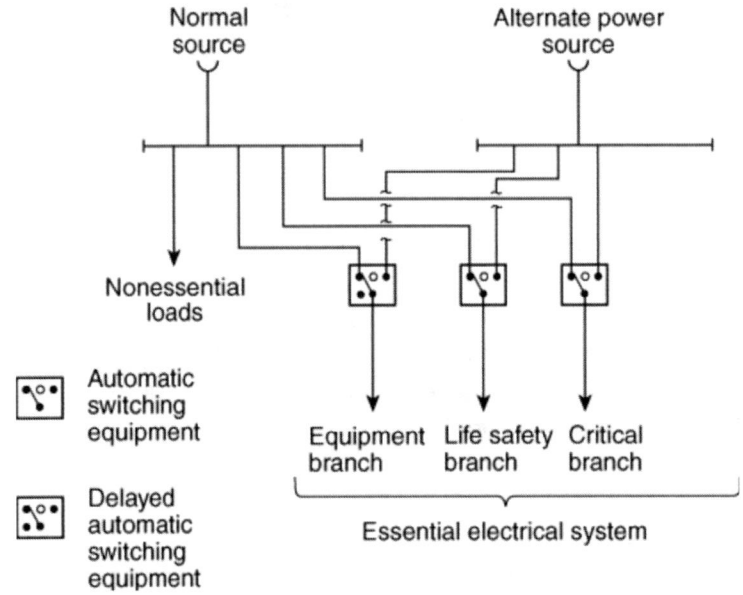

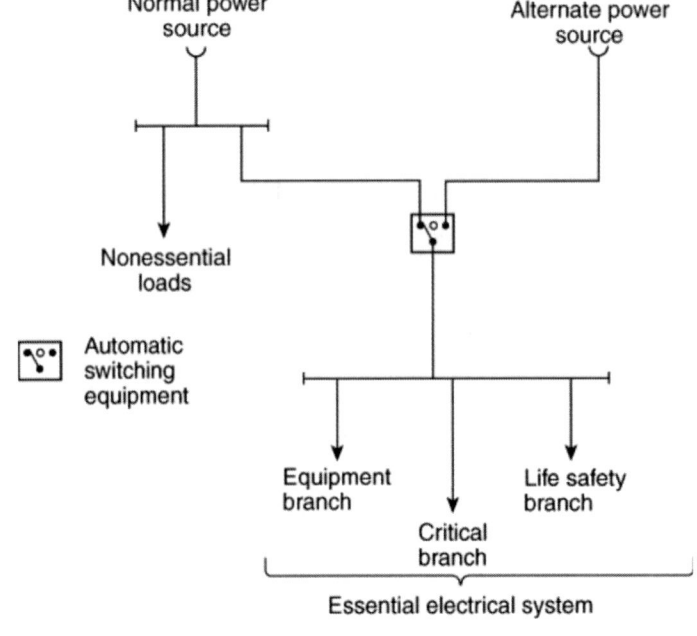

517.31(B)(1). Transfer switches shall be in according with one of the following:
(1) The number of transfer switches to be used shall be based on reliability and design. Each branch of the essential electrical system shall have one or more transfer switches.
(2) One transfer switch shall be permitted to serve one or more branches in a facility with a continuous load on the switch of 150 kVA (120 kW) or less.

517.31(B)(2). Hospital power sources and alternate power sources shall be permitted to serve the essential electrical systems of contiguous (have contact with) or same site facilities.

517.31(C). **Wiring Requirements.**

517.30(C)(1). The life safety branch and critical branch of the emergency system shall be kept entirely independent (separated) of all other wiring and equipment and shall **not** enter the same raceways, boxes, or cabinets with each other or other wiring.

Wiring of the life safety branch and critical branch shall be permitted to occupy the same raceways, boxes, or cabinets of other circuits not part of the branch where such wiring complies with one of the following:

(1) Is in transfer equipment enclosures.

(2) Is in exit or emergency luminaires supplied from two sources.

(3) Is in a common junction box attached to exit or emergency luminaires supplied from two sources.

(4) Is for two or more emergency circuits supplied from the same branch and same transfer switch.

The wiring of the equipment system shall be permitted to occupy the raceways, boxes, or cabinets of other circuits that are **not** part of the emergency system.

517.31(C)(2). Where isolated power systems are installed in any of the areas in any areas in 517.33(A)(1) and (A)(2), each system shall be supplied by an individual circuit serving no other load.

Definition: **Isolated Power System**. A system comprising an isolation transformer or its equivalent, a line isolation monitor, and its ungrounded circuit conductors.

Definition: **Isolation Transformer**. A transformer of the multiple winding type, with the primary and secondary windings physically separated, which inductively couples its secondary winding to the grounded feeder systems that energize its primary winding.

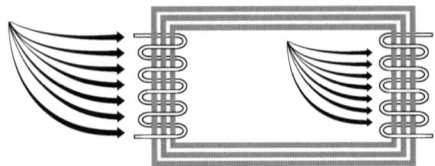

517.31(C)(3). The wiring of the life safety and critical branches shall be mechanically protected. Where installed as branch circuits in patient care areas, the installation shall comply with the requirements of 517.13(A) and 517.13(B) and 250.18. The following wiring methods shall be permitted:

(1) Nonflexible metal raceways, MI cable, or Schedule 80 PVC. Nonmetallic raceways shall **not** be used for branch circuits that supply patient care areas.

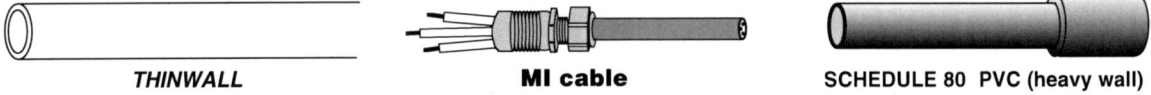

| THINWALL | MI cable | SCHEDULE 80 PVC (heavy wall) |

(2) Where encased in not less than 2" of concrete, Schedule 40 PVC, flexible nonmetallic or jacketed metallic raceways, or jacketed metallic cable assemblies listed for installation in concrete. Nonmetallic raceways shall **not** be used for branch circuits that supply patient care areas.

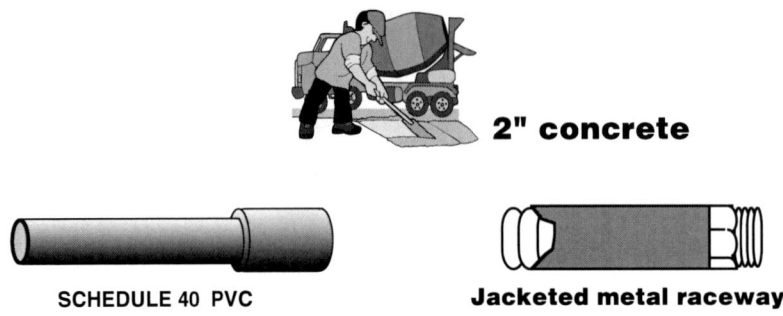

2" concrete

SCHEDULE 40 PVC   Jacketed metal raceway

(3) Listed flexible metal raceways and listed metal sheathed cable assemblies in any of the following:

(a) Where used in listed prefabricated medical headwalls

(b) In listed office furnishings

(c) Where fished into existing walls or ceilings, not otherwise accessible and not subject to physical damage

(d) Where necessary for flexible connection to equipment

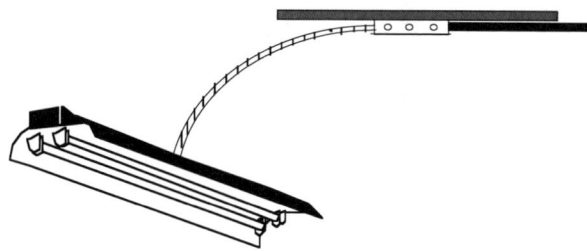

(e) For equipment that requires a flexible connection due to movement, vibration, or operation

(f) Luminaires installed in ceiling structures.

(4) Flexible power cords of appliances or other utilization equipment connected to the emergency system.

(5) Cables for Class 2 or Class 3 systems permitted by Part VI of this article, with or without raceways.

Informational Note: For additional grounding requirements see *517.13*:

517.13(A). All branch circuits serving patient care spaces shall be provided with a ground path in the metal raceway or metal cable armor or sheath that qualifies as an **equipment grounding conductor** per 250.118.

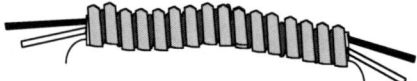

517.13(B). The grounding terminals of all receptacles metal boxes and enclosures containing receptacles and all non-current carrying conductive surfaces of fixed electric equipment likely to become energized that are subject to personal contact, operating at over 100 volts, shall be grounded by an **insulated copper equipment grounding conductor**.

Copper - Insulated Equip. Grounding conductor

517.31(D). The essential electrical system shall have adequate capacity to meet the demand for the operation of all functions and equipment to be served by each system and branch.

Feeders shall be sized per Articles 215 and 220. The generator set(s) shall have sufficient capacity and proper rating to meet the demand produced by the load of the essential electrical system(s) at any given time.

 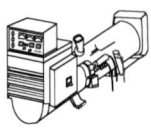

Demand calculations for sizing of the generator set(s) shall be based on any of the following:
(1) Prudent demand factors and historical data
(2) Connected load
(3) Feeder calculation per Article 220 Calculations
(4) Any combination of the above

The sizing requirements in 700.4 and 701.4 shall **not** apply to alternate sources.

517.31(E). The cover plates for receptacles or the receptacles themselves supplied from the life safety and critical branches shall have a distinctive color or marking so as to be readily identifiable.

517.31(F).A single feeder supplied by a local or remote alternate source shall be permitted to supply the essential electrical system to the point at which the life safety, critical, and equipment branches are separated.

517.31(G). Overcurrent protective devices serving the essential electrical system shall be coordinated for the period of time that a fault's duration extends beyond **0.1 second**.

517.32(A). Those functions of patient care depending on lighting or appliances that are connected to the emergency system shall be divided into two mandatory branches: the life safety and the critical branch, described in 517.33 and 517.34.

517.32(B). The branches of the emergency system shall be installed and connected to the alternate power source so that all functions specified herein for the emergency system shall be automatically restored to operation within **10 seconds** after interruption of the normal source.

517.33. Life Safety Branch. The life safety branch shall be limited to circuits essential to life safety.

(A) Illumination of means of egress, lighting corridors, passageways, stairways, and landing at exit doors. Switching from patient corridor lighting to night lighting is permitted, provided only one of the two circuits can be selected and both circuits cannot be extinguished at the same time.

(B) Exit signs and exit directional signs.

(C) Alarm and alerting systems include:
(1) Fire alarms

(2) Alarm and alerting systems (other than fire alarms) shall be connected to the life safety branch or critical branch.

(3) Alarms required for systems used for the piping of nonflammable medical gas.

(4) Mechanical, control, and other accessories required for effective life safety systems operation shall be permitted to be connected to the life safety branch.

(D) Hospital communication systems, where used for issuing instructions during emergency conditions.

(E) Generator set locations as follows:
(1) Task illumination
(2) Battery charger for emergency battery-powered lighting unit(s)
(3) Select receptacles at the generator set location and essential electrical system transfer switch locations

   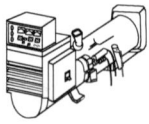

(F) Generator set accessories as required for generator performance.

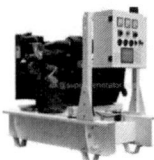

(G) Elevator cab lighting, control, communication, and signal systems.

(H) Automatically operated doors used for building egress.

517.34. Critical Branch.

517.34(A). The critical branch shall supply power for task illumination, fixed equipment, selected receptacles, and special power circuits serving the following areas and functions related to patient care:

(1) Category 1 Critical care areas that utilize anesthetizing gases - task illum., selected recept., fixed equip.

(2) Task illumination and select receptacles in the following:

a. Infant nurseries, select acute nursing areas, psychiatric bed areas, and ward treatment rooms.

b. Medication preparation areas

c. Pharmacy dispensing areas

d. Nurse's stations (unless adequately lighted by corridor lights)

(3) Additional specialized patient care task illumination and receptacles where needed.

(4) Nurse call systems

(5) Blood, bone, and tissue banks

(6) Telecommunications entrance facility, telecommunications equipment rooms, and Telecommunications rooms and equipment in these rooms.

(7) Task illumination, selected receptacles, and selected power circuits for the following areas:

a. Category 1 Critical care or Category 2 general care (at least one duplex receptacle in each patient bedroom).

b. Angiographic labs

c. Cardiac catheterization labs

d. Coronary care units

e. Hemodialysis rooms or areas

f. Emergency room treatment areas (selected)

g. Human physiology labs

h. Intensive care units

i. Postoperative recovery rooms (selected)

(8) Clinical IT-network equipment

(9) Wireless phone and paging equipment for clinical staff communications

(10) Additional task illumination, receptacles, and select power circuits needed for effective facility operation, including single-phase fractional horsepower motors, which are permitted to be connected to the critical branch.

517.34(B). It shall be permitted to control task illumination on the critical branch.

517.34(C). It shall be permitted to subdivide the critical branch into two or more branches.

Informational Note: It is important to analyze the consequences of supplying an area with only critical care branch power when failure occurs between the area and the transfer switch. Some proportion of normal and critical power or critical power from a separate transfer switches may be appropriate.

517.35. The equipment system shall be installed and connected to the alternate power source such that the equipment described in 517.35(A) is automatically restored to operation at appropriate time-lag intervals following the energizing of the life safety and critical branches.

The arrangement of the connection to the alternate power source shall also provide for the subsequent connection of equipment described in 517.35(B).

Exception: For essential electrical systems under 150 kVA, deletion of the time-lag intervals feature for delayed automatic connection to the equipment system shall be permitted.

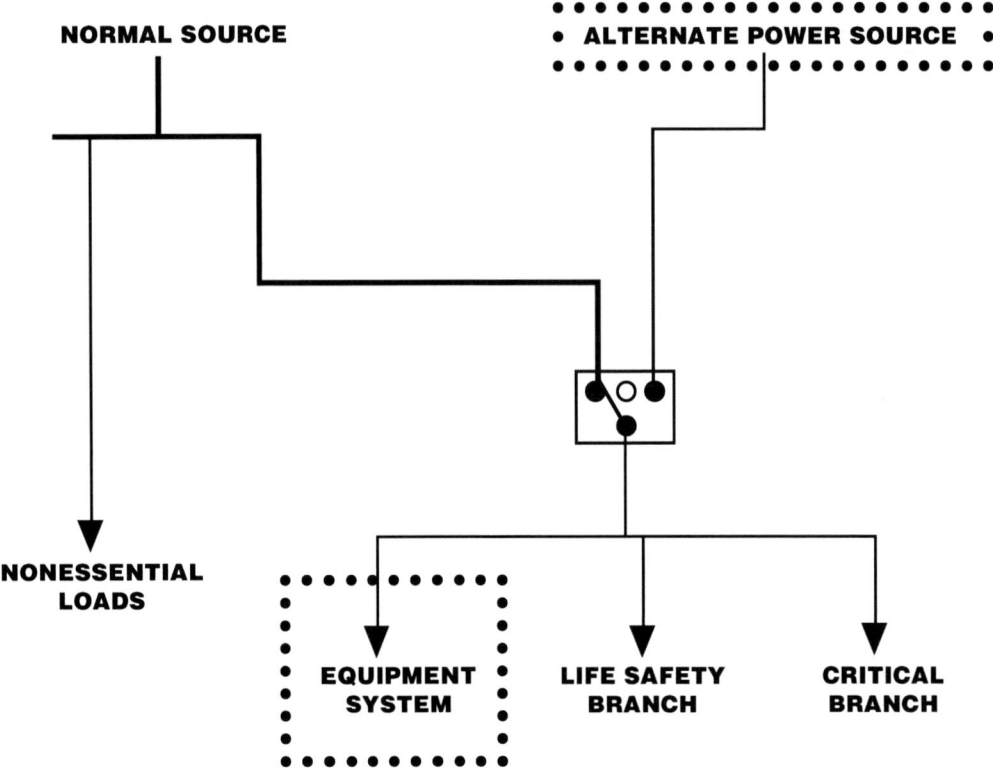

517.35(A). The following equipment shall be arranged for delayed automatic connection to the alternate power source:

 **Delayed automatic switching equipment**

(1) Central suction systems serving medical and surgical functions, including controls. Such suction systems shall be permitted on the critical branch.

(2) Sump pumps and other equipment required to operate for the safety of major apparatus, including associated control systems and alarms.

(3) Compressed air systems serving medical and surgical functions, including controls. Such air systems shall be permitted on the critical branch.

(4) Smoke control and stair pressurization systems, or both.

(5) Kitchen hood supply or exhaust systems, or both, if required to operate during a fire in or under the hood.

(6) Supply, return, and exhaust ventilating systems for airborne infectious/isolation rooms, protective environment rooms, exhaust fans for laboratory fume hoods, nuclear medicine areas where radioactive material is used, ethylene oxide evacuation and anesthesia evacuation. Where delayed automatic connection is not appropriate, such ventilation systems shall be permitted to be placed on the critical branch.

(7) Supply, return, and exhaust ventilating systems for operating and delivery rooms.

(8) Supply, return, and exhaust ventilating systems and/or air conditioning systems serving telephone equipment rooms and closets and data equipment rooms and closets.

Exception: Sequential delayed automatic connection to the alternate power source to prevent overloading the generator shall be permitted where engineering studies indicate it is necessary.

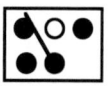 **Delayed automatic switching equipment**

517.35(B). The following equipment shall be arranged for either delayed automatic or manual connection to the alternate power source:

(1) Heating equipment to provide heating for operating, delivery, labor, recovery, intensive care, coronary care, nurseries, infection/isolation rooms, emergency treatment spaces, and general patient rooms and pressure maintenance (jockey or make-up) pump(s) for water based fire protection systems.

Exception: Heating of general patient rooms and infection/isolation rooms during disruption of the normal source shall not be required under any of the following conditions:

(1) The outside design temperature is higher than 20°F.

(2) The outside design temperature is lower than 20°F, and where a selected room(s) is provided for the needs of all confined patients, only such room(s) need be heated.

(3) The facility is served by a dual source of normal power.

 **Author's note**: A dual source of normal power consists of two or more electrical services fed from a separate generator sets or a utility distribution network that has multiple power input sources and is arranged to provide mechanical and electrical separation so that a fault between the facility and the generating sources is not likely to cause an interruption of more than one of the facility service feeders.

(2) An elevator(s) selected to provide service to patient, surgical, obstetrical, and ground floors during interruption of normal power. In instances where interruption of normal power would result in other elevators stopping between floors, throw-over facilities shall be provided to allow the temporary operation of any elevator for the release of patients or other persons who may be confined between floors.

(3) Hyperbaric facilities.
(4) Hypobaric facilities.
(5) Automatically operated doors.
(6) Minimal electrically heated autoclaving equipment shall be permitted to be arranged for either automatic or manual connection to the alternate source.
(7) Controls for equipment listed in 517.35.
(8) Other selected equipment shall be permitted to be served by the equipment system.

517.35(C). AC Equipment for Nondelayed Automatic Connection. Generator accessories, including but not limited to, the transfer fuel pump, electrically operated louvers, and other generator accessories essential for generator operation, shall be arranged for automatic connection to the alternate power source.

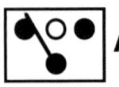 **Automatic switching equipment**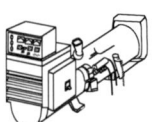

517.40 Type 2 Essential Electrical Systems for Nursing Homes and Limited Care Facilities.

517.40(A). The requirements of Part III, 517.40(C) through 517.44, shall apply to Category 2 general care spaces.

Exception: The requirements of Part III, 517.40(C) through 517.44, shall **not** apply to freestanding buildings used as nursing homes and limited care facilities, provided the following apply:

(1) Admitting and discharge policies are maintained that preclude the provision of care for any patient or resident who may need to be sustained by electrical life-support equipment.

(2) No surgical treatment requiring general anesthesia is offered.

(3) An automatic battery-operated system(s) or equipment is provided that shall be effective for at least 1 1/2 hours and is otherwise in accordance with 700.12 and that shall be capable of supplying lighting for exit light, exit corridors, stairways, nursing stations, medical preparation areas, boiler rooms, and communication areas. This system shall also supply power to operate all alarm systems.

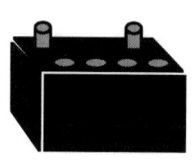  **1 1/2 Hours**

517.40(B). Category 1 Critical Care Spaces, Inpatient Hospital Care Facilities. Nursing homes and limited care facilities that provide inpatient hospital care shall comply with Part III, 517.29 through 517.35.

517.40(C). Nursing homes and limited care facilities that are contiguous (touching along a boundary) or located on the same site with a hospital shall be permitted to have their essential electrical systems supplied by the hospital

Informational Note: For performance, maintenance, and testing requirements of essential electrical systems in nursing homes and limited care facilities, see NFPA 99-2018, *Standard for Health Care Facilities*.

517.41. Required Power Sources

517.41(A). Essential electrical systems shall have a minimum of the following two independent sources of power: a normal source generally supplying the entire electrical system and one more alternate source for use when the normal service is interrupted.

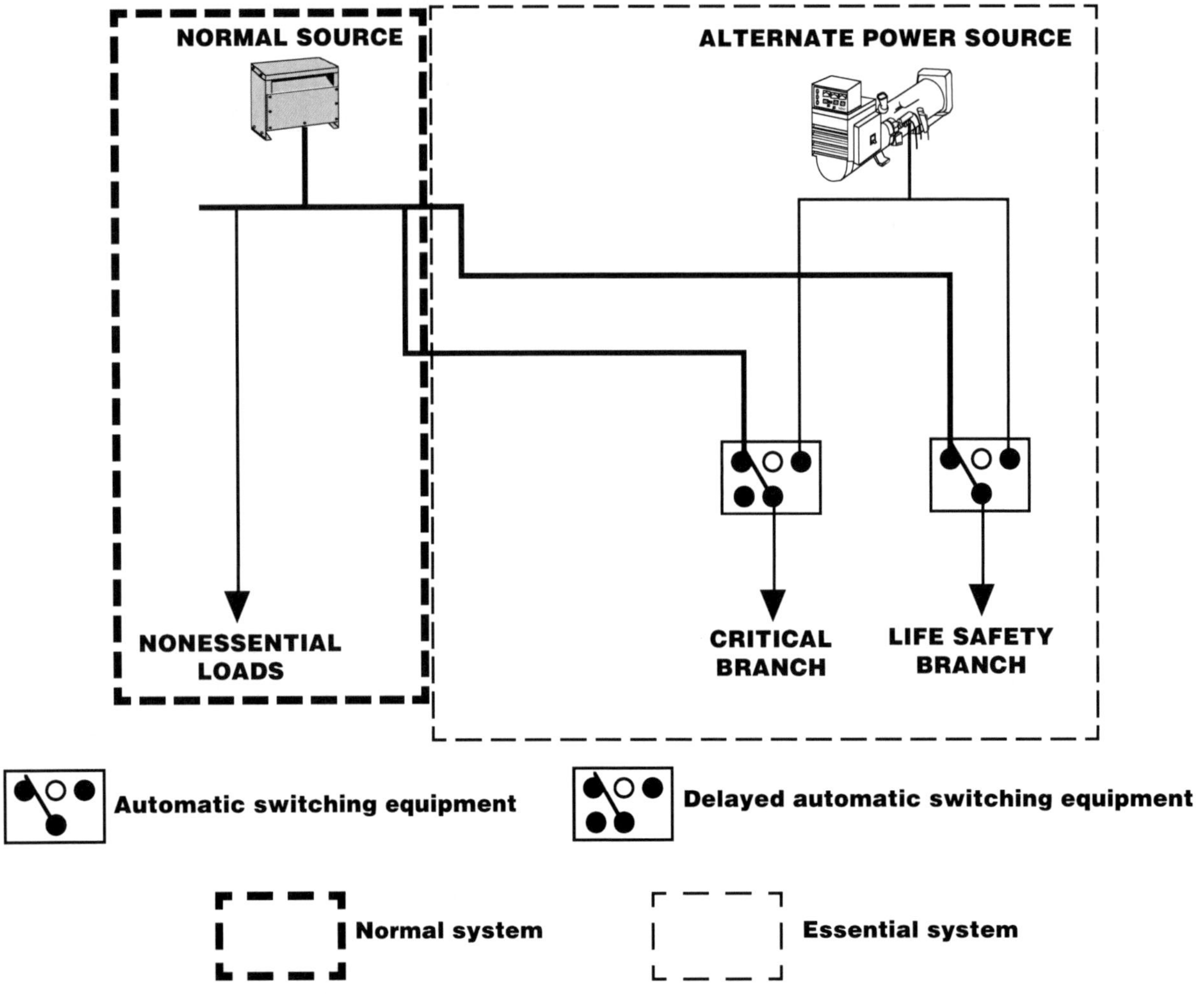

```
NORMAL SOURCE                    ALTERNATE POWER SOURCE




NONESSENTIAL          CRITICAL        LIFE SAFETY
LOADS                 BRANCH          BRANCH
```

◖○◉ **Automatic switching equipment**   ◖○◉ **Delayed automatic switching equipment**

⌐ ⌐ **Normal system**   ⌐ ⌐ **Essential system**

517.42 Essential Electrical Systems

(A) Essential electrical systems for nursing homes and limited care facilities shall be divided into the following two branches, the life safety branch and the equipment branch.

The division between the branches shall occur at transfer switches where more than one transfer switch is required.

517.42(B). The number of transfer switches to be used shall be based on the reliability, design, and load considerations.

(1) Each branch of the essential system shall have one or more transfer switches.

(2) One transfer switch shall be permitted to serve one or more branches or systems in a facility with a continuous load on the switch of 150 kVA or less.

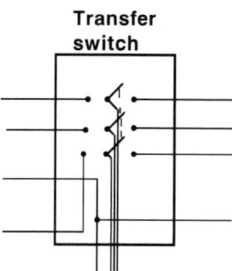

517.42(C). The essential electrical system shall have adequate capacity to meet the demand for the operation of all functions and equipment to be served by each branch at one time.

517.42(D). The life safety branch and equipment branch shall be kept entirely independent (separated) of all other wiring and equipment and shall **not** enter the same raceways, boxes, or cabinets with other wiring except as follows:

(1) In transfer switches.

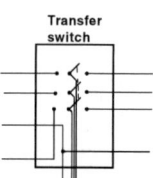

(2) In exit or emergency light fixtures supplied from two sources.

(3) In a common junction box attached to exit or emergency light fixtures supplied from two sources.

517.42(E). The cover plates for receptacles or the receptacles themselves supplied from the life safety or equipment branches shall have a distinctive color or marking so as to be readily identifiable.

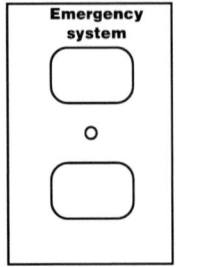 

517.43. The life safety and equipment branch shall be installed and connected to the alternate power source so that all functions specified herein for the emergency system shall be automatically restored to operation within 10 seconds after interruption of the normal source. No functions other than those listed in 517.43(A) through (G) shall be connected to the life safety branch.

(A) Illumination of means of egress, lighting corridors, passageways, stairways, and landing at exit doors. Switching from patient corridor lighting to night lighting is permitted, provided only one of the two circuits can be selected and both circuits cannot be extinguished at the same time.

(B) Exit signs and exit directional signs.

(C) Alarm and alerting systems include:
(1) Fire alarms

(2) Alarms required for systems used for the piping of nonflammable medical gas.

(D) Hospital communication systems, where used for issuing instructions during emergency conditions.

(E) Task illumination battery charger for emergency battery-powered lighting unit(s) and selected receptacles at the generator set location can be connected to the life safety branch.

 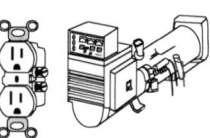

(F) Elevator cab lighting, control, communication, and signal systems.

517.44. The equipment branch shall be installed and connected to the alternate power source such that the equipment described in 517.35(A)(6) is automatically restored at appropriate time-lag intervals following the restoration of the life safety branch to operation. Its arrangement shall also provide for the subsequent connection of equipment described in 517.44(B).

Exception: For essential electrical systems under 150 kVA, deletion of the time-lag intervals feature for delayed automatic connection to the equipment system shall be permitted.

517.44(A). The following equipment shall be connected to the equipment branch and shall be arranged for delayed automatic connection to the alternate power source:

 **Delayed automatic switching equipment**

(1) Task illumination and selected receptacles in the following:
a. Patient care spaces
b. Medication preparation spaces
c. Pharmacy dispensing areas
d. Nurse's stations (unless adequately lighted by corridor lights)

(2) Supply, return, and exhaust ventilating systems for airborne infectious isolation rooms.

(3) Sump pumps and other equipment required to operate for the safety of major apparatus, including associated control systems and alarms.

(4) Smoke control and stair pressurization systems.

(5) Kitchen hood supply or exhaust systems, or both, if required to operate during a fire in or under the hood.

(6) Nurse call systems

517.44(B). The following equipment shall be arranged for either delayed automatic or manual connection to the alternate power source:

(1) Heating equipment to provide heating for patient rooms.

Heating of general patient rooms during disruption of the normal source shall not be required under any of the following conditions:
(a) The outside design temperature is higher than 20°F.
(b) The outside design temperature is lower than 20°F, and where a selected room(s) is provided for the needs of all confined patients, only such room(s) need be heated.
(c) The facility is served by a dual source of normal power as described in 517.30(C), *Informational Note.*

 **Author's note**: The *Informational Note* states: A dual source of normal power consists of two or more electrical services fed from a separate generator sets or a utility distribution network that has multiple power input sources and is arranged to provide mechanical and electrical separation so that a fault between the facility and the generating sources is not likely to cause an interruption of more than one of the facility service feeders.

(2) Elevator service - in instances where disruption of power would result in elevators stopping between floors, throw-over facilities shall be provided to allow the temporary operation of any elevator for the release of passengers. For elevator cab lighting, control, and signal requirements, see 517.43(G).

(3) Additional illumination, receptacles, and equipment shall be permitted to be connected only to the critical branch.

CRITICAL
BRANCH

517.45. Essential Electrical Systems for Other Health Care Facilities.

(A) The essential electrical distribution if required by the governing body, the essential electrical distribution system for basic care (Category 3) patient care spaces shall be comprised of an alternate power system capable of supplying a limited amount of lighting and power service for the orderly cessation of procedures during time normal electrical service is interrupted

517.45(B). Where electrical life support equipment is required, the essential distribution system shall be as described in 517.29 through 517.30.

517.45(C). Where Category 1 critical care areas are present, the essential distribution system shall be as described in 517.29 through 517.30.

517.45(D). Where general care (Category 2) patient care spaces are present, the essential electrical distribution system shall be as described in 517.40 through 517.45.

Author's note: The essential system contains names of locations and equipment not familiar to the electrician. 517.34(7)(b) mentions *angiographic labs*, **angiography** is the visualization of the blood vessels after injection of a radiopaque substance. 517.34(7)(e) mentions *hemodialysis rooms or areas*, **hemodialysis** is the process of removing blood from an artery (as of a kidney patient), purifying it by dialysis, adding vital substances, and returning it to a vein.

517.35(B)(3) mentions *hyperbaric facilities*, hyper means above, hyperbaric means utilizing a greater than normal pressure (such as oxygen). 517.35(B)(4) mentions *hypobaric facilities*, hypo means lower, it would be a lower pressure in the room.

Part IV. Inhalation Anesthetizing Locations

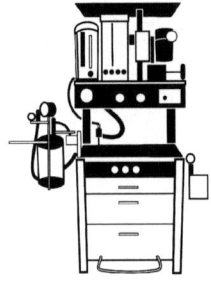 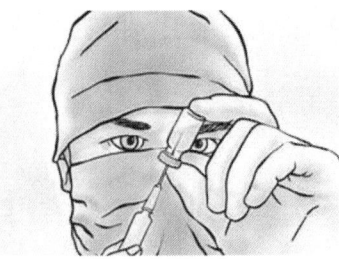

517.60 Anesthetizing Location Classification.

Informational Note: If either of the anesthetizing locations in 517.60(A) or 517.60(B) is designated a wet location, refer to 517.20.

517.60(A). Hazardous Location.

(1) In a location where flammable anesthetics are employed, the entire area shall be considered a Class I, Division 1 location that extends upward to a level 5' above the floor. The remaining volume up to the structural ceiling is considered non-hazardous.

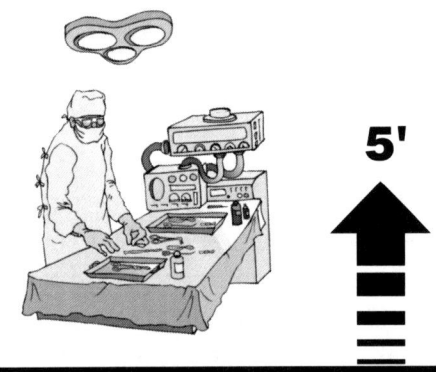

5'

(2) Any room or location in which flammable anesthetics or volatile flammable disinfecting agents are stored shall be considered to be a Class I, Division 1 location from floor to ceiling.

DANGER
HIGHLY FLAMMABLE

Floor to ceiling

HAZARDOUS
Class I
Division1

517.60(B). Unclassified. Any inhalation anesthetizing location designated for the exclusive use of **nonflammable** anesthetizing agents shall be considered to be an unclassified location.

517.61 Wiring and Equipment.

517.61(A). Within Hazardous Anesthetizing Locations.

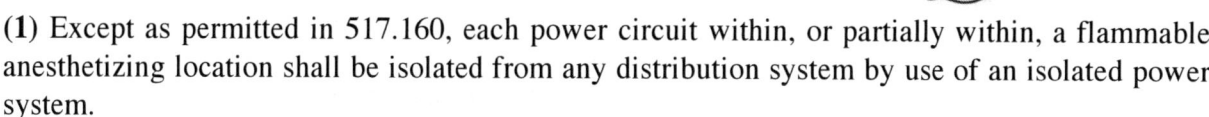

(1) Except as permitted in 517.160, each power circuit within, or partially within, a flammable anesthetizing location shall be isolated from any distribution system by use of an isolated power system.

Definition: **Isolated Power System.** A system comprising an isolating transformer or its equivalent, a line isolation monitor, and its ungrounded circuit conductors.

(2) Where an isolated power system is utilized, the isolated power equipment shall be listed as isolated power equipment, and the isolated power system shall be designed and installed per 517.160.

(3) All fixed wiring and equipment in anesthetizing locations, including lamps and other utilization equipment, operating at more than 10 volts shall be specifically approved for the hazardous atmospheres involved in the Class I, Division 1 location.

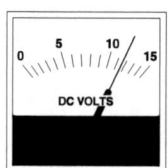   **More than 10 volts**

(4) If a box or fitting is not entirely above the 5' level, the Class I Division 1 area is considered to the top of the box or fitting. The box or fitting is considered entirely within the hazardous area, and a seal is required in the conduit entering the enclosure from either above or below.

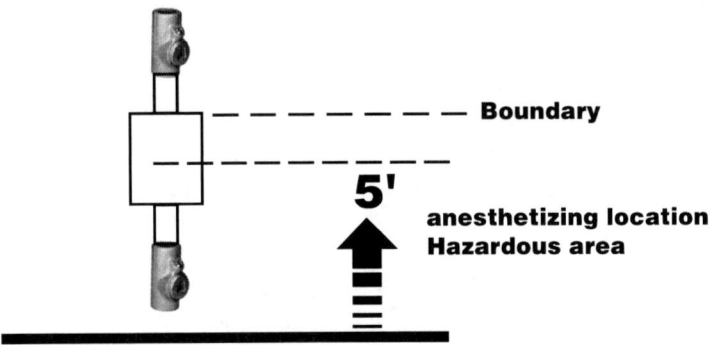

Boundary

5'

anesthetizing location
Hazardous area

(5) Requires explosionproof receptacles and plugs within the hazardous anesthetizing location.

(6) Flexible cords used to connect portable utilization equipment, including lamps at 8 volts or more, shall be approved for extra hard usage, including an **equipment grounding conductor**.

(7) A storage device for flexible cord shall be provided and shall not subject the cord to a bending radius of less than 3".

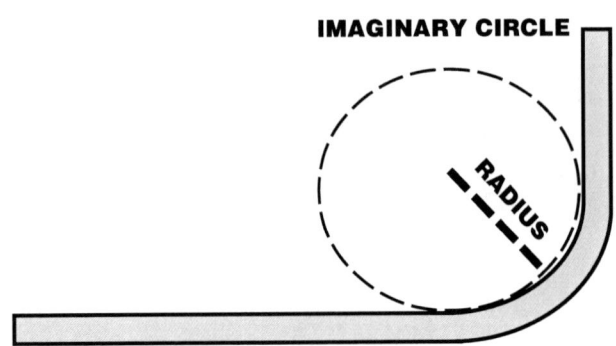

IMAGINARY CIRCLE

RADIUS

517.61(B). Wiring Above Hazardous Anesthetizing Locations.

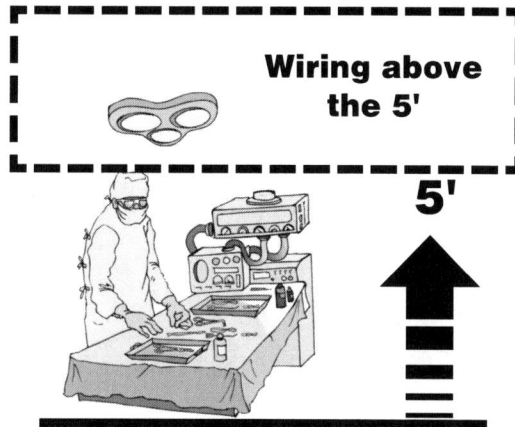

(1) The wiring above the 5' anesthetizing classified area shall be in rigid metal conduit, EMT, IMC, MI cable, or MC cable that employs a continuous gas/vaportight metal sheath.

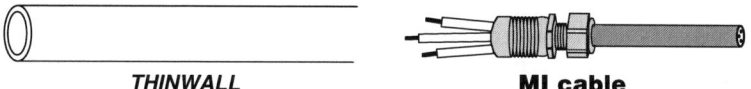

THINWALL   **MI cable**

(2) Installed equipment that may produce arcs, sparks, or particles of hot metal, such as lamps for fixed lighting, switches, motors, etc. or other equipment having make-and-break or sliding contacts, shall be totally enclosed.

(3) Surgical and other light fixtures shall conform to 501.130(B).

501.130(B)(1). Class I, Division 2, where lamps are of a size and type that may reach a surface temperature under normal operating conditions exceeding 80% of the ignition temperature (in°C) of the gas or vapor involved, fixtures that are *identified* for a Class I, Division 1 location shall be installed.

Exception 1: The surface temperature limitations set forth in 501.130(B1) shall not apply.

Exception 2: Integral or pendant switches that are located above and cannot be lowered into the hazardous location shall not be required to be explosionproof.

(4) Approved seals shall conform per 501.15, and 501.15(A)(4) shall apply to horizontal as well as to vertical boundaries of hazardous locations.

(5) Receptacles and plugs above hazardous anesthetizing locations shall be listed for hospital use.

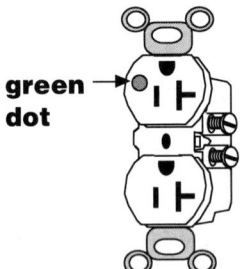

green dot →

Listed "Hospital Grade" receptacle green dot

(6) 250 volt rated receptacles and plugs, for connection of 50 amp and 60 amp medical equipment above hazardous locations, shall be arranged so that the 60 amp receptacle will accept either the 50 amp or 60 amp plug. 50 amp receptacles shall be designed so as not to accept the 60 amp plug. The plugs shall be 2-pole, 3-wire with a third contact connecting to the equipment grounding conductor.

**2 pole 3 wire
50A 250V**

517.61(C). Unclassified Anesthetizing Locations.

(1) Wiring serving unclassified locations, shall be installed in a metal raceway or cable assembly. The metal raceway or cable assembly shall qualify **as an equipment grounding return path** per 250.118. MI and MC cable shall have an outer metal armor or sheath that is identified as an acceptable grounding path.

IDENTIFIED

Exception: Pendant receptacle installations that employ listed Type SJO or equivalent hard usage or extra hard usage, flexible cords suspended not less than 6' from the floor shall not be required to be installed in a metal raceway or cable assembly.

(2) Receptacles and plugs in unclassified locations shall be listed for hospital use.

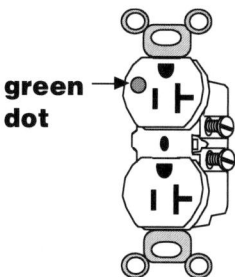

green
dot

(3) 250 volt rated receptacles and plugs, for connection of 50 amp and 60 amp medical equipment in unclassified locations, shall be arranged so that the 60 amp receptacle will accept either the 50 amp or 60 amp plug. 50 amp receptacles shall be designed so as not to accept the 60 amp plug. The plugs shall be 2-pole, 3-wire with a third contact connecting to the **equipment grounding conductor**.

**2 pole 3 wire
50A 250V**

517.62. Grounding. In any anesthetizing area, all metal raceways and metal-sheathed cables and all non-current carrying conductive portions of fixed electrical equipment shall be grounded per 501.30.

Exception: Equipment operating at not more than 10 volts between conductors shall not be required to be connected to an equipment grounding conductor.

517.63. Grounded Power Systems in Anesthetizing Locations.

(A) One or more battery-powered emergency lighting units shall be provided and shall be permitted to be wired to the critical lighting circuit in the area and connected ahead of any local switches.

(B) Branch circuits supplying only listed, fixed, therapeutic and diagnostic equipment, permanently installed above the hazardous location and in unclassified locations, shall be permitted to be supplied from a normal grounded service, single or three phase, provided the following apply:
(1) Wiring for grounded and isolated circuits does not occupy the same raceway or cable.

Grounded circuits   **Isolated circuits**

SEPARATE RACEWAYS

(2) All conductive surfaces of the equipment are connected to an equipment grounding conductor.

(3) Equipment (except enclosed X- ray tubes and the leads to the tubes) are located at least 8' above the floor or outside the anesthetizing location.

(4) Switches for the grounded branch circuit are located outside the hazardous location.

Exception: Sections 517.63(B)(3) and (B)(4) shall not apply in unclassified locations.

517.63(C). Branch circuits supplying only fixed lighting shall be permitted to be supplied by a normal grounded service, provided:
(1) Such light fixtures are located at least 8' above the floor.

(2) All conductive surfaces of the fixtures are connected to an **equipment grounding conductor**.

(3) Wiring for circuits supplying power to light fixtures does not occupy the same raceway or cable for circuits supplying isolated power.

 **Lighting circuits**    **Isolated circuits**

(4) Switches are wall-mounted and located above hazardous locations.

Exception: 517.63(C)(1) and (C)(4) shall not apply in unclassified locations.

517.63(D). Wall-mounted remote-control stations for remote-control switches operating at 24 volts or less shall be permitted to be installed in any anesthetizing location.

24 volts or less

517.63(E). Isolated power system equipment and its supply circuit is permitted to be located in an anesthetizing location, provided it is installed above the hazardous location or in an unclassified location. Isolated power equipment shall be listed as such.

517.63(F). Except as permitted above, each power circuit within, or partially within, a flammable anesthetizing location shall be isolated from any distribution system supplying other-than-anesthetizing locations.

FLAMMABLE

517.64. Low-Voltage Equipment and Instruments.

(A) Low-voltage equipment that is frequently in contact with the bodies of persons or has exposed current-carrying elements shall comply with one of the following:

(1) Operate on an electrical potential of 10 volts or less.

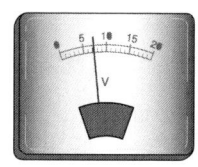 **10 VOLTS or LESS**

(2) Approved as intrinsically safe or double-insulated equipment.
(3) Be moisture resistant.

517.64(B). Power shall be supplied to low-voltage equipment from one of the following:
(1) An individual portable isolating transformer (autotransformers shall not be used) connected to an isolated power circuit receptacle by means of an appropriate cord and attachment plug.
(2) A common low-voltage isolating transformer installed in an unclassified location.

(3) Individual dry-cell batteries

(4) Common batteries made up of storage cells located in an unclassified location.

517.64(C). Isolating-type transformers for supplying low-voltage circuits shall have both of the following:
(1) Approved means for insulating the secondary circuit from the primary circuit.

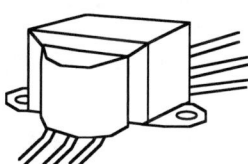

(2) The core and case are connected to an **equipment grounding conductor**.

517.64(D). Resistance or impedance devices shall be permitted to control low-voltage equipment but shall not be used to limit the maximum available voltage to the equiment.

517.64(E). Battery-powered appliances shall not be capable of being charged while in operation unless their charging circuitry incorporates an integral isolating-type transformer.

517.64(F). Any receptacle or plug used on low-voltage circuits shall be of a type that does not permit interchangeable connection with circuits of a higher voltage.

Informational Note: Any interruption of the circuit, even circuits as low as 10 volts, either by any switch or loose or defective connections anywhere in the circuit, may produce a spark that is sufficient to ignite flammable anesthetic agents.

Part V. X-Ray Installations

517.70. Nothing in this part shall be construed as specifying safeguards against the useful beam or stray X-ray radiation.

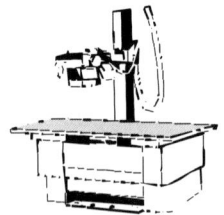  

Informational Note 1: Radiation safety and performance requirements of several classes of X-ray equipment are regulated under Public Law 90-602 and are enforced by the Department of Health and Human Services.

Informational Note 2: In addition, information on radiation protection by the National Council on Radiation Protection and Measurements is published as *Reports of the National Council on Radiation Protection and Measurement*. These reports are obtainable from NCRP Publications, P.O. Box 30175, Washington, DC 20014.

517.71 Connection to Supply Circuit.

(A) Fixed and stationary X-ray equipment shall be connected to the power supply by means of a wiring method that meets the Code.

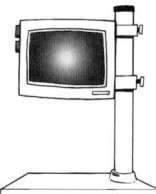

Exception: Equipment properly supplied by a branch circuit rated at not over 30 amps shall be permitted to be supplied through a suitable attachment plug and hard service cable or cord.

(B) Individual branch circuits shall not be required for portable, mobile, and transportable medical X-ray equipment requiring a capacity of not over 60 amps.

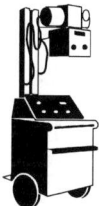

(C) Circuits and equipment operated on a supply circuit of over 1000 volts shall follow the rules of Article 490 for high-voltage.

517.72 Diconnecting Means.

(A) A disconnecting means rated for at least 50% of the input required for the momentary rating or 100% of the input required for the long-time rating of the X-ray equipment, whichever is greater, shall be provided in the supply circuit.

(B) The disconnecting means shall be operable from a location **readily accessible** from the X-ray control.

Accessible, Readily: (readily accessible)
Capable of being reached quickly. The General Rule Section 240.24 states that overcurrent devices shall be readily accessible. This means you can reach them without having to move obstacles or to climb a ladder to reach them.

517.73. Rating of Supply Conductors and Overcurrent Protection.

(A) Diagnostic Equipment.

(1) The ampacity of supply branch circuit conductors and the current rating of overcurrent protective devices shall not be less than 50% of the momentary rating or 100% of the long-time rating, whichever is greater.

(2) The ampacity of supply feeders and the current rating of overcurrent protective devices supplying two or more branch circuits supplying X-ray units shall not be less than 50% of the momentary demand rating of the largest unit plus 25% of the momentary demand rating of the next largest unit plus 10% of the momentary demand rating of each additional unit. Where simultaneous biplane examinations are undertaken with the X-ray units, the supply conductors and overcurrent protective devices shall be 100% of the momentary demand rating of each X-ray unit.

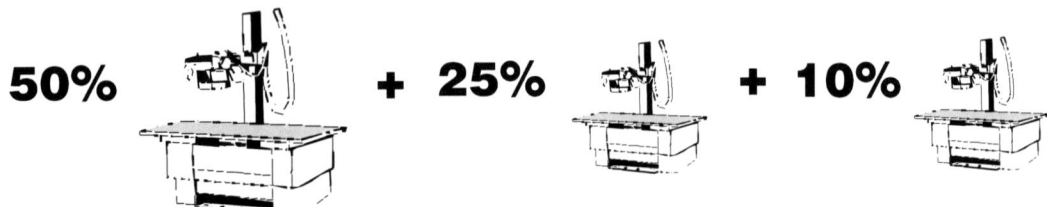

Informational Note: The minimum conductor size for branch and feeder circuits is also governed by voltage regulation requirements. For a specific installation, the manufacturer usually specifies minimum distribution transformer and conductor sizes, rating of disconnecting means, and overcurrent protection.

517.73(B). Therapeutic Equipment. The ampacity of conductors and rating of overcurrent protective devices shall not be less than 100% of the current rating of medical X-ray therapy equipment.

Informational Note: The ampacity of the branch-circuit conductors and the ratings of disconnecting means and overcurrent protection for X-ray equipment are usually designated by the manufacturer for the specific installation.

517.74 Control Circuit Conductors.

(A) The number of control circuit conductors installed in a raceway shall be per 300.17.

300.17. The number and size of conductors in any raceway shall not be more than will permit dissipation of heat and ready installation or withdrawal of conductors without damage.

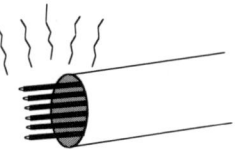

(B) Minimum size #18 or #16 fixture wires per 725.49 and flexible cords shall be permitted for the control and operating circuits of X-ray and auxiliary equipment where protected by not larger than 20 amp overcurrent devices.

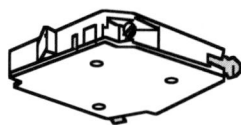 **20 amp maximum**

517.75. All equipment for new X-ray installations and all used or reconditioned X-ray equipment moved to and reinstalled at a new location shall be of an approved type.

517.76. Transformers and capacitors that are part of X-ray equipment shall **not** be required to follow Articles 450 and 460.

Capacitors shall be mounted within enclosures of insulating material or grounded metal.

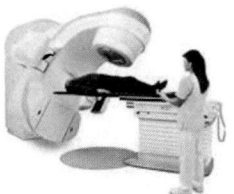 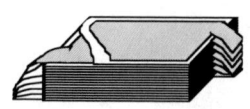 

517.77. Cables with grounded shields connecting X-ray tubes and image intensifiers shall be permitted to be installed in cable trays or cable troughs along with X-ray equipment control and power supply conductors without the need for barriers to separate the wiring.

 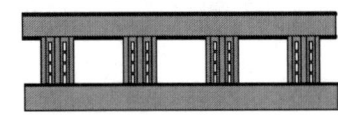

517.78 Guarding and Grounding.

(A) All high-voltage parts, including X-ray tubes, shall be mounted within grounded enclosures. Air, oil, gas, or other suitable insulating media shall be used to insulate the high-voltage from the grounded enclosure. The connection from the high-voltage equipment to X-ray tubes and other high-voltage components shall be made with high-voltage shielded cables.

(B) Low-voltage cables connecting to oil-filled units that are not completely sealed, such as transformers, condensers, oil coolers, and high-voltage switches, shall have insulation of the oil-resistant type.

(C) Noncurrent-carrying metal parts of X-ray and associated equipment such as controls, tables, X-ray tube supports, transformer tanks, shielded cables, X-ray tube heads, etc. shall be grounded per Article 250 Part VII and as modified by 517.13(A) and (B).

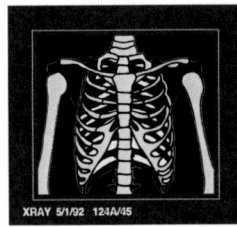 

 **Author's note**: Article 660 also covers X-Ray equipment operating at any frequency or voltage for industrial or other nonmedical or nondental use.

660.2 lists the definitions of long-time rating, mobile X-ray, momentary rating, portable, transportable.

Part VI. Communications, Signaling Systems, Data Systems, Fire Alarm Systems, and Systems Less Than 120 Volts, Nominal.

517.80. Equivalent insulation and isolation to that required for the electrical distribution systems in patient care areas shall be provided for communications, signal systems, data system circuits, fire alarm systems, and systems less than 120 volts, nominal.

517.81. In other-than-patient-care spaces, installations shall be made in accordance with the applicable provisions of other parts of this *Code*.

517.82(A). Permanently installed signal cabling from an appliance in a patient location to remote appliances shall employ a signal transmission system that prevents hazardous grounding interconnection of appliances.

Informational Note: See 517.13(A) for additional grounding requirements in patient care spaces.

517.82(B). Common signal grounding wires such as the chassis ground for single-ended transmission shall be permitted to be used between appliances all located within the patient vicinity, provided the appliances are served from the same reference grounding point.

VII. Isolated Power Systems.

517.160(A)(1). Each isolated power circuit must be controlled by a switch or circuit breaker that has a disconnecting pole in each isolated circuit conductor to simultaneously disconnect all power. Conductors of isolated power circuits shall **not** be installed in cables, raceways, or other enclosures containing conductors of another system.

(2) Any transformer used to obtain the ungrounded circuits must have its primary rated at not more than 600 volts between conductors and must have proper overcurrent protection.

600 volts or less

(3) Isolating transformers, motor generator sets, batteries and battery chargers, and associated primary or secondary overcurrent devices shall not be installed in hazardous locations. The isolated secondary circuit wiring extending into a hazardous anesthetizing location shall be installed per 501.10.

(4) An isolation transformer shall not serve more than one operating room except as covered in (A)(4)(a) and (A)(4)(b).

For the purpose of this section, anesthetic induction rooms are considered part of the operating room or rooms served by the induction rooms.

(a) Induction rooms. Where an induction room serves more than one operating room, the isolated circuits of the induction room shall be permitted to be supplied from the isolation transformer of any one of the operating rooms served by that induction room.

(b) Higher Voltages. Isolation transformers shall be permitted to serve single receptacles in several patient areas where the following apply:
(1) The receptacles are reserved for supplying power to equipment requiring 150 volts or higher, such as portable X-ray units.

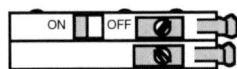

150 volts or higher

(2) The receptacles and mating plugs are not interchangeable with the receptacles on the local isolated power system.

517.160(A)(5). The isolated circuit conductors shall be identified as:

(1) Isolated Conductor #1 - Orange with at least one distinctive colored stripe other than white, green, or gray along the entire length of the conductor.

(2) Isolated Conductor #2 - Brown with at least one distinctive colored stripe other than white, green, or gray along the entire length of the conductor.

For three-phase systems, the third conductor shall be identified as yellow with at least one distinctive colored stripe other than white, green, or gray along the entire length of the conductor. Where isolated circuit conductors supply 125 volt, single-phase, 15 and 20 amp receptacles, the orange conductor(s) shall be connected to the terminal(s) on the receptacle that are identified with 200.10(B) for connection to the grounded circuit conductor.

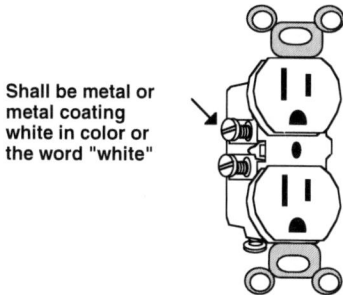

Shall be metal or metal coating white in color or the word "white"

517.160(A)(6). Wire-pulling compounds that increase the dielectric constant shall **not** be used on the secondary conductors of the isolated power supply.

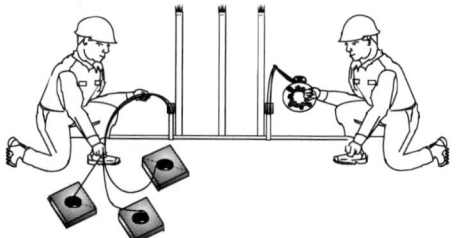

***Informational Note 1*:** It is desirable to limit the size of the isolation transformer to 10 kVA or less and to use conductor insulation with low leakage to meet impedance requirements.

***Informational Note 2*:** Minimizing the length of branch-circuit conductors and using conductor insulations with a dielectric constant less than 3.5 and insulation resistance constant greater than 6100 megohm-meters (20,000 megohm-feet) at 60°F reduces leakage from line to ground, reducing hazard current.

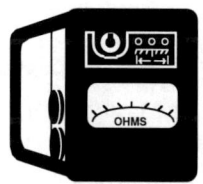

517.160(B). Line Isolation Monitor.

(1) Each isolated power system shall be provided with a continually operating line isolation monitor that indicates total hazard current. A green signal lamp remains lighted when the system is adequately isolated from ground. A red signal lamp with an audible warning signal will be energized when the total hazard current reaches 5 mA under normal line conditions.

Exception: A system shall be permitted to be designed at a lower threshold value of total hazard current. A line isolation monitor for such a sytem when approved is permitted to be reduced not less than 35% of the corresponding threshold value of the total hazard current, and the monitor hazard current is to be correspondingly reduced to not more than 50% of the alarm threshold value of the total hazard current.

(2) The line isolation monitor shall be designed to have sufficient internal impedance such that, when properly connected to the isolated system, the maximum internal current that can flow through the line isolation monitor, when any point of the isolated system is grounded, shall be 1 mA.

Exception: The line isolation monitor shall be permitted to be of the low-impedance type such that the current through the line isolation monitor, when at any point of the isolated system is grounded, will not exceed twice the alarm threshold value for a period not exceeding 5 milliseconds.

Informational Note: Reduction of the monitor hazard current, provided this reduction results in an increased "not alarm" threshold value for the fault hazard current, will increase circuit capacity.

(3) An ammeter calibrated in the total hazard current of the system shall be in a visible place on the line isolation monitor.

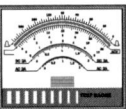

Exception: The line isolation monitor shall be permitted to be a composite unit, with a sensing system cabled to a separate display panel section on which the alarm or test functions are located.

Informational Note: It is desirable to locate the ammeter so that it is conspicuously visible to persons in the anesthetizing location.

 **Author's note**: The purpose of the monitor is to provide a warning of the danger of shock or a fault in the system due to accidental grounding of more than one conductor. If one conductor of an isolated system becomes grounded, the fuse or breaker will not operate because there is no return path. However, if an accidental ground occurs on the other conductor, a short will occur, and could cause a spark to create ignition of ether vapors or a lethal shock to personnel.

Articles 515 - 517   Quiz #1   -   Open Book

•*Circle your choice of answer and* **write the Code section where it was found**.

1. The minimum number of receptacles in each patient bed location of a hospital general care area should be ____.

(a) one   (b) two   (c) four   (d) eight

2. The disconnecting means for portable X-ray equipment operating on 120v, 30 ampere or less branch circuits may be a ____.

I. general duty snap switch loaded not more than 80%
II. grounding type attachment plug and receptacle

(a) I only   (b) II only   (c) both I and II   (d) neither I nor II

3. Where there is no patient equipment grounding point, it is important that the distance between the reference grounding point and the patient vicinity be ____ to minimize any potential differences.

(a) 6 feet   (b) 8 feet   (c) 10 feet   (d) as short as possible

4. The hazardous area in a pit of a spray operation without proper vapor stop is classified as a ____ location.

(a) Class I,   Division 1   (b) Class I,   Division 2
(c) Class II,   Division 1   (d) Class III, Division 1

5. Although it is permitted to run the grounding conductor outside of the conduit, it is safer to run it with the power conductors to provide better protection in case of ____.

(a) mechanical damage   (b) a lightning strike
(c) a ground fault   (d) a second ground fault

6. Health care low voltage equipment frequently in contact with bodies of persons shall not exceed ____ volts.

(a) 50   (b) 115   (c) 10   (d) 8

7. Where Type PVC conduit is used as a raceway system in bulk storage plant wiring, the raceway shall include ____.

(a) sunlight resistant listing   (b) an equipment grounding conductor
(c) a bushing with double locknuts   (d) PVC raceway is not permitted

8. Each patient bed in a critical care area shall be provided with a minimum of ____ receptacle(s).

(a) one duplex   (b) single   (c) two duplex   (d) fourteen

9. Which of the following are **not** classified patient care areas?

I. Waiting rooms II. Lounges   III. Utility rooms

(a) II only   (b) II and III only   (c) III only   (d) I, II and III

10. Any room or location in which flammable anesthetics are stored shall be considered to be a ____ location from floor to ceiling.

(a) Class I, Division 1   (b) Class I, Division 2
(c) Class II, Division 2   (d) nonhazardous

11. Above ground storage tanks shall be classified ____ when the space between 5 feet and 10 feet from open end of vent extends in all directions.

(a) Class I, Division 1   (b) Class I, Division 2
(c) Class II, Division 1   (d) Class II, Division 2

12. A nursing home is a building or part thereof used for the lodging, boarding and nursing care, on a 24-hour basis, of ____ or more persons.

(a) 4   (b) 12   (c) 50   (d) 100

Articles 515 - 517   Quiz #2 - Open Book

•*Circle your choice of answer and* **write the Code section where it was found.**

1. It is desirable to limit the size of the isolation transformer to _____ kVA or less and to use conductor insulation with low leakage to meet impedance requirements.

(a) 10   (b) 15   (c) 20   (d) 30

2. Mobile x-ray equipment is mounted on a _____ base with wheels and/or casters for moving while completely assembled.

(a) portable   (b) transportable   (c) permanent   (d) temporary

3. It is desirable to locate the ammeter so that it is conspicuously visible to persons in the _____ location.

(a) Class I   (b) Class II   (c) Class III   (d) anesthetizing

4. In fixed electrostatic spray zones, signs shall be conspicuously posted to ___.

I.   restrict access to qualified personnel only
II. identify emergency exit routes
III. designate the zone as dangerous with regard to fire and accident
IV. identify the grounding requirements for all electrically conductive objects in the spray area

(a) I only   (b) I and II only   (c) I, III, and IV only   (d) I, II, III, and IV

5. A system of feeders and branch circuits supplying power for lighting, receptacles, and equipment essential for life safety that is automatically connected to alternate power sources by one or more transfer switches during interruption of the normal power source is the _____.

(a) essential system   (b) critical branch   (c) life safety branch   (d) line isolation monitor

6. Any interruption of the circuit, even circuits as low as ___ volts, either by any switch, or loose or defective connections anywhere in the circuit, may produce a spark sufficient to ignite flammable anesthetic agents.

(a) 10   (b) 12   (c) 24   (d) 30

7. Wall mounted remote control stations for remote control switches operating at ___ or less shall be permitted to be installed in any anesthetizing location.

(a) 12 volts   (b) 24 volts   (c) 30 volts   (d) 60 volts

8. In health care facilities, where ground fault protection is provided for operation of the service disconnecting means or feeder disconnecting means, an additional step of ground fault protection shall be provided in the next level of feeder disconnecting means downstream toward the load. The additional levels of ground fault protection of equipment shall not be installed ___.

I.   on electrical systems that are not solidly grounded wye systems with greater than 150 volts to ground.
II. on the load side of an essential electrical system transfer switch.

(a) I only   (b) II only   (c) I and II   (d) none of these

9. A building or part thereof used on a 24 hour basis for the housing of four or more persons who are incapable of self preservation because of age, physical limitation due to accident or illness, or mental limitations, such as mental retardation/developmental disability, mental illness or chemical dependency is a/an ___.

(a) limited care facility   (b) nursing home
(c) psychiatric hospital   (d) ambulatory health care center

10. 15 and 20 ampere receptacles located in pediatric areas shall be ____.

(a) listed and identified tamper resistant   (b) isolated   (c) GFI   (d) specification grade

11. In patient care areas of a hospital, the **equipment grounding** terminal buses of the normal and essential branch circuit panelboards shall be bonded together with an insulated continuous copper conductor not smaller than ____.

(a) #8   (b) #6   (c) #10   (d) #12

12. Essential electrical systems for hospitals shall be comprised of a minimum of two independent sources of power. These systems are the ____.

I. normal source II. one or more alternate source(s)   III. only one generator source

(a) I and II only   (b) II and III only   (c) I and III only   (d) none of these

Articles 515 - 517   Quiz #3   -   Open Book

•*Circle your choice of answer and **write the Code section where it was found**.*

1. For spraying operations confined to an enclosed spray booth or room, the Division 2 area extends ____ in all directions from any opening.

(a) 3'   (b) 10'   (c) 900'   (d) unlimited

2. A feeder is to be installed in a health care facility which has a large 120/208v wye service. The service equipment main has ground-fault protection installed. Which of the following best decribes Code requirements for this new feeder?

(a) The feeder must have ground-fault protection.
(b) The feeder must have fully selective ground-fault protection.
(c) A new feeder is not permitted to be installed in an old building.
(d) Ground-fault protection is only required on 480v wye systems.

3. Each patient bed location shall be supplied by at least ___ branch circuits, equally supplied by the critical branch and one from the normal system.

(a) two   (b) four   (c) six   (d) eight

4. Fixed luminaires for anesthetizing locations shall be at least ____ feet above the floor.

(a) 12   (b) 10   (c) 8   (d) 5

5. A/an ___ is a jack or terminal bus that serves as the collection point for redundant grounding of electric appliances serving a patient vicinity or for grounding other items in order to eliminate electromagnetic interference problems.

(a) hazard current   (b) exposed conductive surface
(c) isolated power system   (d) patient equipment grounding point

6. The color coding for single-phase isolated circuits within a hazardous anesthetizing location is ____.

(a) Isolated Conductor No.1 -- Black
    Isolated Conductor No.2 -- Blue
(b) Isolated Conductor No.1 -- Black
    Isolated Conductor No.2 -- Red
(c) Isolated Conductor No.1 -- Orange
    Isolated Conductor No.2 -- Brown
(d) Isolated Conductor No.1 -- Yellow
    Isolated Conductor No.2 -- Brown

7. Underground wiring for bulk storage plants shall be installed in ____.

(a) threaded rigid metal conduit
(b) threaded steel intermediate metal conduit
(c) Type PVC conduit buried not less than 24"
(d) Any of the above

8. For spray application operations confined to an enclosed spray booth or room, the area within ____ feet of any opening shall be classified as Class I, Division 2.

(a) 3   (b) 8   (c) 10   (d) 12

9. Open containers, supply containers, waste containers, and solvent distillation units that contain Class I liquids shall be located in _____.

(a) wet rooms   (b) rooms identified   (c) areas ventilated   (d) non conductive rooms

10. The definition of an isolated power system is: A system comprising of _____.

I.   its ungrounded circuit conductors
II. a line isolation monitor
III. an isolating transformer

(a) II and III only   (b) I and III only   (c) I and II only   (d) I, II and III

11. In an unenclosed paint spraying area, electrical wiring and utilization equipment located outside but within ____ horizontally and 10 feet vertically of an enclosed spray area and not separated from the spray area by partitions extending to the boundaries of the area designated as Division 2 shall be suitable for Class I, Division 2.

(a) 8'   (b) 15'   (c) 20'   (d) unlimited

12. In a hospital electrical system, the Critical Branch of the Emergency System shall supply power for ____.

(a) coronary care units   (b) human physiology labs
(c) anesthetizing locations   (d) all of these

FINAL EXAM

FINAL EXAM 50 Questions - Open Book

•*Circle your choice of answer and* **write the Code section where it was found.**

1. Color coding shall be permitted to identify _____ conductors where they are colored light blue and where no other conductors colored light blue are used.

(a) fire alarm   (b) elevator   (c) intrinsically safe   (d) electrolytic cell

2. All of the following motors are permitted in a Class III, Division 1 area except _____.

(a) totally enclosed pipe ventilated   (b) non-ventilated
(c) totally enclosed fan cooled   (d) water cooled

3. Class III locations are those that are hazardous because of _____.

(a) the presence of combustible dust
(b) over 8' depth of water
(c) flammable gases or vapors may be present in the air
(d) the presence of easily ignitible fibers or flyings

4. Sealing compound is employed with mineral-insulated cable in a Class I location for the purpose of _____.

(a) preventing passage of gas or vapor   (b) excluding moisture
(c) limiting a possible explosion   (d) preventing escape of powder

5. A point located 24" above grade level and 20 feet from the edge of an indoor remote gas pump is considered _____.

(a) Class I, Group D, Division 2   (b) Class I, Group D, Division 1
(c) Class I, Group C, Division 2   (d) Class I, Group C, Division 1

6. Which of the following about an aircraft hangar is true?

I. Any area below the floor level shall be considered a Class I, Division I location up to the floor level.
II. The area within 5' horizontally of aircraft power plants or fuel tanks shall be considered a Class I, Division II location extending from the floor to a level 5' above the upper surface of wings and engine enclosures.

(a) I only   (b) II only   (c) both I and II   (d) neither I nor II

7. Lighting fixtures installed over vehicle lanes inside a commercial garage shall be installed a minimum of ____ feet.

(a) 8 (b) 10 (c) 12 (d) 15

8. The disconnecting means for portable X-ray equipment operating on 120v, 30 ampere or less branch circuits may be a ____.

I. general duty snap switch loaded not more than 80%
II. grounding type attachment plug and receptacle

(a) I only (b) II only (c) both I and II (d) neither I nor II

9. In minor repair garages, entire space within any pit, below workgrade work area is classified as ____ if not ventilated.

(a) Class I, Division 1 (b) Class I, Division 2 (c) Class II, Division 2 (d) Class II, Division 1

10. The minimum thickness of the sealing compound in Class I, Division 1 and 2 locations shall not be less than the trade size of the conduit and in no case less than ____.

(a) 3/16" (b) 3/8" (c) 1/2" (d) 5/8"

11. Locations where combustible dust is normally in heavy concentrations are designated as ____.

(a) Class I, Division 2   (b) Class II, Division 1
(c) Class II, Division 2   (d) Class III, Division 1

12. The minimum depth of oil over the power contacts in an oil immersion type switch for use in a Class I Division 2 location is ___ inches.

(a) 1 (b) 1 1/2 (c) 2 (d) 3

13. No transformer or capacitor shall be installed in a Class II, Division 1, ____ location.

(a) Group A   (b) Group C
(c) Group B   (d) Group E

14. Zone equipment is required to have flanged openings placed a certain minimum distance away from steel, walls, weather guards, mounting brackets, pipes, etc. unless the equipment is listed for a smaller distance of separation. This distance provides for the expanding gases flowing out through the flanged opening. The minimum distance for IIB gas group is ____.

(a) 5/8" (b) 25/64" (c) 1 3/16" (d) 1 1/2"

15. Fixed wiring, which is to provide external power to aircraft hangers, shall be installed at least ____ above floor level.

(a) 12" (b) 18" (c) 24" (d) 30"

16. In a major repair garage, the pit shall be classified ____ unless provisions are made for ventilation.

(a) Class I, Division 2 (b) Class II, Division 2 (c) Class II, Division 1 (d) Class I, Division 1

17. Underground wiring for a motor fuel dispenser shall be installed in ____.

(a) threaded rigid metal conduit
(b) threaded steel intermediate metal conduit
(c) Type PVC conduit buried not less than 24"
(d) Any of the above

18. Any room or location in which flammable anesthetics are stored shall be considered to be a ____ location from floor to ceiling.

(a) Class I, Division 1   (b) Class I, Division 2
(c) Class II, Division 2   (d) nonhazardous

19. Above ground storage tanks with a fixed roof shall be classified ____ when the space between 5 feet and 10 feet from open end of vent extends in all directions.

(a) Class I, Division 1   (b) Class I, Division 2
(c) Class II, Division 1   (d) Class II, Division 2

20. A building or part thereof used on a 24 hour basis for the housing of four or more persons who are incapable of self preservation because of age, physical limitation due to accident or illness, or mental limitations, such as mental retardation/developmental disability, mental illness or chemical dependency is a/an ____.

(a) limited care facility   (b) nursing home
(c) psychiatric hospital   (d) ambulatory health care center

21. For spraying operations confined to an enclosed spray booth or room, the Division 2 area extends ____ in all directions from any opening.

(a) 3' (b) 10' (c) 900' (d) unlimited

22. At a gasoline dispensing, self service station which is unattended, the emergency disconnect for a circuit leading to dispensing equipment, must be located more than ___ feet from the dispensers.

(a) 3 (b) 5 (c) 10 (d) 20

23. Parking garages used for parking or storage and where no repair work is done, open flame, welding, or the use of volatile flammable liquids are ____.

(a) Class I (b) Class II (c) Class III (d) not classified

24. In a Class II location, there shall be no uninsulated exposed part that operates at more than ____ volts (15 volts in wet locations).

(a) 10 (b) 12 (c) 24 (d) 30

25. To reduce the danger of spontaneous combustion in Class III locations, the Code limits the surface temperature of electrical equipment used in these locations. The temperature for motors, transformers, etc. that can operate while overloaded is ____.

(a) 212°F (b) 248°F (c) 304°F (d) 329°F

26. Which of the following would **not** be approved in all Class II locations?

(a) flexible connections   (b) threaded bosses
(c) dust-tight boxes   (d) EMT

27. In a Class III location, each luminaire shall be clearly marked to show the ____.

(a) ballast rating (b) voltage (c) maximum lamp wattage (d) current

28. Rooms and areas containing ammonia refrigeration systems that are equipped with adequate mechanical ventilation may be classified as ____ locations.

(a) unclassified (b) Group D (c) Division 2 (d) Class III

29. In commercial garages using electrical hand tools, portable lights, etc., ground fault protection shall be provided for _____.

(a) receptacles in pits below floor level only
(b) receptacles located in adjacent bathrooms only
(c) receptacles within 18" above the floor only
(d) personnel

30. Gasoline stations shall have emergency disconnects to shut off all power to dispensing equipment. Such devices shall be located more than ___ feet but less than ___ feet from the dispensers.

(a) 20 - 100   (b) 20 - 50   (c) 10 - 100   (d) 10 - 50

31. In commercial garages, all 125v single-phase, 15 and 20 amp receptacles where _____ are to be used, shall provide GFCI protection for personnel.

I. portable lighting equipment
II. electrical hand tools
III. electrical automotive diagnostic equipment

(a) I only   (b) II only   (c) III only   (d) I, II and III

32. What is the minimum burial depth for Type PVC conduit in a dispensing station Class I, Division 1 location?

(a) 18"   (b) 24"   (c) 30"   (d) cannot be used in Class I, Division 1 location

33. Where there is no patient **equipment grounding** point, it is important that the distance between the reference grounding point and the patient vicinity be _____ to minimize any potential differences.

(a) 6 feet   (b) 8 feet   (c) 10 feet   (d) as short as possible

34. The hazardous area in a pit of a spray operation without proper vapor stop is classified as a _____ location.

(a) Class I,   Division 1   (b) Class I,   Division 2
(c) Class II,   Division 1   (d) Class III, Division 1

35. A nursing home is a building or part thereof used for the lodging, boarding and nursing care, on a 24-hour basis, of _____ or more persons.

(a) 4   (b) 12   (c) 50   (d) 100

36. Where are conduit seals **NOT** required in a Class I installation?

(a) Where metal conduit passes completely through the Class I area with no fittings less than 12" outside any classified area.
(b) Where a conduit less than 36" in length connects two enclosures.
(c) Where the conduit enters an explosion-proof motor.
(d) Where the conduit exits the Class I area.

37. For limited flexibility for motor connections in a Class I, Division 2 location, flexible conduit
_____.

(a) must be explosionproof
(b) must be liquidtight flexible conduit or equal
(c) may be standard flexible metal conduit
(d) shall not be used

38. In Class I, Division 1 locations, the Code requires conduit seals adjacent to boxes containing splices if the conduit is equal to or larger than _____.

(a) 3/4"   (b) 1 1/2"   (c) 1"   (d) 2"

39. In Class II locations _____ dust may dehydrate or carbonize making them even more dangerous.

(a) plastic   (b) coal   (c) organic   (d) metallic

40. Where Type PVC conduit is used as a raceway system in bulk storage plant wiring, the raceway shall include _____.

(a) sunlight resistant listing   **(b) an equipment grounding conductor**
(c) a bushing with double locknuts   **(d) PVC raceway is not permitted**

41. In patient care areas of a hospital, the equipment grounding terminal bars of the normal and essential electrical system panelboards shall be bonded together with an insulated continuous copper conductor not smaller than _____.

(a) #8   (b) #6   (c) #10   (d) #12

42. In an open paint spraying area, the Division 2 area extends _____ horizontally outside of the Division 1 location.

(a) 8'   (b) 15'   (c) 20'   (d) unlimited

43. All fixed wiring above Class I locations in a repair garage shall be in _____.

I. flexible nonmetallic conduit   II. rigid nonmetallic conduit   III. TC cable

(a) I only   (b) II only   (c) I and II only   (d) I, II and III

44. Conductors and cables of intrinsically safe circuits not in raceways or cable trays shall be separated at least _____ and secured from conductors and cables of any nonintrinsically safe circuits.

(a) 24"   (b) 12"   (c) 6"   (d) 2"

45. A/an _____ circuit is a circuit in which any spark or thermal effect is incapable of causing ignition of a mixture of flammable or combustible material in air under prescribed test conditions.

(a) low voltage   (b) intrinsically safe   (c) hazardproof   (d) explosiveproof

46. Which wiring method is **not** permitted in a Class II, Division 1 location?

(a) MI cable   (b) cable tray   (c) IMC   (d) rigid metal conduit

47. A propane-dispensing unit is located outdoors, 50 feet from an office in which the branch circuit supplying the unit originates. Conduit seals shall be required _____.

(a) where the conduit emerges from the earth at the office only
(b) where the conduit emerges from the earth at the dispensing unit only
(c) where the conduit emerges from the earth at both the dispensing unit and at the office
(d) No seals are required for propane gas

48. An approved seal shall be provided in each conduit run entering or leaving a dispenser or any cavities or enclosures in direct communication therewith. The sealing fitting shall be _____ .

(a) concrete-tight
(b) 3/4" minimum thickness
(c) the last fitting after the conduit emerges from the earth or concrete
(d) the first fitting after the conduit emerges from the earth or concrete

49. A system of feeders and branch circuits supplying power for lighting, receptacles, and equipment essential for life safety that is automatically connected to the alternate power sources by one or more transfer switches during interruption of the normal power source.

(a) essential system   (b) critical branch   (c) life safety branch   (d) line isolation monitor

50. In a Class I, Division 2 area, bonding can be accomplished by _____.

I. double locknuts   II. locknut-bushings

(a) I only   (b) II only   (c) both I and II   (d) neither I nor II

ANSWERS

To grade your exam:

Count the number of correct answers
and divide by the number of questions 20.

Example: 15 correct answers   = 75%
            20 questions

Articles 500 - 501   Quiz #1   -   Open Book

1. (a) dust — 500.5(C)
2. (d) neither — 501.30(A)
3. (a) 12" outside — 501.15(A)(4) ex.1
4. (d) neither — 501.130(A)(3)
5. (d) fibers — 500.5(D)
6. (d) 5/8" — 501.15(C)(3)
7. (c) gases or vapors — 500.5(B)
8. (c) flexible metal — 501.10(B)(2)(2)
9. (c) Class III, Div.1 — 500.5(D)(2)
10. (d) 2" — 501.15(A)(1)(2)
11. (a) rigid metal — 501.10(A)(1)(1)
12. (b) Class II, Div.2 — 500.5(C)(1)(1)

Articles 500 - 501   Quiz #2   -   Open Book

1. (b) moisture — 501.15
2. (b) 80% — 501.125(A)(4)
3. (b) either side — 501.15(B)(2)
4. (b) NPT — 500.8(E)(1)
5. (a) 18" — 501.15(A)(1)
6. (c) 2" — 501.115(B)(1)(2)
7. (c) organic — 500.8(D)(2)
8. (c) I,II,III — 501.105(B)(6)
9. (b) Group E — 500.5(C)(3)
10. (a) 25% — 501.15(C)(6)
11. (a) general type — 501.115(B)(2)
12. (d) no Groups — 500.6

Articles 502 - 506   Quiz #1   -   Open Book

1. (d) at least 3" — 504.30(A)(2)(1)
2. (d) not allowed — 502.100(A)(3)
3. (b) not likely — 505.5(B)(3)(1)
4. (c) intrinsically — 504.80(C)
5. (b) enclosure — 502.115(A)
6. (b) Class II — 502.115(B)
7. (b) closed containers — 506.5(B)(3)
8. (d) three groups — Article 503
9. (d) glass or quartz — 100 Part III DEF
10. (c) Qualified persons — 505.7(A)
11. (c) 1 3/16" — T. 505.7(D)
12. (d) water cooled — 503.125

Articles 502 - 506   Quiz #2   -   Open Book

1. (b) external — 505.25(B)
2. (c) grounded — 504.50(B)
3. (d) long periods — 506.5(B)(1)(2)
4. (d) 30 volts — 502.25
5. (c) listed — 504.4 ex.
6. (b) 248°F — 503.5
7. (d) 2" — 504.30(A)(3)
8. (c) dusttight — 503.10(A)(2)
9. (d) EMT — 502.10(A)(1)
10. (b) intrinsically safe — 100 Part III DEF
11. (d) maintenance — 505.5(B)(2)(2)
12. (c) arcing parts — 100 Part III DEF

Articles 502 - 506   Quiz #3   -   Open Book

1. (c) Article 504 — 505.15(A)
2. (d) not allowed — 502.100(A)(3), 500.6(B)(1)
3. (c) long periods — 505.5(B)(1)(2)
4. (d) identified — 502.5
5. (c) max. wattage — 503.130
6. (c) Splices — 505.16(D)(4,5)
7. (b) cable tray — 502.10(A)(1)
8. (c) documented — 505.4
9. (d) dusttight — 502.10(A)(4)
10. (a) frequently — 506.5(2)(2)
11. (d) 329°F — 503.5
12. (a) unclassified — 505.5(A)

ANSWERS

Articles 510 - 514   Quiz #1   -   Open Book

1. (a) Group D Div.2   T. 514.3(B)(1)
2. (b) 18"   513.10(C)(1)
3. (d) all   511.12
4. (c) office   514.1 & 514.9(A)
5. (b) broken   513.4(A)
6. (d) Class I, Div.1   Table 511.3(C)
7. (b) 20', 100'   514.11(A)
8. (a) handle   511.4(B)(2)
9. (a) charged   513.10(A)(2)
10. (d) Any of the above   514.8 ex.2
11. (a) readily accessible   514.11(B)
12. (d) I,II and III   511.7(A)(1)

Articles 510 - 514   Quiz #2   -   Open Book

1. (d) unclassified   511.3(A)
2. (a) individual island 514.11(C)
3. (c) delineate   514.3(B)(1)
4. (d) I,II and III   511.12
5. (c) both I and II   513.3 (A,C)
6. (d) shall not   513.3(D)
7. (d) first fitting   514.9(A)
8. (b) Class I, Div.2   Table 511.3(C)
9. (b) 24"   514.8 ex.2
10. (c) 12 feet   511.7(B)(1)(b)
11. (b) I and III only   513.7(B)
12. (b) 511 through 517   510.1

Articles 515 - 517   Quiz #1   -   Open Book

1. (d) eight   517.18(B)(1)
2. (b) II only   517.72(C)
3. (d) short   517.19(D) I.N.
4. (a) Class I, Div.1   516.4(5)
5. (d) second   517.19(G) I.N.
6. (c) 10 volts   517.64(A)(1)
7. (b) equip. grounding   515.8(C)
8. (d) fourteen   517.19(B)
9. (d) I,II and III   517.2 DEF I.N.
10. (a) Class I, Div.1   517.60(A)(1)
11. (b) Class I, Div.2   T. 515.3
12. (a) 4 or more   517.2 DEF

Articles 515 - 517   Quiz #2   -   Open Book

1. (a) 10 kVA   517.160(A)(6) I.N. 1
2. (c) permanent   517.2 DEF
3. (d) anesthetizing   517.160(B)(3) I.N.
4. (c) I,III and IV   516.10(A)(8)(1,2,3)
5. (c) life safety   517.2 DEF
6. (a) 10 volts   517.64(F) I.N.
7. (b) 24 volts   517.63(D)
8. (c) I and II   517.17(B)   230.95
9. (a) limited care   517.2 DEF
10. (a) tamper resistant   517.18(C)
11. (c) #10   517.14
12. (a) I and II only   517.30(A)

Articles 515 - 517   Quiz #3 - Open Book

1. (a) 3'	516.5(D)(4)	7. (d) any of the above	515.8(A)
2. (b) selective	517.17(C)	8. (a) 3 feet	516.5(D)(4)(1)
3. (a) two	517.18(A)	9. (c) ventilated	516.36
4. (c) 8 feet	517.63(C)(1)	10. (d) I,II and III	517.2 DEF
5. (d) grd. point	517.2 DEF	11. (c) 20'	516.5(D)(1)
6. (c) orange-brn.	517.160(A)(5)(1,2)	12. (d) all of these	517.34(A)(1)(7)(d & g)

FINAL EXAM   50 Questions - Open Book

1. (c) intrinsically	504.80(C)	26. (d) EMT	502.10(A)(1)(1,2 3)
2. (d) watter cooled	503.125	27. (c) max. wattage	503.130(A)
3. (d) fibers	500.5(D)	28. (a) unclassified	505.5(A)
4. (b) moisture	501.15	29. (d) personnel	511.12
5. (a) Group D, Div.2	T. 514.3(B)(1)	30. (a) 20 - 100 feet	514.11(A)
6. (c) both I and II	513.3(A,C)	31. (d) I,II and III	511.12
7. (c) 12 feet	511.7(B)(1)(b)	32. (b) 24"	514.8 ex.2
8. (b) II only	517.72(C)	33. (d) short as possible	517.19(D) I.N.
9. (b) Class I, Div.2	511.3(B)	34. (a) Class I, Div.1	516.4(5)
10. (d) 5/8"	501.15(C)(3)	35. (a) 4 or more persons	517.2 DEF
11. (b) Class II, Div.1	500.5(C)(1)(1)	36. (a) no fittings	501.15(A)(4) ex.1
12. (c) 2"	501.115(B)(1)(2)	37. (c) flexible metal	501.10(B)(2)(2)
13. (d) Group E	502.100(A)(3)	38. (d) 2"	501.15(A)(1)(2)
14. (c) 1 3/16"	T. 505.7(D)	39. (c) organic	500.8(D)(2)
15. (b) 18"	513.10(C)(1)	40. (b) equip. grounding	515.8(C)
16. (d) Class I, Div.1	T. 511.3(C)	41. (c) #10	517.14
17. (d) Any of the above	514.8 ex.2	42. (c) 20'	516.5(D)(1)
18. (a) Class I, Div.1	517.60(A)(1)	43. (d) I,II and III	511.7(A)(1)
19. (b) Class I, Div.2	T. 515.3	44. (d) 2"	504.30(A)(3)
20. (a) limited care facility	517.2 DEF	45. (b) intrinsically safe	100 Part III DEF
21. (a) 3'	516.5(D)(2)	46. (b) cable tray	502.10(A)(1& 2)
22. (d) 20 feet	514.11(A)	47. (c) at both	514.9(A)
23. (d) not classified	511.3(A)	48. (d) first fitting	514.9(A)
24. (d) 30 volts	502.25	49. (c) life safety branch	517.2 DEF
25. (b) 248°F	503.5	50. (d) neither I nor II	501.30(A)

THE PREVIEW OF THE ELECTRICAL EXAM

Tom Henry states the electrical exam should contain questions in the field which the electrician is working, need specialized exams. This book contains examples of exam questions and how to prepare for the open and closed book exam questions.

•Book #1 The Preview of the Electrical Exam is **FREE** when purchased with at **least two other books** from The Henry Electrical License Exam Series.

This book contains a 100 Question Exam which you can work and e-mail to Tom Henry and he will personally grade it and return to you the **correct answers** and give you a review on how to improve your score on any weakness you may have.

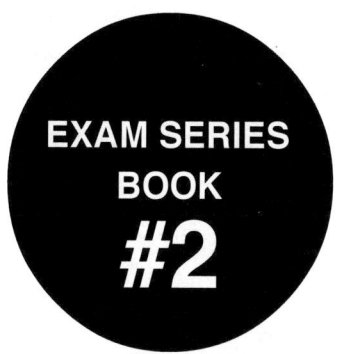

The Behavior of Electricty
Theory - Ohm's Law - Transformers

OTHER THAN CODE BOOK QUESTIONS -
•NO BOOK QUESTIONS:

General knowledge categories such as the behavior of electricity, theory, Ohm's Law, ac-dc power, voltage drop, power factor, efficiency, cost, tools, safety, plan reading, specifications, etc.

There is no NEC section to locate for **general knowledge** questions, you must select the correct answer by **memory**. These are the questions where **formulas** come into play.

Book #2 contains 6 practice exams and examples with **correct answers**.

OTHER THAN CODE BOOK QUESTIONS -
•NO BOOK QUESTIONS:

General Knowledge - Tools - Safety - Plan Reading - Specifications - Maintenance - Controls - Meters

The **general knowledge** categories test your knowledge of what you have learned from the years spent in the electrical field to **qualify** to take the exam. How much can you remember from your training?

The NEC is updated each 3 years, **general knowledge** categories remain the same over the years in most cases.

Book #3 contains 8 one hour practice exams with **correct answers**.

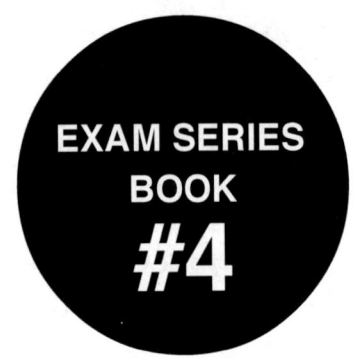

The National Electrical Code Chapter One

ARTICLE 90 thru 110

Introduction, Definitions, Requirements for Electrical Installations.

Preparing for the exam, common sense will tell you to **study an hour a night** for a week is better than an all day cram.

The difficulty occurs when you say **National Electrical Code book**. Most applicants taking an exam are **not** familiar enough with the Code book and it's easy to understand why only 30 out of 100 pass an electrical exam. Many are *unsuccessful* because they failed to *read* the question correctly.

Your score on the open book exam depends on how familiar you are with the **National Electrical Code book**. Most exam applicants run out of time and are not able to find all the answers to the questions within the limited time.

You must understand Article 100 Definitions. If you don't understand the definition, you will have trouble with answering the questions correctly.

In writing these books on OPEN BOOK questions for **locating the section** of the NEC, I'm using a different format. *I want you to write down what section of the NEC that states the fact.* This will help you in using your memory cells and eliminate guessing. **I'll give you the correct answer**.

EXAMPLE: Each meeting room of not more than _____ sq. ft. in other than dwelling units shall have outlets for nonlocking-type, 125 volt, 15 or 20 ampere receptacles.

(a) 250   (b) 500   (c) 750 |(d) 1000|

Section ___**210.71(A)**___ .

Book #4 contains 6 one hour practice exams with **correct answers** and **section** where found.

The National Electrical Code Chapter Two

ARTICLE 200 thru 285

Wiring and Protection. Calculations of Demand Factors, Services, Overcurrent Protection, Grounding, etc.

Chapter Two is a big one! Article 220 is Load **Calculations.**

Article 220 - Branch-Circuit, Feeder, and Service Load Calculations.

EXAM SERIES BOOK #6

EXAM SERIES BOOK #7

EXAM SERIES BOOK #8

EXAM SERIES BOOK #9

EXAM SERIES BOOK #10

The National Electrical Code   Chapter Three

ARTICLE 300 thru 399

Chapter Three Wiring Methods and Materials is big! It contains 8 exams on boxes, NM cable, conduits, PVC, cable trays, open wiring, etc.

The National Electrical Code   Chapter Four

ARTICLE 400 thru 490

Chapter Four Equipment for General use contains 8 exams on cords, fixture wires, switches, appliances, space heating, luminaires, motors, transformers, batteries, equipment over 1000 volts, etc.

The National Electrical Code   Chapter Five

ARTICLE 500 thru 590

Chapter Five Special Occupancies contains 8 exams on hazardous locations, commercial garages, air craft hangers, bulk storage plants, health care facilities, assembly occupancies, carnivals, TV studios, mobile homes, marinas, etc.

The National Electrical Code   Chapter Six

ARTICLE 600 thru 690

Chapter Six Special Equipment contains 8 exams on signs, elevators, welders, X-ray, swimming pools, solar, fuel cell system, wind electric, etc.

The National Electrical Code Chapters 7-8-9 Calculations

ARTICLE 700 thru Chapter 9

Book #10 contains 5 exams on special/conditions, communication systems. And examples on Tables most used, cooking equipment demand factors, box fill calculations, motor calculations, etc.

Pricing as of November 2019 •Subject to change in 2020.

•Book #1 The Preview of the Electrical Exam is **FREE** when purchased with at **least two other books** from The Henry Electrical License Exam Series.

Example: Purchase books #2 and #3 and receive Book #1 Free!

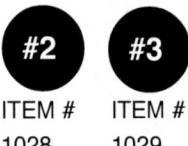

#2
ITEM #
1028

#3
ITEM #
1029

Each book is $19 and you are receiving 3 books for $38 + Shipping or $12.66 a book!

The BEST BUY is all 10 books The Henry Electrical License Exam Series
ITEM # 1037 $171 + Shipping   ($17.10 per book)

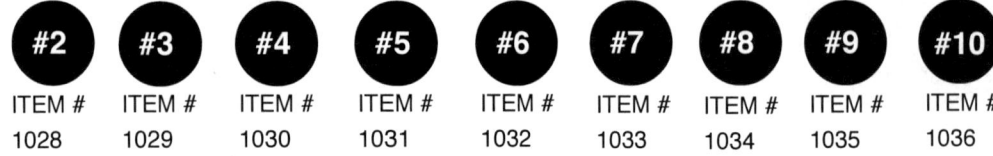

#2	#3	#4	#5	#6	#7	#8	#9	#10
ITEM #	ITEM #	ITEM #	ITEM #	ITEM #	ITEM #	ITEM #	ITEM #	ITEM #
1028	1029	1030	1031	1032	1033	1034	1035	1036

Tom Henry's
Code Electrical Classes Inc.
and Bookstore
7449 Citrus Avenue
Winter Park, Florida 32792

THE ELECTRICIANS BOOKSTORE
1-800-642-2633

SAME DAY SHIPPING...
 Call 1-800-642-2633
OR FAX
(407) 671-6497

7 DAYS MAX

EASTERN TIME
MONDAY - FRIDAY 8am - 5pm
ANSWERING MACHINE, FAX, or
www.code-electrical.com
24 HOURS - 7 DAYS A WEEK

 **Call 1-800-642-2633 today!**

•Note: Call Monday thru Friday 8 am to 5 pm Eastern time and a person will answer the phone and eliminate pressing all the buttons only to get a recording. *It's called the personal touch*. Without the customer we don't exist!

READ THE BOOKS THE ELECTRICIAN'S READ

WORLDWIDE LEADER IN ELECTRICAL EDUCATION

1-800-642-2633
E-mail tomhenry@code-electrical.com
ONLINE SHOPPING AT
http://www.code-electrical.com

Tom Henry's Code Electrical Classes Inc.

Since 1979 we have taught electrical exam preparation classes in 21 states, 84 cities and St. Croix in the Virgin Islands.

Schedule a class in your city by calling 1-800-642-2633.

Alabama
Birmingham, Huntsville, Mobile, Montgomery

Arkansas
Little Rock

Connecticut
Hartford

Florida
Fort Myers, Fort Lauderdale, Lakeland, Tampa, St. Petersburg, Bradenton, Sarasota, Winter Haven, Jacksonville, Ocala, Leesburg, Daytona Beach, Orlando, Kissimmee, Winter Park, Haines City, Cocoa Beach, Ft. Pierce. Naples

Georgia
Atlanta, Macon, Gainesville

Hawaii
Honolulu

Indiana
Fort Wayne, Indianapolis, South Bend, Evansville, Muncie, Kokomo, Michigan City, Elkhart

Iowa
Des Moines, Cedar Rapids

Kansas
Wichita, Manhattan, Topeka, Salina, Dodge City

Kentucky
Louisville, Owensboro, Lexington

Louisiana
New Orleans, Shreveport, Baton Rouge, Covington

Michigan
Detroit, Grand Rapids

Mississippi
Jackson

Missouri
St. Louis, Kansas City, Springfield, Joplin, St. Joseph

North Carolina
Raleigh

Ohio
Columbus, Cincinnati, Akron

Oklahoma
Oklahoma City

Pennsylvania
Allentown

South Carolina
Columbia, Greenville, Spartanburg

Tennessee
Chattanooga, Memphis, Knoxville, Johnson City, Nashville, Jackson

Texas
Dallas, Lubbock, Amarillo, Wichita Falls, Waco, Odessa, Corpus Christi, Abilene, Longview, Plainview, San Angelo, Houston, San Antonio, College Station

http://www.code-electrical.com